"In this passionate call to live life fully with joy, play, and authenticity, Carla Hannaford awakens us to a new and emerging paradigm of reality. She offers the science of quantum physics to support her conclusions that each of us, as part of the unified whole, affects each other. By living with an intention to create coherence in our lives, we create the possibility of personal fulfillment for all."

—Paul Dennison, author of **Brain Gym and Me** and co-originator of the Brain Gym® Program

"An inspiring vision of our vast potential for growth when we drop our notions of limitation and open up to life with awareness, passion, and empathy. Carla Hannaford's insights from science and traditional wisdom emphasize why we must own our power, realize our interconnectedness and raise our children to inherit a world of greater consciousness and compassion."

—Zen Master Dennis Genpo Merzel, author of **Big Mind, Big Heart**

"What a beautiful work Carla Hannaford has created. This is another prize. Carla has done a masterful job of weaving together story and information and deep wisdom."

—Bob Sornson, author of **Creating Classrooms Where Teachers Love to Teach and Students Love to Learn**

"I totally enjoyed reading this book. I have been 'putting my toes into this water' for a very long time. ever since reading Gary Zukov's **The Dancing Wu Li Masters**. Carla Hannaford's book is fantastic."

—Ronn Langford, author of **Inner Speed Secrets**

"Carla Hannaford is unique, creative and visionary. She leads the way for 21st century educators to rethink the science of mind, memory and learning. **Playing in the Unified Field** brings rich new realities to our heart, mind and possibilities."

—Don Campbell, author of **The Mozart Effect** and **Rhythms of Learning**

Playing

in the Unified Field

Raising & Becoming

Conscious, Creative Human Beings

*

Carla Hannaford, Ph.D.

Foreword by William A. Tiller, Ph.D.

GREAT RIVER BOOKS
SALT LAKE CITY

Cover Design by M.M. Esterman
Foreword Illustration and Figure 4.2 © 2009 William A. Tiller
Figure 3.8 designed by Bonnie Hershey
Figures 2.2 and 3.4 designed by Jerry Phoenix Williams

For information contact:

Great River Books
161 M Street
Salt Lake City, Utah 84103
www.greatriverbooks.com

Library of Congress Cataloging-in-Publication Data

Hannaford, Carla, 1944-

Playing in the unified field : raising and becoming conscious, creative human beings / Carla Hannaford.

p. cm.

Includes bibliographical references.

Summary: "Presents findings from quantum physics, chaos theory, biology, and neuroscience that support a new conception of human potential. It includes practical suggestions for enhancing family, school and social environments"–Provided by publisher.

ISBN 978-0-915556-39-7

1. Consciousness. 2. Creative ability. I. Title.

BF311.H3357   2010   2009032511

150—dc22

Printed in the United States of America   10 9 8 7 6 5 4 3 2 1

My heartfelt thanks go first to my publishers Margaret and Mark Esterman for their generous help in deepening and editing the ideas in this book, and enthusiastically supporting its completion. And to my friends, Nancy Rose and Chris Brewer, and my brave husband Ahti, who took time out of their lives to expertly edit my English and clarify my ideas.

A special thanks to the following who were such an inspiration to me as friends and leaders in the field of consciousness, physics, music, play and love: William and Jean Tiller, Rollin McCraty, Lynn McTaggart, Joseph Chilton Pearce, James Prescott, Candace Pert, Hazrat Inayat Khan, Catherine Warrick, Dee Coulter, Dennis Genpo Merzel, Joe Smith, Susan Kovalik, Chris Brewer, Don Campbell, Robert Sylwester, Bob and Nancy Sornson, Paul and Gail Dennison and all those who have challenged me to play passionately in the unified field.

My love and appreciation go to three of my most important spiritual teachers: my daughter Breeze, my husband Ahti Mohala and Breeze's dad Jim Hannaford.

Contents

List of Illustrations

Foreword

William A. Tiller, Ph.D.

Orthodox science has spent the last 400 years building a "space/time" reference frame in order to consistently and quantitatively make sense of our apparent reality. In this scientific model of reality, everything travels at velocities slower than the speed of light and is subject to four accepted fundamental forces: gravity, electromagnetism, long-range nuclear force and short-range nuclear force. Einstein was the first to seriously try and unify these four fundamental forces into one all-encompassing force. Many others followed, some even audaciously claiming theories of everything.

These theories of everything, however, have failed – in my view because they have totally neglected the probable existence of finer levels of substance that are not accessible to our familiar five senses. I propose the existence of four finer levels of substance that all function reciprocally in the physical vacuum, all travel at velocities faster than the speed of light (and thus are invisible to our physical senses and our current instrumentation) and all function in the potential field of spirit. It is my belief that this is the unified field in which Dr. Carla Hannaford has chosen to play!

Once we acknowledge the limitations of our physical senses and open up to the idea of a much greater unified reality, we can start to appreciate and validate the degree of influence we humans can individually exert on the whole. We are, each of us, agents of causation in this universe and each of us matters. It can be bracing to discover our power to affect one another in hidden ways – it brings about a new sense of responsibility for our personal actions. At the same time, glimpsing a greater reality and the intimate place we hold within it broadens our conception of who we are and what our personal capacities may be!

Much of what we may dislike in our present society cannot be effectively changed from the outside because such exterior conditions merely reflect that which is collectively within us. We must each first intentionally change ourselves within, then the outer collective, congruent manifestations in space/time will naturally occur. If we perform high quality inner work, our outer materialized transformations can also be of high quality.

We cannot assume however, that our inner work can proceed single-handedly. We also must understand that, at the reciprocal space (magnetic information-wave) level of physical reality, we are all subtly entangled with each other. We are all one at the higher levels of self that "pull the strings" in this world and we need to be aware of the fact that we evolve alongside one another. The evolution of all is ultimately necessary for the evolution of the one. It is a family task as well as an individual task and it must ultimately be solved at the family level (the group coherence level). As all families know, the most effective working fluid is love. Love seems strange because, the more one gives of it the more one has of it. My personal experience has been that, when applied intentionality is focused through the human heart into daily life processes, a greater rate of internal coherent infrastructure develops and thus the more rapidly does one's consciousness expand.

Let us visualize ideal behavior expressions for our personal selves as well as for our communities and then let us radiate these perfected expressions with every thought, attitude and action of our lives. Every action, no matter how small, influences others and contains the potential to enhance the level of benevolent radiation around us. The quiet radiation of inner joy is as nurturing to human life as food upon the table. As we become more and more our own person, we will find that we can profoundly perceive and enjoy the beauty of the world and lift our environment wherever we go — then, all those lives we touch are enriched by our having been there, as we are enriched by them being there as well.

In her new book, Carla Hannaford gathers a large mass of scientific findings that she explains in an easily comprehensible style to challenge and even shatter the conventional and limited world view of our collective physical reality. In its place she offers a more reflective perspective on life that leads towards greater human capacity and manifested capability. As we can see from the many stories she tells of her own experiences and experiments, Dr. Hannaford has devoted her life to understanding what we humans are and to exploring better ways to relate with one another as parents, teachers, co-workers and citizens of this planet. Her personal stories richly illustrate the experience of a human being open to all the life-learnings available to us. There is great heart in this book as she invites us to live more passionately and more consciously in order to discover and unlock our greatest potential as human beings and human societies.

My primary working hypothesis is that we are all spirits having a physical experience as we ride the "River of Life" together. Our spiritual parents dressed us in these biobodysuits and put us in this playpen that we call a universe to grow in coherence, develop our gifts of intentionality and become what we were intended to become — co-creators with them!

I like to think of this playpen (or classroom if you prefer) as being constructed from a variety of different basic materials, the coarsest substance being electric charge based stuff we currently label as matter and antimatter, and the finest being Spirit.

My current metaphor for the "whole person" may be visualized as a sphere comprised of three concentric zones that are at least weakly coupled to each other as illustrated in the following figure. The outermost zone consists of two concentric layers of very different kinds of substance (electric particles and magnetic information waves) and constitutes the personality self. The middle zone consists of three concentric layers, each constructed from three still different kinds of substance. I call this the **soul self**. The third, and inner zone, I call the high spirit self, the God Self or the source self, whichever label one wishes to use. Thus, the whole person is made up of three very different selves.

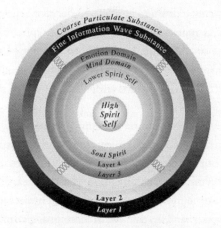

A metaphor for the "whole person"

In the personality, self interfaces with what we call the outer world — the earth, our solar system, etc. via our physical senses. In the adjacent, magnetic information wave material layer, some type of sensory system must exist through which our personality self interfaces with our soul self. Certainly parts of this system include what we call the human unconscious, the "acupuncture" meridian/chakra system, and a part that encompasses all the psychic senses. However, there is undoubtedly a great deal more that we will learn about in this century. Finally, as we all know, although our collective personality selves are all stewards of this planet, they have only a brief temporal existence.

The soul self, consisting of the still higher dimensional domains of emotion (9th dimension), mind (10th dimension) and an aspect of spirit (11th dimension and above), is thought to be the entity that is importantly evolving in this overall process. It is much more durable than the personality self and is the repository of all the key experiences from a long succession of personality selves. When the various outer world classrooms have little more to teach the soul self, it graduates to the high spirit domain and is thought to transfer all of its essential information to the source self which is continuously expanding.

This overall construct looks like a type of two-stage step-down transducer/transformer between what we call God or the source, and one of its inventions, "evolving humans — space/time nature perturbed by the presence of free-will". Consciousness exists at each stage with much more existing at the soul self stage than at the personality self stage. My working hypothesis is that consciousness is a **byproduct**, or emergent property, of spirit entering dense matter. Further, I posit that spirit can only attach to dense matter if new infrastructure has been developed to which it may attach. This appears to be one of the main jobs of living our daily lives — to build infrastructure into the various individual layers of our whole person self.

As this new infrastructure is being continuously built, additional spirit is being continuously transferred from our high spirit self to these various layers of our whole person self. In the process, we come to see concepts, perspectives, opportunities and possibilities that we had never seen before; we become more conscious and thus more capable! It is really important for us to remember, that **we are the product of our process and we are built by our process**. So now we see a larger perspective on both our playing field and the players.

As we become more and more inner self-managed, we increase our coherence at the various levels within self and sustain it via the infrastructure we have built. The more coherence we have developed, the more we can change the properties of materials both inside and outside the human body via our sustained strongly focused intentions. In this way, we can significantly influence our environment and physical reality.

As much as anything, the enterprise of transforming our world takes place in daily actions: in the nursery, at the kitchen table, the school yard, the office water cooler and everywhere else. All of our relationships matter, as do those currencies through which our relationships are built: our thoughts, attitudes, emotions, actions and especially our intentions. In these areas, Dr. Hannaford's book offers much practical advice. She provides many powerful ideas and suggestions for improving the quality of our daily interactions and ways to come to greater coherence of heart and mind. She shows us that humans can indeed attune to the transmission frequencies of others and thus develop a positive interaction force between them, especially through heart-to-heart interactions.

William A. Tiller, Ph.D.
Professor Emeritus, Stanford University
Department of Materials Science and Engineering

Books By Dr. William Tiller

- W. A. Tiller. *Psychoenergetic Science: A Second Copernican-Scale Revolution.* Pavior Publishing, Walnut Creek, CA, 2007.

- W. A. Tiller, W. E. Dibble, Jr. and J. G. Fandel. *Some Science Adventures with Real Magic.* Pavior Publishing, Walnut Creek, CA, 2005.

- W.A. Tiller, W. E. Dibble, Jr. and M. J. Kohane. *Conscious Acts of Creation: The Emergence of a New Physics.* Pavior Publishing, Walnut Creek, CA, 2001.

- Recent essays collected in the White Papers, at www.tillerfoundation.com.

Preface

Though it wasn't always so, whenever I experience chaos in my life
now, I feel a spark of possibility, a chance for the new to emerge, the phoenix
to rise from the ashes.

As we approach the times ahead, we may view our life as wondrous,
tenuous or dangerous depending on our paradigm, our perception of the
world and our power to live deeply and consciously. I now realize we have a
choice; we can choose our interpretations and our responses to events instead
of unconsciously repeating old patterns and referencing old paradigms of
the way things are. Great masters and children in their natural state seem to
yield and flow with life, willing to see everything as a process for growth, and
every situation a doorway to higher consciousness, higher order. I consider
these masters and children my greatest teachers.

These teachers have challenged me to honestly question how I choose
to live my life. Does curiosity drive me to fully explore nature, or a new
technology or a new relationship? Do I become so engrossed in a project
(art, music, poetry, dancing, building, gardening) that only the present
moment seems to exist? Do I experience the thrill of a new idea and take
the risk to do something really *out of the box*, for the excitement of it? Do I
understand that something frightening or challenging in my past has been
the catalyst for the amazing events of my life now?

A world of awareness and enthusiasm, finding meaning and growth
from each moment is the reality that children and masters live in. When we
allow children to fully explore their natural world and watch them without
interfering, we see that everything they do furthers their understanding of
relationships with their own body, other people and all of nature. With
each new experience and challenge, their sensory receptors become more
attuned, their muscles strengthen, their nerves and nerve networks change
and elaborate, and their pleasure and creativity expand.

I feel this masterful child-like nature is the key to a life well lived.
It is not limited to children or synonymous with the natures of the very
young, for sadly, many children have been denied this priceless possession.

Conversely, I know many magnificent people in their golden years that possess such a nature in abundance. To all those who choose to live fully, this world is our natural inheritance and completely accessible. It seems that we manifest not only the joy, but the challenges as well, in order to grow in understanding, explore our mistakes, live passionately and create something richer and deeper, not as victims, but as masters of our lives.

How do we experience daily the wonder and beauty of life in these times that seem so tenuous and out of our control? How do we feel the awe and wonder as the worldwide economy degenerates, as wars destroy thousands of lives, as global warming changes the world's climates? From an understanding of the new sciences, and more clarity about what we truly are, I believe we can come home to ourselves and passionately live the mystery that is life while maintaining a place of peace, enthusiasm, and even joy, thereby promoting a shift of consciousness that is beneficial to all.

In the places where I have traveled and taught, I have sensed a common longing in the people I've met for deeper personal connection and a sense of oneness with all beings. In these times there appears to be an intrinsic awareness surfacing that we are more, much more creative and powerful than our family or societal conditioning would have us believe.

A combination of experiences over the past forty years has forced me to seriously question my inherited beliefs about the world and myself. These include: experiencing the wonder of my daughter Breeze as she took on life; the proliferation of new information in the biological and physical sciences that radically changed my assumptions; my longing for deeper spiritual experience; the astonishing changes I saw working with educational and energy-related modalities; and the synchronicities that have taken me to more than thirty countries and connected me to phenomenal teachers, wisdom seekers and paradigm pioneers.

The current paradigm, still prevalent in much of Western culture perceives living organisms as ordered, consistent atomic conglomerations, taking structural form based upon function and the need to survive and reproduce as separate entities. Discoveries in quantum physics, chaos theory, complexity theory and other sciences are radically altering that paradigm to include the understanding that we are in fact dynamic, vibrational patterns, highly malleable, connected to (entangled with) and both affected by and affecting everything. Research on intentionality claims we condition our environment and in so doing are creators of our reality. To challenge traditional thinking even further, these new areas of science have arisen in the West contemporaneously with the infusion of Eastern thought and practices that emphasize energy more than matter.

This emerging paradigm has many champions in indigenous cultures, mystical philosophies, the noetic sciences and the fields of homeopathy, chiropractic, naturopathy, qigong, healing touch, tai chi, yoga, Hellinger work, and movement/music work, to name a few. All of these powerful people and practices are asking us to become aware of our vibrational, malleable nature, to claim our power again as loving, creative masters of our lives, and fully experience the mystery of life individually as well as collectively. Science is showing us this greater picture of ourselves, but the information is only slowly percolating through our society, and many of us are still operating from outmoded paradigms.

My interest in the new sciences, the neurophysiology behind how we learn and grow, and my spiritual quest has compelled me to explore the connectedness of these various interests. The connections I find have led me to view the world differently, reminding me of who I truly am and how to more readily access joy in my life. There is an understanding of my responsibility for the unfolding journey of my life and an awareness of my desires and how to obtain them. This search, and the connectedness I discovered through this seeking, has brought great value to my existence and deeply challenged me to grow in greater consciousness and creativity. This book is an attempt to explore and share that connection and ways that assist and enrich the life journey we have embarked upon.

Exploring our nature, what we essentially are, is both a profound scientific inquiry and a deeply personal journey for me as a scientist and seeker of meaning in my life. As a scientist, I marvel at the way physicists, biologists, cardiologists, cognitive scientists, sociologists, neuroscientists, academicians and a host of others are drawing closer to the mystical insights of truth seekers who have claimed for thousands of years that we are dynamic, malleable, non-linear beings. Through the rich traditions of inner seekers we have a wealth of testimony that human beings are vastly endowed with the potential to grow in consciousness and benevolence. Our bodies and minds hold an inherent capacity to experience ourselves as energetic fields united with everything, and scientific interest in mapping the physiological patterns of these non-mundane states has grown significantly. So has public interest in them.

According to the New York Times, in 2008 more than two million people viewed a talk given by Dr. Jill Bolte Taylor on the TED (Technology

Entertainment Design) website. She speaks of her own experience of a boundary-less state and great peace while undergoing a stroke in the left hemisphere of her brain. At the time of her stroke, Dr. Taylor was a neuroscientist at Harvard's brain research center and she was able to follow and remember her progression of sensations. She noted that the suppression of left-brain function caused multiple changes in her perception. In her own words, "The energy of my spirit seemed to flow like a great whale gliding through a sea of silent euphoria."[2] Current research suggests that the left hemisphere of the brain is responsible for control of well-established patterns of behavior under familiar conditions, while the right hemisphere is sensitive to a wide range of novel and unexpected stimuli, thus opening us to new perceptions.[3] The boundary-less state that Jill Bolte Taylor experienced is similar to the ideas presented by Plato, indigenous peoples all over the planet, the mystical branches of most religions and what quantum physicists are telling us about the unified information field, and ourselves as vibrational interference patterns with unlimited potential.

Over the past hundred years, scientific understanding has challenged and expanded our view of reality. In light of new evidence I am awed by the mystery and potential that we all have available to us. Quantum physics, as it stepped from beneath the ordered cloak of Newtonian physics and Descartes' dualistic principles, and further, the research on the information field, have opened a whole new perspective of who we are and how we are affected by, and affect our reality.

Honoring Subjective, Empirical Information

"…if the scientific study of consciousness is ever to grow to full maturity…
it will have to incorporate a fully developed and rigorous
methodology of first-person empiricism." —The Dalai Lama[4]

For me to consciously understand the complexities of quantum physics, chaos theory, reciprocal space, entanglement, and myself as a vibrational interference pattern, I had to relate these concepts directly to personal experiences in my life. Western science has placed primary importance on the objective, third person perspective, but I agree with the Dalai Lama that third-person analysis is inadequate to fully explain the first person, subjective experiences of consciousness and life itself. There must be a methodology that accounts not only for what is occurring at the neurological, biochemical, and quantum level, but also within the introspective experience of consciousness itself. Though I will be sharing current scientific findings on the neurobiology and chemical changes within the brain, these alone cannot explain happiness, insight, or creativity. Consequently, this exploration will integrate third-person scientific research with subjective first-person stories to illustrate how these new discoveries can be shown to manifest in reality.

Some of the stories I present are personal, involving family and friends. Fortunately, I enjoy their support to use our collective and individual struggles and epiphanies to illustrate how our lack of knowledge about our authentic nature, as well as our nurturing and miraculous experiences, can affect our lives.

In the next chapter we will take a look at several underlying factors that affect our ability to learn and grow in consciousness. Then we will explore factors that shape our view of reality and how that relates to our true nature as vibrational patterns in this universe of vibrational patterns. In further chapters we will review the fascinating new research about the heart and its effect on our brain. We will examine the underpinnings of quantum physics and chaos theory that point toward our full potential from conception onward. We will then explore the ways that emotions, communication, music and play enhance our lives, and how to incorporate these forces for greater connection and consciousness with ourselves and others. And finally, we will explore the human spirit, and its potential for a dynamic, growth-filled future, full of joy and creativity.

May this book be of some value for remembering the beauty and wonder of your authentic nature, as we explore together current scientific findings that shed light on the mystery of what we truly are. I believe that all of us, from the newly conceived embryo to the wisest elder, are here in this life to learn and grow in consciousness, altruism, joy and love. To that end, I offer my best thinking and research, which I hope will serve children, parents, business people, health professionals, artists, teachers, and all who seek to live a more fulfilling, passionate life.

1

Changing Paradigms

In the last hundred years or so, scientists examining the most fundamental units and processes of the material world discovered a subatomic realm where the processes they sought to understand were not governed by the separateness of things, but rather by the wholeness of existence. If we think about it, the simple observation that the world operates through universal laws, and the success of science in discovering these laws, point to this fundamental wholeness. Some scientists now propose that we and everything else are the physical manifestations of a unified field of information. This is not to say that we aren't also active as agents within this field. We influence the field and each other in myriad ways — overtly with our actions and direct communications, but also in ways we do not see. For instance, our bodies, especially our hearts and brains radiate electromagnetic fields that communicate our true state to others. Beyond this, it also appears that our intentions and thoughts are somehow entangled with the whole.

I begin this book where I hope to end, by emphasizing the choices we have as we play together in the unified field. We can choose to be coherent, we can choose to be conscious and present to life's situations, and we can choose our responses from moment to moment. Human beings are elegantly constituted to learn how to be human through a mirroring process. What we choose to do will be mirrored back to us, whether we wish it or not. Conditions in the field where we play, create, and grow to greater coherence and consciousness are largely up to us through the choices we make.

In Search Of Coherence

Brain research shows that the natural pleasure of play, curiosity, creativity, human interaction, and reflective time, grows our brains, keeps us healthy, and allows us to effectively handle what arises in our lives moment by moment.[5,6] Natural pleasure can't exist, however, without a coherent, unencumbered heart that empowers us to change reality and assist in the establishment of coherence in those with whom we are entangled.

Coherence is a touchstone term throughout this book and the understanding of how I define it is vital to understanding all the rest of the experiences and information I will be presenting.

The dictionary defines coherence as:

> *logical connection, consistency, and congruity,*
> *the act or fact of holding together as with cohesion,*
> *harmonious connection of the parts of a discourse.*[7]

In the broad sense, coherence simply means an ordered, consistent, congruent, harmonious functioning within any system. I also define the term "coherence" as the state or experience of being aligned with one's purpose and consciously connected to everyone and everything in the environment at each moment, with the awareness that every experience is a step toward growth. When in a coherent state, there is a feeling of wholeness, a sense of being fully integrated within the present moment, which can lead to the euphoria and boundary-less state experienced by Jill Bolte Taylor.

I remember my own childhood as full of warm, magical, expansive summer days, flowing into one another with sweet smells and constant wonder as I nestled in the sensuous, fully leafed branches of a quiet tree or played elaborate imaginative games with the neighborhood kids. I was so present in the moment that only the prolonged shrill whistle of my father could bring me back home in the evening. My life was secure in the embrace of a neighborhood community, surrounded by guardians who knew how precious each child was. Even the first few years of school in the early 1950's were an extension of my play, providing a cornucopia of natural pleasures and an abundance of coherence.

I was fortunate to grow up in such a supportive early environment with the essential factors of development coming together to encourage my mental, physical, social, emotional and spiritual growth. Coherence allowed me to be creative, constantly curious, taking risks to explore and experience all of life and live passionately, the most natural state for early learning.

It wasn't until the third grade that multiplication tables and my inability to read made me question my invincibility, diminishing my joy. Then with adolescence came alienation from my father and an eroding sense of trust in my self. I was experiencing the difference between coherence and incoherence, and each shaped my confidence to be creative and authentic, and live and learn with pleasure and passion.

Vibrational Coherence

According to quantum physics, everything we perceive as matter is actually energy existing as vibration; therefore, we are, in essence, vibration existing in a sea of vibration. In relationship to one another, vibrations can be coherent or incoherent. The difference between coherence and incoherence can be understood by comparing the light vibrations emitted from a simple light bulb with those emitted by a laser. A regular 25-watt light bulb gives off photons of light in a very diffuse, scattered, incoherent manner with no set pattern. This incoherent light will illuminate the page we read and give off a little heat but nothing more.

However, if we take that same light bulb and get all the photons vibrating at the same frequency in a unified pattern (coherence), we produce a powerful, efficient laser that can cut through steel. The light is now pure, focused, and far more efficient and powerful than when it was incoherent. In fact, if you could get the photons from a 60-watt light bulb to resonate in harmony with each other, the energy density would be thousands to millions of times higher than that of the surface of the sun.[8] Similarly, personal coherence provides us with focus, power and brilliance in our lives.

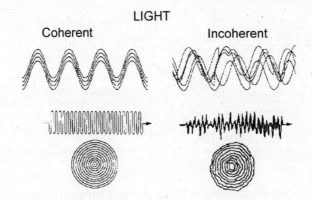

Figure 1.1 Coherent and incoherent light

The ancient Hawaiians believed that all humans are born as bowls of pure coherent light with great power to live harmoniously and creatively. If, however, they interrupt that pure light by putting stones or *pohaku* (incoherent thoughts, words and actions that disconnected their true nature from that of others and their environment) in their bowls, their light becomes diffuse, making their lives less harmonious and powerful. The Hawaiians felt that through reconnection and congruity with their light nature, they could simply turn over their bowls, causing the stones to drop out and bring their lives back to that coherent pure light.

In the 1970's, Fritz-Albert Popp, a German physicist, discovered that all living things emit tiny waves of light that are mainly stored and emitted from the DNA of the cells. He felt these "biophoton emissions" were the driving force coordinating all cellular processes in the body because they could transfer information across the organism almost instantaneously.[9] Gary Schwartz and Kathy Creath at the University of Arizona, using a super-cooled charge-coupled device (CCD) camera that can pick up very faint light, recorded "full images" of light emanating from living organisms.[10] According to the Standard Model of particle physics, photons of light are involved in the interactions between the subatomic particles that make up all matter from atoms on up. The generation of electromagnetic force (attraction and repulsion) between electrons and quarks is mediated by the exchange of a photon, back and forth between these charged particles.

Recently, Popp found that when coherent, biophotons act like a single super-powerful frequency that creates subtle harmonious relationships. This frequency could be the laser or "master tuning fork" of the body that connects us with ourselves and the world around us.[11,12] Light as a mediating force between subatomic particles and Popp's findings on biophotons present an interesting parallel with the Hawaiian belief.

The terms *enlightenment* and *illumination* have taken on new meaning for me, that of my human nature returning to coherence, and reconnecting harmoniously to my pure light form. However, it is all too easy to lose coherence in reaction to circumstances that appear dangerous or disconcerting. The resultant incoherence can shift us out of the balanced state where we can consciously choose our responses into more reactive, survival-oriented, primal brain functioning.

Survival Or Just Plain Stress (Incoherence)

"But however much the neocortex assumes control, the primal brain
will still be primal in the sense of being first in importance.
It is the primal brain which gives us the urge to survive as an individual..."
—Michelle Odent[13]

From a biological perspective, our body's primary function is survival. Our elegant survival mechanisms get set up in utero, so that we can keenly monitor the world around us for danger. We are equipped to sense and respond to every potentially dangerous sound, light change, or movement in our environment, alerting us to actions or people that are unsafe, and orchestrating our lightning-quick reactions. Our survival mechanisms are geared for an acute, fast fight or flight response that determines whether we will survive or die.

In the 1950's, Swiss researcher, Hans Selye discovered that people were exhibiting the survival response in a chronic way to non life-threatening situations. He termed this incoherent state "stress." and claimed it was an aberrant, inefficient use of our survival mechanisms.[14] Though very little if anything in our daily lives is truly life threatening, the body reacts as if it were whenever we become fearful, anxious, confused, frustrated, out of balance, or critical of others or ourselves.[15]

In my workshops and presentations I ask if people experience stress in their lives, and they all answer, "yes." Then I ask about daily stress and they also answer, "yes," as if that were natural. I also ask how many of them have been in a life-threatening situation that day, and they unanimously admit they have not. Chronic stress that produces high levels of adrenaline and cortisol and greatly decreased levels of dopamine (possibly our most important learning chemical) on a regular basis is not natural. Adrenaline increases heart rate and muscle tension and decreases deep breathing, digestive function, eye teaming, and whole brain functioning. Cortisol inhibits the immune system, uptake of protein for cellular growth, learning and memory, and increases the transport of fat molecules that can clog vessels going to the heart and other organs, resulting in heart attacks, high blood pressure and death of organ tissues. Unfortunately, stress has become normal, being stimulated by common life situations, and setting the stage for the emotional, physical and social ailments in our lives, those of our children and of the world in general. For more in depth information on the physiology of stress, please consult Chapter 12 on stress in my book, *Smart Moves, Why Learning Is Not All In Your Head.*[16]

CHRONIC STRESS:

- Inhibits our resilience to life's challenges[17]

- Inhibits our freedom to risk and grow physically, emotionally, spiritually and intellectually

- Contributes to depression, hyperactivity, memory loss, learning difficulties, allergies and diseases like AIDS, cancer, multiple sclerosis, diabetes, Alzheimer's and Parkinson's

- Causes alienating behaviors that isolate us from love, belonging and altruism

- Detracts from our natural drive to explore, learn, and add to the beauty and wonder of our world through pleasure and creative endeavor

Why on earth do we make stress such a center-post of our lives? I honestly ask myself this question often as I fall from coherence into old stress habits. How do we get off track, misusing our elegant survival mechanisms for everything in our daily lives?

Developing Coherent Or Incoherent Patterns

Already in utero, signals from the mother's physical and emotional state set up intricate patterns in the brain that will assure survival. However, they also set an internal pattern of how we will respond to situations in our life and whether we are resilient, easily maintaining coherence or not. If the mother is relaxed, able to coherently handle the conditions in her life, and only reacts with high levels of cortisol and adrenaline during life-threatening situations, the child will mirror that coherence. If the pregnant mother is chronically stressed, the high levels of survival hormones will cross the placental barrier and cause the developing embryo and fetus to also be in survival mode. This early pattern of chronic stress can lead to poor development and incoherent patterns of response.

"Today's child has become the unwilling, unintended victim of overwhelming stress. The stress borne of rapid, bewildering social change and constantly rising expectations."[18] — *David Elkin*

According to the Australian Aborigines, people originally had nothing to fear. They knew they were forever, their souls immortal and that any pain, discomfort, or loss was only temporary and part of their journey toward higher understanding. Now some Aboriginal groups sense that fear and stress have become major energy forces surrounding the planet.[19] In a fear state, we lose our ability to share our passion and essence and model them to our waiting children, family, friends and others.

The ancient Greek philosopher Epictetus reminds us: "Man is troubled not by events themselves but by the views he takes of them." Everything in life is just an event. We have the choice to explore and learn from events with childlike wonder, wide open to the mystery of life, or to fear change and struggle with life through incoherent stress. Our health, wellbeing, and creativity depend upon our cultivating coherent perceptions and responses.

If I am going to really be present and free in every moment to be authentically myself, I have to become consciously coherent, stepping out of the grip of stress into the presence and genuineness of my authentic nature. I must experience each event as a part of my adventure and an opportunity for growth. Profound and easy ways to remain coherent and enjoy the journey are an integral part of the following chapters.

The Powerful Mirror

Another aspect that plays a key role in how we grow in and creativity has to do with how we mirror the world around us. Mirror neurons in specific areas of the brain are responsible for how we learn to be human in our birth culture. Just observing someone else making a physical movement, or expressing an emotion, causes the same areas in our own brains to be activated and mirror that action or emotion.[20,21] Mirror neurons have been a hot topic in science over the past decade. They are thought to be responsible for our empathetic responses that form the roots of social behavior, as well as hand gestures and facial expressions that allow us to develop language and comprehend other people's emotions.

Even before birth, we learn to mirror our mother's responses (joy, stress, musical preferences, movement, etc). Until about fifteen months after birth, our children see themselves as us, mirroring every movement and emotion, reflecting us back to ourselves. At approximately fifteen months, children begin to perceive themselves as separate, and then they mirror us to be like us. When our children are hyperactive or withdrawn, they may be picking up our fear and frustration. When they are joyful, they may be picking up our joy. Parents remain the most significant people in children's lives until ages fourteen or fifteen when they more fully embrace their peer culture.[22] With socialization, they begin to mirror the people they value or are heavily exposed to as models — their friends, teachers, other adults and media personalities.

When we truly understand the importance of mirroring or mimicry, we will consciously remain open, enthusiastic, playful, willing to experience all of our emotions, curious, present in the moment, and experience life as a mystery to be lived rather than a business to be managed. We will set the necessary humane boundaries early to make our children safe, respectful and empathetic toward the earth, toward living organisms, and toward all humans by embracing those qualities in ourselves. And we will model willingness to take risks to learn, and confidence in our ability to direct our journey and create our reality.

Understanding how we develop from conception on has given me a far deeper respect for the sensitivity and wisdom of children in mastering the lessons of their life. As a mother and educator, I suffer under a burden of regret for all I didn't know about how powerfully my actions and ideas were being mirrored by my daughter and my students. It is now clear to me that we must partner with our children and students, rather than act as ultimate authorities. I send up sighs of relief that miraculously, my daughter Breeze and other beautiful young adults have managed to survive the unwitting muddling of their well-intentioned parents and teachers and remain flexible and open to possibilities for themselves. As mirrors in which our children and others in our lives know their wisdom and see themselves, we either reflect their authenticity as beings of wonder and infinite potential — or we do not.

Along with the understanding of mirroring goes the realization that everyone is right where they need to be for the lessons that will grow their souls, and that they know, far better than I, what they need. My challenge is to remain coherent, live my own lessons deeply, see everyone in my life, young and old, as my teacher, and come home to my authentic, passionate self while fully supporting the wisdom of all sentient beings.

"I asked for strength — and was given difficulties to make me strong.
I asked for wisdom — and was given problems to solve.
I asked for prosperity — and was given brain and brawn to work.
I asked for courage — and was given danger to overcome.
I asked for love — and was given troubled people to help.
I asked for favors — and was given opportunities.
I received nothing I wanted — I received everything I needed."
— Analects of Confucius

Consciousness

Being conscious of whether we are coherent or incoherent is an important step toward becoming more authentic. We cannot move toward coherence until we become aware of our incoherence. At this point in time, however, there is no scientific consensus about what consciousness is, where it resides, or how it operates. Because it appears to be so elusive and can't be directly studied, consciousness is considered the Holy Grail of scientific research today.

Antti Revonsuo, at the University of Turku, Finland, points out some reasons why it is so hard to study consciousness. Current research technology, such as functional Magnetic Resonance Imaging (fMRI) generates images too slowly to capture the lightning-quick changes in the electrical properties of thousands or even millions of neurons associated with consciousness. Also, fMRI and Positron Emission Tomography (PET scans) check changes in blood flow rather than the neural activity directly involved in conscious thought. And scientists researching this area are dealing with experimental conditions rather than immediate functional consciousness.[23]

Nonetheless, a panel of researchers in a worldwide study on consciousness, using both objective and subjective research and theories, put together a definition for consciousness that seems to cover part of its mystery:

"Consciousness itself is a psychological phenomenon, in that it is the direct experience by the individual of his or her own being. Consciousness enables the individual to reflect upon and interpret experience (including the experience of personal cognition), to construct a sense of self, and to predict and deliberate upon the future. Through these psychological processes, the individual is empowered to pose fundamental ontological and metaphysical questions about reality and individual existence, and potentially construct a sense of meaning and purpose in relation to them. Such construction allows the individual to place a value upon his or her life and the life of others, an activity which is augmented by the ability of consciousness to respond reflectively to the individual's personal world of emotions and feelings, and to conceptualize it in terms of positive or negative effect."[24]

From this statement, it appears that consciousness arises from the awareness of our physical bodily experiences when we encounter environmental information and manmade symbols that we then analyze and act upon. However, it seems that higher consciousness alone is not what sets us apart from other animals and allows us to come to coherence.[25]

Underlying and closely tied to the conscious mind is the subconscious, the intuitive mind that plays a crucial role in many of the mental faculties we prize as uniquely human, including creativity, memory, learning and even language. Our subconscious is not an unthinking autopilot that needs to be subjugated by rationality, but purposeful, active and an independent guide to our actions and emotional coherence.[26] It constantly monitors our internal and external environment so that when a sensation becomes important enough, the subconscious awakens and engages the conscious mind and we become aware of what the subconscious considers important. When required to make difficult decisions based on hard-to-assess information, people are happier with their decisions when acting on intuition rather than rationally thinking through their choices. In social interactions, subconscious processing appears to allow us to integrate complex information in a more holistic, non-judgmental way than the rational conscious mind could. The subconscious appears to also be our source of inspiration and creativity.[27]

More than ever it is time to come home to our child-like nature, opening up new dimensions of ourselves, practicing coherence and modeling it for those around us as we consciously gain an understanding of our vast creative potential and live deeply life's mystery, for the sake of all humanity and this precious planet we share.

Our experiences, both conscious and subconscious, set the groundwork for how we shape our reality and live our lives, AND, we have the choice and dynamic ability, as continually developing individuals, to change our reality. In the next chapter we will explore this idea in depth. We are all woven from the same fabric with the same need to return to coherence. It seems to me that to become more coherent — consciously and subconsciously — is the greatest gift anyone can give to the world; it assures increased connection, pleasure, integrity, creativity, understanding, and compassion.

2

Shaping Reality

*"The only reason we're different is because of different experiences.
These create the software of our souls."*[28] —*Deepak Chopra*

We can live our whole lives unaware of our conditioning and self-imposed patterns that limit our growth. Conceding our aspirations and goals to impossibility because "that's the way things are" or the "way I am" confines us within preconceived ideas of what's possible for us and for our children. Yet each of us begins life open to all the possibilities for growth and development. We start out fully equipped and open to a world of vibrations and the sensations we receive from them. When we realize that we are, in large part, constructing our own reality through our experiences, our interpretations, and our belief systems, we gain some distance from our ideas and the neutrality to assess them. In this chapter we'll look at the many factors that shape us, and shape our views of reality. It starts at the very beginning.

Beginnings

Childhood took on new meaning as I re-experienced it as a mother to my daughter Breeze. She was conceived in a beautiful Colorado mountain meadow, brilliant with August columbine, cinquefoil, rockrose, lupine, and Indian paintbrush. Jim and I, lost in the fresh mountain air, the beauty of the majestic mountainside and each other, had joyously celebrated our union. It was a perfectly coherent way to honor a new soul into existence.

However, Breeze was an "accident," rekindling Jim's fears of having to give up his two daughters when his first marriage failed. His wounding was deep and he hadn't wanted another child that he might have to give up too. I, on the other hand, loved and trusted him deeply, and I wanted this baby. In the 1960's, I gave up a baby for adoption, one of the hardest decisions I had ever made. Though Jim and I were experiencing different emotions, we loved each other and chose to raise this child in a committed, married relationship.

Besides the joy and connection we felt, as my pregnancy progressed, some of the fears and uncertainties reemerged, leading to incoherent days with troubled emotions. Neither of us had any idea that our past individual wounds would be affecting our unborn child who was already developing survival patterns that she would draw upon throughout her life.

From the moment she was born, on the eclipse of the full moon, my image of her was that of a red balloon, explorer of the universe, my guide to worlds forgotten or not yet experienced. Breeze, this miracle that has so blessed my life, was far more than she initially appeared to be. Born to us, was this exquisite being, so small, and so sensitively aware. In her beautiful perfection, she was like an alien exploring a new planet, alert and fascinated by everything.

I observed in awe as she explored new sounds, different and crisper than the sounds of her former watery environment. She listened intently to our voices, those of the dogs and cats who shared her home, the birds of summer who gathered in the trees outside the house, the new voices of friends and Grandma, the cacophony of traffic, sirens, airplanes, and children playing next door.

She welcomed the rich, vibrant array of smells, carried through her now airy environment, from fresh garden flowers, next door's dinner, rain, furry animals exploring close to her nose, and the external scent of joy, frustration and love. She remembered my smell as she nursed on milk, spiced with my recent meal, while we rocked in the big rocking chair, undisturbed by time, space or other beings.

Her undeveloped eyes perceived brilliant new light patterns, scattered through the vaporous prism of morning dew to present her with light in all its visible and invisible forms. She elegantly sensed the light radiating from objects and people that swam as vibrational waves across her visual field, unmodified by conditioning.

Her now unbounded limbs experienced space and the touch of admirers who stroked and prodded her hands, face and feet, welcoming her to the outside world. She received a good dose of movement and touch during family baths and jostling in the soft fabric carrier that held her close to my heart.

The shaping of her reality came from a combination of nature (genetics) and nurture (experience), though I am beginning to believe that nurture is more profound and can override genetics. All these experiences she absorbed with her highly sensitive system, perfectly designed to take in everything and learn at warp speed. She was acutely aware of sensations (vibrations) that I had long ignored or forgotten to be aware of.

The awareness of vibrations and the shaping of our reality actually begins, not with birth, but with conception. A wide range of experiences bombards the developing embryo and fetus in a fairly random, chaotic manner. However, as the unborn child cues into (amplifies) the mother's patterns, the pressure of the mother's body, the mother's heartbeat, and the chemicals delivered from the mother, the child's perceptual world begins to take on some structure and order.

Sentient Life in the Womb

"There is no period of parenthood with a more direct and formative effect on the child's developing brain than the nine months of pregnancy leading to the birth of a full term baby"— Marian Diamond [29]

Hundreds of studies show the vulnerability of the unborn child, its sensitivity, impressionability and ability to relate to the mother's emotional state.[30,31,32] According to psychologist Wendy Ann McCarty, we are sentient beings, having a sense of self prior to, during and after our human life, and we perceive, communicate and learn from the moment we are conceived. Her research shows that embryos and fetuses are aware of their parents' and other people's thoughts, feelings and intentions and their own needs to be wanted, safe, nourished, included, heard and connected with. Through these womb experiences, we form adaptive strategies that shape our perception of the world and our view of reality.[33]

I am only now beginning to understand how deeply everything I felt as an uncertain, newly married, pregnant professional woman influenced Breeze in those nine months that we shared my body. Every thought and action gave rise to hormones and other biochemicals that created a pleasurable or an incoherent fetal environment for Breeze. She was influenced by my joy, my stress, loud sounds, movement, my heartbeat and electro-magnetic fields. Her entire world, the way she now perceives it and the way she adjusts to it, was shaped, to some degree, by what happened in the womb.[34,35]

A mother's attitude appears to have the single greatest effect on how an infant will turn out.[36,37] Breeze represented a second chance for me to fully embrace being a parent, to somehow make up for the child I gave up for adoption, and I was very grateful for this new life developing in mine. For many women, an unexpected pregnancy carries less positive feelings, and often, major stress. Any conflict, ambivalence, or rejection the mother feels toward her unborn child can be reflected in the fetus's increased activity (hyperactivity) and in continuing difficulties throughout his or her life.[38,39,40] In chronically anxious mothers-to-be, the levels of hyperactivity in the fetus can be 10 times that of fetuses in relaxed mothers.[41]

Dr. Lester W. Sontag's studies during WWII were the first to make us aware of the effects of maternal anxiety on the fetus. Babies whose mothers were highly stressed during pregnancy later exhibited reduced resistance to disease, sleep and feeding disorders, and in extreme cases, as much as 60% delays in their normal development.[42,43,44,45,46]

In many cultures worldwide, conception and pregnancy has been a sacred time to embrace the miracle of new life, to welcome a valued sentient being. It is a time of joy and discovery. In Bali, when a woman learns she is pregnant, she immediately starts telling her unborn child about the wonders of the world it is about to enter, and about the family that will embrace it. She consults with the village healer to help her enter into a dialogue with her unborn child in order to discover its identity and purpose in life. The whole family and village can then best assist the incarnating soul to fulfill its destiny. Her communication and empathy with the unborn child nurtures and protects the embryo and fetus.[47] During my time in Bali, I never saw a hyperactive or stressed out Balinese child.

In Australian Aboriginal societies, the child appears in the father's dream before conception and the mother joyfully becomes a temporary haven for this special being with its own pre-existing spiritual identity. Again, they value and nurture the unique identity and purpose of this new life.[48] These cultures have lived in a way maximally conducive to valued, loved, healthy, bright, joyful children.

The strength and quality of the fundamental cord of love spun between mother and child determines a person's emerging tapestry of relationships: person-to-person, person to society, person to the environment, and ultimately the global connection. It all starts in the womb.

The Outside World

After a child is born, her world starts to be shaped by an array of new experiences. Her sense of reality is powerfully influenced by the vividness of her life. Intense, extended, focused experiences can actually alter her neural networks and brain activity.[49] These experiences further structure her physical, mental, emotional and spiritual perceptions that will determine how she will respond to the world, and which experiences she will be attracted to.[50] As most parents do, Jim and I subjected Breeze to experiences we felt would make her happy, brilliant, secure, and able to fit into society. As Breeze voraciously took in all the sensations of her world, we were unconsciously shaping which ones she would make a part of her reality. Our combined passion for biology, nature, music, dance, exploring different cultures, and our love of teaching are all an integrated part of her reality. The same shaping of reality continues to occur throughout a person's lifetime.

Though we are all humans on this same home planet, we are each so unique. Even identical twins have differences due mainly to different experiences. My mother, born in 1905, was raised in a family of eight, on a farm with no electricity, phone or motorized vehicles until later. She experienced vast changes in her life, giving her a reality very different from mine as a post-war baby boomer, or Breeze's as a child of the 70's and 80's.

Conditioning Our Reality

"There is no clear boundary between the self and society, and this may be particularly true at the automatic level. Growing up in a culture where some people are valued more than others is likely to permeate our private orientations, no matter how discomforting the fact." —Laurie A. Rudman[51]

Unborn humans start with full awareness, sensitivity, and connection with all potentiality. As adults, our dogma, belief systems, habits, and life experiences narrow our connections with the full potential of our true nature, and we may have a hard time seeing beyond our perceived material world or our learned judgments.

For an understanding of how this narrowing occurs, it only takes looking at our own beliefs, biases, habits, language and physiology. Life experiences, as intangible as culture, can reorganize our neural pathways, change the priority of brain functions and determine how we interpret what we see with regards to cultural convention.[52] The development of preferred moral/ethical values in children is a central task for a society that hopes to maintain its specific identity in a world of diversity.[53,54] Then, in order to bolster our acquired values and beliefs, we tend to join with others who share them, and seek converts. Many of our implicit (subconscious) associations regarding people different from ourselves in race, religion, economic status, and age, form as mirrors of our environment before we are old enough to think rationally.[55] Fortunately we are malleable and these biases can change in a conscious, coherent, egalitarian environment.[56]

Below is a list of experiences that help determine our reality. For each item, you might want to list how it has developed your belief system, habits, use of language, and your physiology and how it might have limited your choices:

- Being male or female
- Place in family of origin
- Main caregivers
- Race
- Specific family beliefs
- Location (urban/rural)
- Societal beliefs
- Country of birth
- Religion or spiritual beliefs
- Early education
- Childhood labels such as: brilliant, dumb, gifted, handicapped, fat, skinny, etc.
- Advanced education
- Cultural involvements (art, music, dance, sports, etc.)
- Media (TV, radio, newspapers, magazines, movies
- Profession
- Status in profession
- Unemployment
- Illness
- Current economic status
- Marital status
- Adult labels such as: yuppie, senior citizen, new-age, red neck, etc.
- Current age
- Travel or contact with other cultures

All of these factors and many more have formulated how we perceive our world and ourselves. We tend to gravitate toward experiences that fit our cultural belief system because they feel comfortable and familiar. This reality helps us interpret what is true, in a particular time and place, among a particular people, and in general what is considered right and wrong. I was born the eldest female at the end of WWII into a white Protestant home. My parents were older and had both been raised on farms in Iowa, a military man and a home-economics teacher. From this background, there was a fairly clear understanding of how I should be trained to fit into the world.

If we become inflexible, closed to any other reality, we are at risk of letting our enculturated reality become the bars on a prison window minimizing our growth. But if we remain open, there may be a time when, through wisdom, curiosity and a thirst for understanding, our enculturated reality becomes the platform from which we leap, in order to come home to our true selves and a far broader understanding of humanity.[57]

In Figure 2.1, the embryo begins as all potentiality. As the pregnancy progresses, the mother is the environment, and factors that affect the mother also affect the embryo and fetus. Birth, itself, plays a huge part in conditioning our reality, and then all the influences from family, culture, and society have a profound effect as well.

Constructing Our Visual Reality

The development of vision gives us a portal of understanding into how our reality gains structure. Visually constructing the material world, as our culture defines it, with full acuity, color vision, and binocularity takes over a year after birth to develop fully, and it's built in association with all the other senses. Only by combining information from all the sensations of our internal and external environment can we truly gain an overall unitary image of our surroundings and ourselves.[58] The newborn is taking in light as a pure waveform, probably experiencing her parents, and the world, as sensations of full spectrum radiant light and pulses of vibration devoid of structure.

We then begin to condition a baby's vision with solid objects from our material reality. The baby's visual system is in large part set up by bodily kinesthetic information gained from touch and movement in space. Babies only begin to perceive components of their world as "objects" in those that move as a coherent unit (i.e. Mom), due either to real motion of the object relative to the background or to the motion of the infant.[59] The ability to study stationary visual scenes doesn't occur until between three and six months.

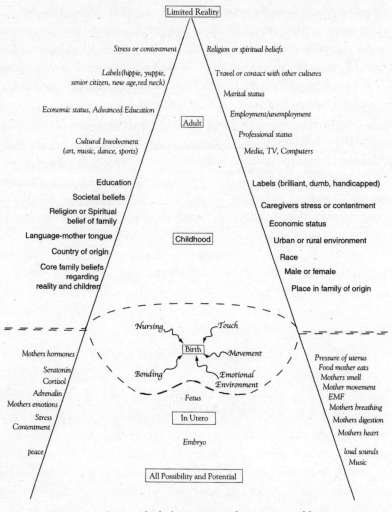

Figure 2.1 Pyramid of what impacts, determines and limits our reality from conception to death

The vestibular system that controls how the eyes will move is tied directly to the ears and the core muscles of the trunk, just below the navel, and supports the child's movement into various positions. This system makes the child able to explore her environment, first by following sounds and later through the reflexes of hand/eye connection. This same system gives her a sense of object, space and density in regards to gravity.[60] All the various touch receptors, especially in her hands and lips, give her the sensations that shape how objects will become stored in visual memory. With a huge part of the sensory and motor cortices in the brain involved with the hand, the hand shapes our cognitive, emotional, linguistic and psychological development. Early childhood experiences using the hand to reach, grasp, and feel objects determine how the baby's brain will develop and how it will visually perceive her world.[61]

Through these physical/sensory experiences we unconsciously orchestrate our vision to focus and organize light in a particular way, according to our belief in the physical world. Only 4% of vision comes as light through the eye. The other 96% is manufactured in the brain as it associates the light with all the senses, especially sound, touch and movement, producing an internal image. These internal images, along with the associated emotions, determine our perception of the world. In adults, it is estimated that more than one half of the brain deals just with processing visual information from the association of light with our emotions and senses. This process takes 1/5 of a second, thus we don't actually get visual reality first hand instantly, but rather with a delay, as it is filtered through our perceptual lenses of emotion.[62,63,64]

Slater demonstrated the illusion of vision in a 1930's experiment with upside-down glasses. Experimental subjects were asked to continually wear glasses that turned their vision upside-down and backwards. It took about two weeks to get past tripping over objects in their environment, until their brains finally made the internal structural change, so they saw things "right side up." What they saw then appeared normal until they took the glasses off, and again, it took some time for their brains to right the image.[65]

"We are led to believe a lie when we see with our eyes." —William Blake

Many people in Eastern cultures naturally see vibrations that are emitted from other people as radiant light — called auras. These people have maintained their receptive sensitivity to pure light vibrations, beyond the learned visual reality of our Western culture. We do perceive pure light vibrations in the radiant light of the sun, moon and a rainbow, which gives us a true window into reality and vibration. These Eastern cultures show us the potential is there if we can get past seeing what we expect to see based on our conditioned reality.

How Language Shapes Reality

The language we learn as children actually changes the structure of the brain and how we will structure our reality. It was discovered that the Japanese brain is quite different from Western brains in where and how linguistic information is processed. The Japanese traditionally have a need to be immersed in natural sounds, such as bird and insect songs, animal cries, snow thudding off tree branches, ocean waves, and the wind in the forest. Their traditional lifestyle, including their language, is based on a deep appreciation and harmony with nature and is, therefore, more reliant on the right brain hemisphere than in Western societies, which rely more on the left hemisphere.[66,67] The implication here is that the very structure of the brain is influenced by our actual experiences of the world.[68]

Newborns and young babies have the ability to distinguish the sounds of all languages on the earth. But over time, the baby adopts the sounds it hears most frequently. A Japanese baby born in Japan will be unable to distinguish between L and R when she begins to speak at about 9 months of age, and throughout her life.[69] However, if that Japanese baby were born in Hawaii and living in the midst of non-Japanese-speaking people she would be able to distinguish between L and R and easily say "R" throughout her life. Thus, language is more a matter of experience than a physical trait. Humans are dependent on what they hear to develop normal vocalization.[70]

Interpreting Experience

Our reality becomes so enculturated and structured that we tend to base every new experience on past experiences. By holding onto that conditioning, we tend to attract the same kind of experiences because they are familiar and predictable, even if we would prefer to have a different reality. In so doing we further narrow the field of understanding and possibilities for ourselves.

> *"Your beliefs become your thoughts*
> *Your thoughts become your words*
> *Your words become your actions*
> *Your actions become your habits*
> *Your habits become your values*
> *Your values become your destiny"*
> —*Mahatma Gandhi*

Throughout life the association areas of the brain that bring together the sensory information to give us our reality are in a dynamic state of equilibrium, constantly changing in response to our changing environment and sensory input.[71] Our brains assemble this information to endow each of us with a unique and irreproducible existence and an internal and external map of who we are.[72]

Our explicit, conscious mind constitutes only a small part of how we put our world together. It is slow, sequential, rational, deliberate, and requires effort to employ. Our behind-the-scenes intuitive, subconscious mind, dominates the gathering of sensory information, editing it and sending on in small bits to the conscious brain to experience, based on what has meaning in consciousness.[73] The subconscious is fast, automatic, effortless, associative, more connected to all potential, whole, implicit (not available to introspection), and often emotionally charged. It only takes six seconds for us to assess another person's warmth and energy. Everything is evaluated as safe/good or not-safe/bad within a quarter of a second. Our neural pathways run from our eyes to the rapid response emotional control areas, bypassing the thinking part of the brain, thus we feel before we analyze. Our gut feelings predict future outcomes better than our rational brain, but sometimes we can develop intuitive fears that don't match up with reality and need to be checked against the facts with mindfulness.[74]

How transient is our reality? We might assume that we know what and where our body is, but we're discovering that our sense of the body is also constructed. Research shows that the brain creates a neural picture or neuro-matrix of our body not only from sensory signals from the body, but also from its own neural pattern that represents the body in its intact state. This pattern inscribes the psyche with a sense of the body's configuration and borders, our body image and sense of self that persists even after the removal of a body part.[75] Researchers are playing with this ephemeral sense of self with video cameras that can induce an out-of-body sensation. One experiment focused two cameras on the back of a volunteer. A headset displayed the images from the left camera on the left eye and the right camera on the right eye. When an experimenter stroked another subject's back within view of the volunteer, while simultaneously stroking the volunteer's back just below the cameras view, the subject reported being overcome with the sensation that he was not in his own body, but sitting where the cameras were, experiencing himself as "out of body".[76]

"What you think you understand is that which
you must challenge first."[77] —Jay Bremyer

Storage Of Our Reality And Human Malleability

Just how our experiences become memory, as a basis for our reality, is still not fully understood. Memory is part of the 99.99% of us that is below the level of consciousness.[78] Our current scientific scenario of how memory occurs states that with all the incoming information (over forty thousand bits per second), our built-in "reality filters" (the reticular activating system in the brain stem, and the thalamus) monitor the strength and nature of the sensory impulses and, in just milliseconds, uses our current reality to determine each input's degree of importance.[79,80,81]

Further sifting occurs in the basal ganglion and amygdala (the spam filters that block physically and emotionally unimportant information) and the prefrontal cortex (the rationalizing, thinking area) that provides details about the relevance of information to our immediate goals and beliefs and then discards it, or sends it on to the hippocampus.[82] The hippocampus, with large populations of neurons acting in concert, monitors abstract, general information, or more selective features of the stimuli.[83] The hippocampus consults the "emotional references" in the amygdala to determine if the information is worth long-term storage in the neocortex of the brain.[84]

The choice in the hippocampus to cement a connection (to remember it) comes only after the importance of the information has been demonstrated by a strong or repeated nerve firing over a period of time. Learning to say one's name, learning to play a musical instrument, learning to drive a car and other learned abilities all require strong, repeated nerve firings over a period of time to anchor the information.

In order to produce the proteins to make new nerve networks, or strengthen appropriate nerve networks within the neocortex, or actually grow new nerve cells, the specific gene on the DNA that encodes the proteins must be unwound and open to map the code onto RNA. This process requires enzymes called histones acetyltransferases (HATs) to attach sufficient numbers of acetyl groups to histones, thereby opening the DNA, allowing the appropriate genes to be available for easy decoding for a specific needed protein.[85] Short-term memory changes to long-term memory through the production of new nerves, or strengthening of nerve connections, or the increase in nerve networks. If the input to the neurons is weak or inconsistent, the nerve nets within the neocortex will dissolve. New information (strong consistent firing of neurons) can cause the nerve networks in the neocortex to reform, thus establishing a new memory.[86]

What we think about, or physically do on a frequent basis, determines our memory. It is generally agreed that it only takes ten years of motivated, consistent action and thought to master any field and become an expert.[87] If we don't use specific nerve nets for a long time, we lose them (hence the popular expression, *use it or lose it*).

Flow Chart On How Memory Might Develop

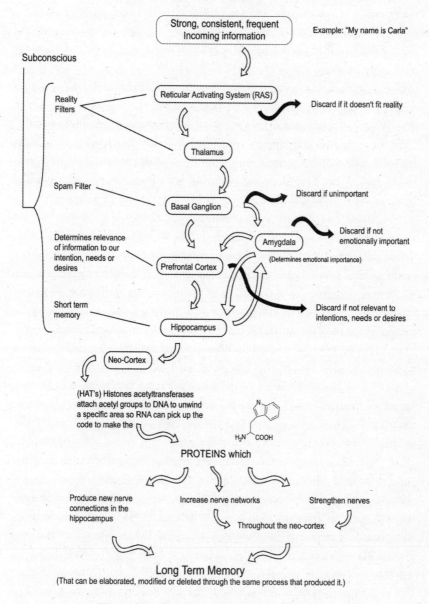

Figure 2.2 *Flow chart on memory development*

Interestingly, both context and time are important factors in memory. Our ability to discern connections among pieces of information encountered in new or novel situations with what we already know is called relational memory and is an important key to flexible decision making and creative insight. The sleeping brain searches for relationships in remembered information as a way to deal with new information and situations. Relational memory does not require conscious thought, but rather time to percolate among the brain's many memory circuits.[88] Thus sleep is very important for anchoring memory.

In the schools I visited in mainland China, all the students (from pre-school through high school) would take a nap in the middle of the school day. What a brilliant idea to help anchor information in the memory circuits. I am constantly picking up new bits of information, but it takes some time for me to put them in context with what I know, and practically apply them to my reality. My best ideas and flashes of insight and inspiration typically occur at about 4:00AM after a good night's sleep. Now I know why.

Stress has a great impact on memory formation. When we are stressed, the acetyl groups that open the DNA are replaced by methyl groups. These cause the DNA to close up and inhibit the expression (decoding) of genes so that proteins are not produced and nerve nets are decreased and weakened. Epigenetics is the study of environmental influences (whether nurturing or stressful) on the production of histones, and whether acetyl or methyl groups will act on the DNA and affect gene expression and ultimately brain activity. We have known for a long time that stress decreases memory significantly. Increased methyl groups on the DNA decrease the production of BDNF — Brain Derived Neurotrophic Factor (nerve growth factor). Increased methyl groups appear to contribute to depression, and are also associated with drug addiction, and are detected in children and adults who are less resilient to stressful events in their life.[89]

The brain monitors old memories looking for a match to the present conditions and whether survival tactics will be required. Our emotional memories of past experiences color our perception and determine how we will react or respond to current situations.[90] In a new relationship, for instance, our new friend may do something that triggers a memory of a previous relationship. Our amygdala will match the old relationship, whether positive or negative, to our new friend and lead us to assume this relationship will be the same. If the old relationship was painful or frustrating, the vigilant amygdala will set in motion our survival reaction causing us to react in a protective way, though the action of the new friend may and probably does have a completely different context.

Looking at my own life, I've been able to see that my difficulties with men came from emotional memories dating back to the abandonment I felt with my father. Faced with a new male relationship, my amygdala would alert me to watch for similar situations or actions. Sure enough, I would find something and could easily make these men into the image of my father through my projections. In so doing, I would totally miss their true selves and the opportunity for a deep, healthy relationship. It's amazing how easily projections from the past shape relationships in the present. No wonder misunderstandings occur. In a study, Susan Anderson, from New York University found that these transference responses not only affect the individual experiencing them, but also alter the behavior of the person who is the target of the transference. Responding from old patterns makes it difficult to truly see and understand another person, and to also be authentically one's self in all situations.

Human Malleability   *Plasticity*

Bad memories or losing one's memory can affect how we structure our reality, keeping us in fear and unable to learn and grow. A group of researchers at the Massachusetts Institute of Technology discovered they could wipe out the bad memories, decrease depression and reinvigorate genetic expression for increased memory. They found that enriched environments with lots of nurturing and integrated movement like walking, swimming, dancing, Brain Gym®, tai chi, yoga, qigong and aerobic activities, increased the acetyl groups on histones, which unmasked the fearful memories and made new connections between healthy neurons.[91]

Memory can be very malleable, causing networks to dissolve, strengthen, or change with new input. It appears that memory occurs throughout the brain, not just in the areas mentioned before. Michael Merzenich at the University of California, while studying memory in the brains of monkeys, found that movement of the hand involved different areas of the brain in different monkeys. He suggested that brain sites for specific fingers are not hardwired to particular neurons but rather exist as a fluid pattern of relationships. And further, that if he damaged or destroyed a finger, electrical activity from an adjacent area would migrate to the area as the monkey learned to compensate with the other fingers.[92]

Karl Lashley, working with rats in the 1940's, in an effort to determine the physical parameters of memory, systematically destroyed parts of their brains to see whether behaviors they had previously learned would be lost when specific parts of the brain were destroyed. He found that the rats could still remember what they had previously learned and react appropriately. He concluded that though certain limited regions of the nervous system may be essential for retention, learning and retrieval, memory is distributed throughout the body/mind system, much like a hologram.[93,94]

The following quotation, written by Karl Lashley in 1950 sums up his years' long search for physical memory traces:

"This series of experiments has yielded a good bit of information about what and where the memory trace is not. It has discovered nothing directly of the real nature of the memory trace. I sometimes feel, in reviewing the evidence of the localization of the memory trace, that the necessary conclusion is that learning is just not possible. It is difficult to conceive of a mechanism that can satisfy the conditions set for it. Nevertheless, in spite of such evidence against it, learning sometimes does occur."[95]

Memories As Holograms

The hologram, invented by Dennis Gabor in 1947 records the vibrational interference patterns of an object subjected to focused light. In making a hologram, a single laser beam is sent through a beam splitter, which creates two beams. One of the beams becomes the reference beam and is deflected by a mirror through a diffusing lens, which diffuses its rays, as it falls upon an unexposed photographic plate. The second beam is also sent through a diffusing lens to illuminate the object being photographed. The light from this beam, "disturbed" by the object, falls upon the photographic plate. These two beams intersect forming an interference pattern that is recorded on the photographic plate as a hologram. You can then shine a laser (pure beam of light), now a "reconstruction beam," through the hologram and get the whole image projected as a three dimensional object.

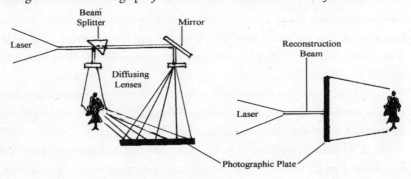

Figure 2.3 Procedure for producing a hologram

You can even walk around some projected images and see them from below and above as if they were real three-dimensional objects.[96] The most familiar depictions of holograms are in the Star Wars films where various characters use this technology to transmit information across long distances.

Each piece of the hologram contains the whole, thus, even when cut into very fine pieces, a single piece when exposed to a laser (reconstruction beam) will recreate the entire object. This principle is analogous to the living cells in our body (except red blood cells, sperm and eggs) that contain the entire DNA code necessary to clone a new us — a hologram of us.

Memories as holograms make sense. When a stimulus (a situation, word, smell, etc.) triggers a memory by focusing a "laser beam" or "reconstruction beam" of attention on our stored hologram, a complete three-dimensional memory with all its aspects is projected on our consciousness.[97] Frank Lake, a 1980's researcher studying trauma in utero, claims that memories from our developmental time in the womb act as holographic templates to orchestrate our perception of reality.[98]

Candace Pert, a molecular biologist, sees the whole body as a chemical hologram, with information molecules being produced and binding to receptor sites on every cell. These information molecules (a variety of transmitters, peptides, hormones, factors and protein ligands) could be the triggers that anchor information in the body as memory, or "reconstruction beams," retrieving memories that will determine our emotions and actions in accordance with the current experiences of our life.[99]

Massage therapists often report the activation of memories as they massage certain areas of a client's body. I have personally experienced this phenomenon. A friend told me that the calf muscle (the gastrocnemius) had to do with "mother issues" according to Applied Kinesiology. Over a year later, a body worker was working on my calf muscle to get it to relax when suddenly I was overwhelmed with memories of my mother who had passed away six months earlier.

We are also discovering an intricate memory in the heart, which has receptor sites for virtually all the neuropeptides.[100] Gary Schwartz calls this memory in the heart, "Systemic Memory."[101] Paul Pearsall, a psychiatrist working with heart transplant patients, wrote about this memory in his book "The Heart's Code." Following heart transplants, new heart recipients report new likes and dislikes of a variety of things, from use of words to food and clothing. They and their cardiologists also noticed personality changes with recipients taking on some of the behaviors, and cravings of the people whose hearts they had received.[102]

Vibrational Immediacy Versus Static Patterns

Because of their dynamic activity, the holographic properties of vibrational interference patterns make them perfect pattern organizers of the complex structures within the body, and assure there is always a biochemical and vibrational potential for change and growth.[103] Focusing our attention and intention on coherence assists us to restructure our memories and organize or reorganize the complex structures within our body.

We memorize the world in context with what we already know. Children experience life with their whole beings and all their senses, as a gestalt. So they build a world whole to which they add all their new findings. When our desire for them is to fit in, to feel a part of our world, the wholeness is often lost. When we begin to take their world of wholeness, and differentiate for them the dualities of what we consider right and wrong, good and evil, us and them, we limit the expansive world they could bring to us if we open to their knowing instead of limiting it to our reality. Naming anything affects the field in which our experiences occur. When we name something, for instance, "attention deficit disorder," or "stupid," or "evil" it will be experienced as such.[104] Children shut down their sensitivity and only take in what will provide them approval. We as humans want to be loved, accepted, and acknowledged, therefore, approval becomes the strongest anchor of behavior. Pressures are great in our society to fit in. It doesn't take much to start limiting the possibilities and block out much of the vibrational field available.

In Plato's *Republic*, he says our senses allow us to see only the shadows of ourselves projected as firelight on the cave wall, thus only seeing a reflection. But the reflected light/shadows inhibit us from seeing the actual being, our true self, our full energetic, vibrational potential.

"You must follow the reflected light until you have found the primary light, that which is so real that you can touch it." —Plato

Until we recognize that the outer world and the inner world reflect each other, and that the line between may be passed in gentleness, acceptance, and care."[105] *—Jay Bremyer*

We can fully nurture ourselves and the precious world around us by dropping the masks we wear, the images we have of ourselves to fit in, to do what our family, religion, society and culture says is good and right, and our ideas of ourselves as limited beings. <u>By using the body through integrated movement, setting strong intentions, and quiet meditative time, research is showing that we have the power to change our conditioning and broaden our perceptions/perspective.</u> Being aware that whatever happens in this moment has never happened before and will never happen again in the same way, I am again able to see the world through "child eyes" as a great adventure. It also helps to remember that I have been responsible for drawing my experiences to me for learning and growth. Even though our previous experiences have structured our realty to a certain extent, we have a vast reservoir of potential to change and re-create ourselves.

It may be time to go back to that child-like state, before the awareness of distinction, and separation, and reestablish consciousness without content, moving past limited vision to insight or inner sight from the heart.[106] Stepping out of our boxes, back into our inherently open nature may be the only way to come home to who we truly are, curious and passionately learning each moment, and connected through altruism to all that is.

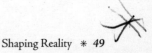

3

VIP – Our True Identity

The brain and nervous system may only be the amplifiers of our perception, consciousness and ultimately our reality, rather than the creators.[107] Many scientists are exploring beyond three-dimensional space/time, and showing us that we are much more than what we can see, touch, taste, smell and hear. We are vibrations of energy, they say, receiving and experiencing our world through sense receptors that filter the vast sea of available vibrations to present us with the reality our family and culture has prepared us to receive. Quantum physicists call this our "attractor basin," information we are attracted to because it has been such a part of our reality, even prior to birth. One of the greatest attributes of being human is that we can and will change our minds in the face of new experiences and information if we are truly open, curious and passionate about a world full of possibilities.

Shattering the Atom

When I was teaching college biology I always began the course with the story of the Big Bang, leading my students through the formation of galaxies and stars and on to the eventual demise of those stars as they formed novas or supernovas. I would dramatically explain that from the intense temperatures, pressures and energy of those dying stars, all the elements (atoms) in the periodic table were formed. These were the same elements or atoms that made up our bodies and the structures of all animate and inanimate things on earth. I would always end by saying "We are children of the universe, connected to everything through atoms." The atom, almost a sacred icon, was believed to be the fundamental unit of matter out of which all things were formed.

Our understanding of the atom changed radically with the advent of particle accelerators that could split the atom and discover its secrets. The spaces within the atom are much greater than we could have imagined. For example: if the nucleus of the atom were the size of a typical California orange in Los Angeles, the first electron orbital with its spinning electrons, would be in Chicago. In between the nucleus and orbital there is SPACE, making our physical structure 99.9999% space. Using sophisticated particle accelerators, with enough beam energy to take apart the atom and study its subatomic particles, scientists discovered that they aren't particles or matter at all, but rather, Vibrational Interference Patterns (VIPs).

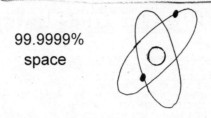

99.9999%
space

Figure 3.1 Sir William Rutherford's model of the Atom

"Subatomic particles, and all matter made therefrom, including our cells, tissues, and bodies, are in fact patterns of activity rather than things."[108] —*Fritjof Capra*

The vibrational patterns that make up our structure would probably appear much like the circle pattern formed when we throw many rocks into a still pond. As the circles move out from the point of impact, they overlap each other forming a pattern. Perhaps the places where they overlap, the interference areas of the pattern, give us a perception of matter. Matter, however, appears to only exist within the perceived context of our reality.[109]

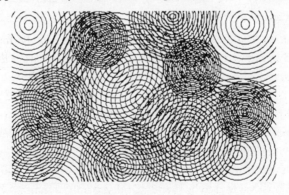

Figure 3.2 Representation of vibrational interference patterns

The German physicist Werner Heisenberg was one of the founding scientists of quantum physics. His most famous contribution was his uncertainty principle in which he found that the more precisely the position of a subatomic particle was determined, the less precisely its momentum was known in any instant, and vice versa. He was one of the first scientists to challenge the simple, linear causality described by classical physics, in which material objects are assumed to be knowable and predictable once you know the forces acting upon them. With Heisenberg's principle, however, causation is not such a simple, linear affair since the exact future motion of a particle cannot be predicted, but only a set of probabilities for its future position and momentum. Large-scale objects like rocks and trees have large probabilities to be in one place or another and thus are quite predictable. The electrons and other infinitesimally small particles making up us and other large objects are randomly jumping from one energy state to another, and can even cross impenetrable boundaries because their energy is momentarily uncertain and indeterminate. Subatomic reality is not solid or reliable, but ephemeral with seemingly infinite options. Indeterminacy may present us with a peculiar feeling about the reality of reality, but quantum physics and the uncertainty principle have been used with great success in electronics and other practical applications of quantum science.[110]

Subatomic particles are ultimately unknowable because they are actually vibrating waves or little knots of energy, redistributing that energy back and forth in dynamic, flexible, open patterns even at the temperature of absolute zero.[111] Paul Dirac, an architect of quantum field theory, suggested that there is no such thing as empty space; it's rather an area teeming with subatomic activity. We can think of space as fields created by exchanges of energy, constantly being redistributed in a dynamic pattern. E. Laszlo noted that if all the energy exchange from this dynamic dance were added up, it would supply an inexhaustible supply of energy, exceeding all energy in matter by a factor of 10 to the 40th.[112] Richard Feynman, winner of the 1965 Nobel Prize in Physics went so far as to say "the energy in a cubic meter of space is enough to boil all the oceans of the world."[113] William Tiller, Professor Emeritus from Stanford University, stated that space is a chaotic sea of boundless energy.[114] So physically we can think of ourselves as mostly boundless energy.

You might take a look at yourself in a mirror right now and see the space in you, filled with vibrating energy, rather than the solid being you've learned to perceive, and then see others that way: it's a mind expanding perspective. For me it is like peering around the corner into another world, much like the picture in Figure 3.3.

"Matter is nothing more than energy vibrating at a frequency low enough that we can perceive it with our senses." —Albert Einstein

Figure 3.3 Alternate reality

The energy Albert Einstein speaks about is measured as the vibrational electromagnetic spectrum, which is enormous, spanning between the slowest brain waves (delta waves) at .5 Hz (cycles/sec.) to cosmic rays at 10 to the 28th (28 zero's behind the 10) Hz (cycles/second). Figure 3.4 shows the complete spectrum.

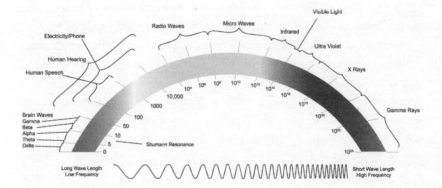

Figure 3.4 Electromagnetic spectrum of vibration in our world

Brain waves lie between .5 – 35 Hz, with sound waves between 3 – 10^4 Hz, electricity at 30 – 10^4 Hz, radio waves at 10^4 – 10^9 Hz, microwaves 10^9 – 10^{13} Hz, infrared 10^{13} – 10^{15} Hz, visible light waves 10^{15} Hz, etc. It is still amazing to me how we can simply turn on a radio or TV and literally pull sound and light vibrations from the space around us like magic.

Amazing also is talking on the phone to someone directly across the world and hearing the warmth and timbre of his or her voice.

Beyond The Five Senses

As vibrations existing in a sea of vibration, our receivers, our senses, seem to be the step-down transducers that slow and break down the vibrational continuum into tiny, discrete pieces. These pieces can then be analyzed, filtered and reassembled into a pattern the brain recognizes according to our paradigm.[115] We have no understanding of the sounds in our environment, or spoken language without the ear receiving it and sending it on to the brain for processing.[116]

The idea of only five senses (hearing, seeing, tasting, smelling and touch), as picked up by five distinct sensory receptors (ears, eyes, tongue, nose and touch receptors in the skin) has been challenged by researchers R. Rivlin and K. Gravelle. They have discovered receptors for at least nineteen senses and possibly many more.[117] Figure 3.5 is a picture of two-year-old Breeze picking up her sensory world using much more than just our believed five senses.

In Western society, we tend to lean heavily on our visual sense. The retina of the eye processes more information than we had previously thought, sending dozens of different movies to the brain. However, these movies simply serve as elementary clues, abstractions, or approximations without feeling, attitude, texture or focus. They are a kind of scaffolding upon which the brain imposes constructs from all the other senses and emotions to give us vision. Only 4% of vision comes from these retinal movies, the other 96% is manufactured in the brain according to input from our other senses and emotions.[118,119] Though visible light waves comprise a very tiny portion of the whole vibrational spectrum, we say "seeing is believing," and thus only believe that tiny reality. Take a moment to look at a picture you have in your office or home. Has your brain made a three dimensional image of it? In reality, it is just light, dark, and color on a two-dimensional piece of paper. Seeing is our last sense to develop and our least accurate sense. Since we perceive the world through the lenses of our emotions and all the other senses, we tend to see only what we expect to see and nothing more.

Everything in our world is always new — the vibrational patterns are constantly shifting, and in each moment we are presented with a whole new set of sensations. Because of our training, we usually experience what we expect to experience, rather than the newness and reality that, I believe, is such a part of the young child's world. And because of our stress, we tend to respond with learned survival patterns that don't allow further exploration, growth and understanding.

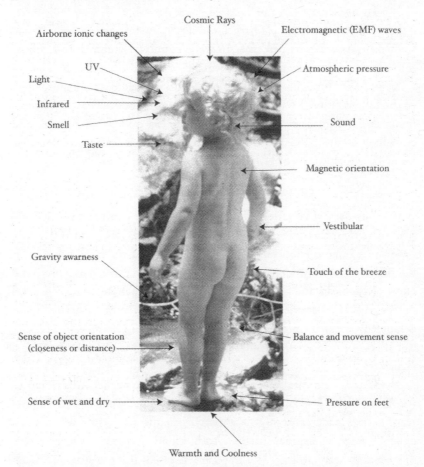

Figure 3.5 Rivlin and Gravelle's nineteen senses

In a coherent open state, embryos, fetuses, newborns and young children seem still to be sensitive to a much larger part of the vibrational spectrum and therefore are able to take in and optimally process more sensory information for a broader more holistic understanding of the world. That is until they are conditioned to filter out some subtle information, or if they exist in so much stress that they filter out anything that doesn't have to do with survival. In a stressed, incoherent state, the polarity across the nerve membranes decreases, making the nerves more reactive to outside disturbances, and thus decreasing the ability to focus and select the information necessary for not only learning, but also creativity.

I am fascinated by the Balinese, some African, and other indigenous cultures, where many people have the ability to openly perceive vibrational frequencies that I can't perceive. In these cultures, parents do everything in their power to provide safety, love and joy from the time the child is conceived and throughout its life. Both adults and children are more open to the full vibrational spectrum and are able to reproduce those spectrums in art, and music. They also readily see light and color around people and trust their instincts to know if a person or situation is safe or not. Intuitive knowing is highly regarded in these cultures.

Earth Fields

The natural vibrational fields emitted by the earth and other living beings, particularly those of extremely low frequencies (less than 100 hertz), have a pronounced effect on virtually all cellular and chemical processes in our bodies. Even tiny fluctuations in these fields from earth, have a profound effect on the heart and brain. Notice how children behave, or how you feel on the days of a barometric pressure shift before a storm, especially if you are already stressed (incoherent). That simple shift of barometric pressure can affect our emotions, learning, and memory, and the ability to perform a skilled task.[120]

Our systems are so sensitive that during geomagnetic disturbances (such as strong winds, lightning storms, volcanic eruptions, tsunamis) researchers see increases in general psychiatric disorders, suicide attempts, epileptic seizures, Sudden Infant Death, blood viscosity, coronary artery disease and heart attacks.[121] If we are stressed, these disturbances can cause a steep rise in adrenaline and cortisol and a decrease in brain function causing us to react rather than reason. Thus we become far more vulnerable to disease, high blood pressure, fear and depression.[122,123] Coherence allows us to take in the details of the disturbance, make appropriate adjustments, and take right, and often creative, action. The stories of animals moving to high ground, even a day before the 2004 Tsunami in Malaysia lead me to believe they were able to maintain a coherent state and take the action that allowed their survival.

By maintaining our coherence, we can consciously retrain our senses to be more available to the rich vibrational fields around and within us, giving us full access to learning, our intuition and high-level reasoning. Coherence leads to creative ways of living again in our authentic nature. The heart produces our largest vibrational field and just might be the key to opening our senses and maintaining that coherent state, no matter what.

> "In oneself lies the whole world and if you know how to look and learn then the door is there and the key is in your hand. Nobody on earth can give you either the key or the door to open except yourself." —Jiddu Krishnamurti

The Masterful Heart

> "And what is as important as knowledge?" asked the mind.
> "Caring and seeing with the heart," answered the soul. —Flavia[124]

The heart and mind are seen as one in traditional Chinese Medicine. The heart is the center of the soul in yogic practice and has long symbolized love and emotions. Western science, until recently, has seen it simply as a complex, tenacious pump. Currently, research is showing that, "The heart is a highly complex, self-organized sensory organ with its own functional 'little brain' that communicates with and influences the brain via the nervous system, hormonal system and other pathways."[125]

I first became interested in the heart's influence on the brain and coherence at the International Consciousness Conference in Tucson, Arizona, in April 1994. I attended a session where Linda Russek from Harvard and Gary Schwartz from the University of Arizona were presenting their amazing research.

Linda Russek had taken over a forty-two year longitudinal study with Harvard students begun in the 1940's. In the study, Harvard students, then in their twenties, were asked a battery of questions. When these same people were interviewed in their mid-sixties, an interesting correlation was found between a question asked of them in their twenties and the percentage that had heart disease in later life. The question was: "Do you have one loving parent, two loving parents or no loving parents"? These were the results:

Percent with Heart Disease 40 years later

Two Loving Parents — 25%
One Loving Parent — 35%
No Loving Parents — 93%

Also, most of the other 7% of the "no loving parents" group had life threatening diseases like cancer or Parkinson's disease, compared to less than half of the other two groups.[126]

Millions of dollars have gone into studying the risk factors of heart disease: high cholesterol diet, high blood pressure, cigarette smoking, obesity, lack of regular exercise, diabetes mellitus and genetic predisposition. However, about half the people who suffer their first heart attack have none of these common risk factors for heart disease. Moreover, more than eight out of ten people with at least three of these risk factors never have a heart attack.[127] From the Harvard study, it appears that the stress of isolation and disconnection from family may be a stronger cause of heart disease than the purported risk factors.

Linda Russek and Gary Schwartz were compelled to further investigate the heart/brain connection. They ran experiments hooking groups of students up to EKGs (to measure the electrical activity of the heart) and EEGs (to measure the electrical activity of the brain). They were fascinated to find that the heart waves were the first to come into a state of entrainment or synchrony with the heart waves of the other students, and that secondarily the brain waves came into entrainment. Entrainment occurs when two or more things come into exact rhythm or synchronicity with each other.

To understand their surprising results, they searched the literature for other research, and the picture of the heart's immense influence on the brain began to take shape.

According to Andrew Armour, a neuro-anatomist, there are more nerves going from the heart to the brain than the other way around, and these nerves have an important regulatory role on the brain and nerve signals from the brain back to the heart and other organs. The heart signals the brain regarding chemical levels, heart rate and pressure, pain, coherence and incoherence within the environment and even emotions. The heart actually appears to have its own sensitivity to the world and exhibits that with intelligence, to the extent that the brain energetically revolves around the heart, not the other way around.[128,129] Armour's observation about the heart led me to delve deeper and change my view of the heart as a simple pump.

All of the information chemicals (neurotransmitters) found in the brain are also found in the heart.[130] The heart is also an endocrine gland, classified as such in 1983, releasing two major hormones that profoundly affect the brain. The first hormone, ANF (Atrial Natriuretic Factor) affects many major organs of the body including the regions of the brain that regulate our emotional state and influence our learning and memory.[131] The second hormone, ICA (Intrinsic Cardiac Adrenergic) affects the synthesis and release of adrenaline and dopamine which play an important role in taking organized, graceful action when exploring our world and learning.[132,133] Thus, the messages between the heart and brain are communicated through neurochemical, electrochemical, and hormonal connections, with the heart's influence being substantial.

Among its characteristics, the heart has automaticity, which means that the beat of the heart resides in each of its cells and is controlled within the heart by a pacemaker, a nerve bundle in the right atrium (the SA or sinoatrial node). Individual heart cells in a petri dish will visibly beat at their own rhythm until they come into close proximity with another cell. They then begin to beat in unison or synchrony with each other, without any kind of message from the brain.[134] During a heart transplant, the new heart's pacemaker (SA or sinoatrial node) will spontaneously start the beat of the heart without external help.[135] The function of the brain is simply to regulate the speed of the heartbeat, speeding it up during stress to supply blood to the muscles for fight or flight, or slowing it down during rest.[136] This ability to operate by itself hints that the heart is a constellation unto itself within the body.

One of the most amazing traits of the heart is that it generates an electrical field with an amplitude sixty times greater than the electrical field produced by the brain. The EMF (electromagnetic field) of the heart, measured externally with a SQUID (superconducting quantum interference device) is at least 1,000 times greater than the field produced by the brain. It is the largest electromagnetic field in the body extending to a currently measurable distance of 8 to 16 feet (more than 5 meters) from the body. People's hearts, as powerful transmitters, are constantly sending out light and electromagnetic field waves. The physical antenna able to pick up these waves is the whole body with its elaborate sensory apparatuses (at least the 19 receptors reported by Rivlin and Gravelle) and the huge heart field, when the antenna is tuned in.[137]

In the years since our first work with the electron microscope we have developed amazing technologies to see beyond the intricate structures of the cell to the vibrational fields. Among these are the MRI (Magnetic Resonance Imaging), (fMRI) Functional MRI, PET (Positron Emission Tomography) scanner, SQUID (Superconducting Quantum Interference

Device), and GDV (Gas Discharge Visualisation) bioelectrography device. Though they give us valuable information and spur us toward deeper exploration, it seems they cannot match the sensitivity of a young child or wild animals for that matter.[138]

Babies are very tuned in, as adults can be when truly present. Dee Coulter, child development specialist teaching at Naropa Institute in Boulder, Colorado, talks of a study with young children on a playground whose parents simply sat on benches around the edge, not interfering with the children. A soccer field lay beyond the playground, and the researchers had child friendly dogs and people walk from the far side of the soccer field toward the playground with no response from the children. However, when a convicted child molester walked toward the playground, though they neither saw nor heard this person, the children immediately left their play and went to their parents.[139]

How did the children know there was a dangerous person walking toward them? It could be the same way dogs know if a person is scared, or dangerous. It may have to do with that person's state of incoherence. The results from the Linda Russek and Gary Schwartz research on heart entrainment lend concrete evidence that we are sensitive to other people's heart fields and may be able to sense their coherence or incoherence subconsciously or intuitively.

Measuring Coherence

The Heart Math Institute is an organization in Boulder Creek, California that studies heart/brain communication and the power of coherence. Using electromagnetic field readings of the heart called a heart rate variability (HRV) pattern, they examined people in states of coherence and incoherence. A wave of electrical current moving across the heart between the atria and ventricles can be picked up by electrodes (called leads) placed in various places on the chest, and fingers. Depending upon the lead, the movement of current is designated by a Q,R,S,T wave on an electrocardiogram(EKG/ECG).

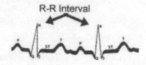

Figure 3.6 EKG pattern showing R-R Interval

Using the lead attached to the middle finger of the left hand that reads the R wave, Heart Math researchers measured the variation in R-R intervals, called the Heart Rate Variability (HRV) pattern. The graph of the interval easily shows if the HRV is coherent or incoherent. This pattern gives important physiological parameters of heart rate changes over time and dynamically reflects the inner emotional state and stress levels of the research subjects as well as external environmental and situational influences.[140,141]

Researchers observed a steady coherent HRV pattern (Figure 3.7) when a person experienced feelings of appreciation and gratitude; was engrossed in joyful, creative work or learning, was meditating, or was truly at play. These findings further showed that a coherent heart pattern determined the brain's ability to optimally receive sensory information from both the internal and external environment. A coherent heart pattern appeared to affect the brain's ability to recognize patterns from sensory information coming in from the environment, remember them, learn from them and act on them in appropriate, effective, and creative ways.

When stressed or frustrated, the heart rate variability pattern was shown to become incoherent, causing the same incoherent, erratic patterns in the brain. These incoherent patterns decreased the brain's ability to take in sensory information, make an understandable pattern of it, remember it, and act on it appropriately.[142] Our coherence or incoherence affects our biochemical reactions, which influence our mental, emotional, physical and spiritual states each moment.

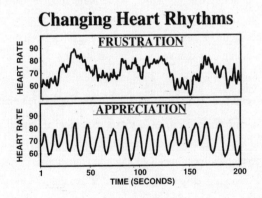

Figure 3.7 Incoherent and coherent Heart Rate Variability (HRV) patterns using the R Lead of an EKG/ECG

The powerful vibrational field around the heart makes it possible for us to be affected by or affect other people and animals and may explain how highly sensitive/receptive children and animals are able to pick up another person's, and even the environment's coherence or incoherence.[143,144]

The Heart As Emotion Generator

"The heart is the source of our intuition which is eventually perceived at the brain/mind level." —Rollin McCraty[145]

The heart has within its structure, specialized nerve cells that monitor hormonal changes, pressure changes and even nervous stimulation originating from within the heart.[146] It also responds to messages sent from the amygdala, one of the storehouses for our emotional memories, and the brain's center for vigilance and fear.[147] But how we react or respond to our world begins with the complex interplay between the heart, the amygdala and the rest of the brain.[148] The heart informs and influences our responses.

Rollin McCraty, Director of Research at the HeartMath Institute, refers to the heart as a "step-down-transducer," slowing external and internal vibrations down enough for us to understand them with our senses. This would imply that the heart is constantly monitoring our entire environment, and setting up a heart rate variability pattern that is either coherent or incoherent.[149,150] This coherent or incoherent pattern is then relayed from the heart to the brain through the vagus nerve (a pathway of sensory neurons) to the medulla oblongata (the brain's switch-board), to the thalamus (the area through which all sensory information except smell is handled), to the basal ganglion (the main spam detector — filter), and the amygdala. There is more nervous information going from the heart to the brain than vice-versa. At the same time, hormones from the heart (ANF and ICA) are also affecting the brain.

Coherence/Incoherence — Vive La Difference

When we are feeling curious, focused, peaceful, joyful, appreciative, enthusiastic and creative, the heart rate variability pattern is coherent, the amygdala decreases its vigilance, and the parasympathetic nervous system becomes active, slowing down heart rate, decreasing blood pressure and relaxing breathing.

A coherent HRV pattern enhances the ability of the thalamus to easily take in all the sensory information from the environment (seeing, hearing, taste, touch, proprioception, etc.) and, through the basal ganglion, filter out unnecessary information,[151] thus maintaining an optimal state for focus and learning.

The Heart/Brain Interface

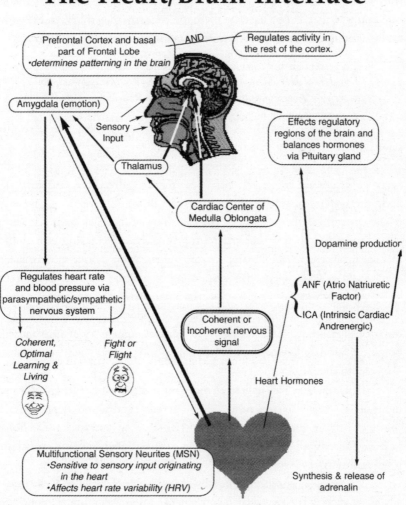

Figure 3.8 *The heart brain interface*

A coherent brain wave pattern is established in the prefrontal cortex of the frontal lobes (considered to be the brain's "thinking", rationalizing part), causing meaning and understanding to come into full consciousness. Coherence allows the brain to easily take in all the diverse sensations from the environment, filter out those not needed, and put the important pieces into patterns that can be used by the brain to learn, remember, and expand understanding to create new ideas. This is the optimal state for learning.

"Human perception and learning arise from synchronized (coherent) activity of clusters of neurons in order to render unified scenes and meaning from diverse sensations."[152] —*Eugenio Rodriques, et al.*

If the heart frequencies are incoherent (as with any threat to our safety, or stress leading to frustration, anxiety, fear, worry and anger), the amygdala, cortico-trophic releasing factor (CRF) and the sympathetic nervous system are triggered. Stress hormones (adrenaline, and cortisol) flood the system causing the person to react in a defensive, protective way to the situation (fight or flight). The thalamus shuts down to any sensory information not directly related to survival, thus decreasing our ability to take in all the available rich sensory information of our environment that would provide deeper understanding of a situation. An incoherent brain wave pattern is set up in the prefrontal cortex and association areas decreasing the brain's ability to combine information in patterns that lead to high-level reasoning, and creativity. The emotional memory of an event will be stored, but detailed memory for reasoning and creativity will be minimal. We react to survive.

This research has challenged me to rethink my whole life. Every event in my life is simply that, an event. How I perceive and act on these events is colored by the memory of my early experiences. Yet I always have a choice in how I receive and interpret each new event, though it takes conscious reprogramming.

Consciously choosing is not always easy, especially when we've made a habit of getting frustrated by inconvenience in our lives, but the long run benefits are worth it. Coherent synchronization of the heart and brain seems to more easily open the doors to greater productivity, creativity, harmony and joy. For instance, I can choose coherence during a traffic jam, using the extra time to look around, come up with new ideas, sing or just be still for a moment. When I practice to develop coherence by consciously focusing on what is right in my life, taking relaxing regular walks in nature, doing slow integrated movements like yoga, tai chi, qigong or Brain Gym*, and connecting to others from my heart, coherence becomes more spontaneous. Remembering the detrimental effects of incoherence assists me to choose coherence.

In addition to Russek and Schwartz's work, several other studies show that our heart and brain pick up the heart fields of others. When several people are within six feet of each other and hooked up to EKG and EEG machines, there is a measurable signal between one person's heart and the other person's heart and then brain. If the heart rate variability pattern of one person is coherent, the other person's brain wave patterns will be in synchrony as measured by an EEG.[153,154] These studies also show that the coherent state is our most natural and powerful state.

The receptor of what we call the subconscious intuitive mind that picks up coherence and incoherence may actually be the whole body. We often refer to gut reactions when we think of intuition. Dean Radin and Marilyn Schlitz, measuring the electrical behavior in the gut using an electrogastrogram (EGG) with 26 paired volunteer students validated that people actually experience gut reactions empathically with others. They discovered that the emotions (anger, calmness, neutrality, positive feelings, negative feelings) in one partner, as elicited by images and music, correlated with readings on the EGG of the other partner. The emotional state of others can register in one's body, and can actually be felt in the gut itself.[155]

Almost thirty years ago, before I had encountered the idea of coherence, I had an interesting experience with an Indian woman named Amma. I had gone to an open concert where she and her devotees were singing bhajans, beautiful and inspiring spiritual chants. At the end of her concert she invited people to come and greet her. When I finally came face to face with her, she smiled, looked into my eyes, took my hands and I was flooded with the most amazing sensations. They were the sensations of coming home, of being absolutely loved, of being completely whole. I experienced magnetism between us, a power surge of energy, a full opening of all my senses and great joy.

The major power transfer of information that occurred between Amma and myself required rugged and robust, energy handling gear (trunk lines, etc.) to transport the information exchange. The heart, with its large coherent electromagnetic field, may fit that description. Her wonderfully coherent heart brought my heart and brain waves into synchrony, opening my system to experience all the rich array of vibrations available to me that I had been unaware of.[156] I certainly felt my heart, and hers, as she simply held my hands. The fact that I felt, even on the conscious level, all that "electricity", that broad spectrum of vibration, shows me it is always possible if we choose to be open and sensitive to it. Since then, that same exquisite feeling of joy and wholeness is occurring more and more often as I choose coherence, am fully present with another, and step into my child-like authentic nature.

Spreading Coherence

Several research studies done at the University of Edinburgh, and by Dean Radin in 2004, found brain wave synchrony with closely bonded people: couples, friends, parents and their children, as well as in matched pairs of strangers. When one partner of the pair sent a focused intention to the other, the partner's EEG mirrored the sender's EEG in a significant number of instances.[157,158]

The new research on heart entrainment inspired me to conduct my own informal studies using *muscle testing* to test for coherence or incoherence in people. Muscle testing has hundred year history of use by osteopaths. Chiropractors, homeopaths, kinesiologists, and even medical doctors have found it a useful tool for accessing subconscious information. In the 1970's I was introduced to muscle testing by a chiropractor that was helping me discover the stress within my body. Since then I have used it extensively in my work.

This simple tool that uses the feedback-feedforward loop between the motor cortex of the frontal lobe of the brain, the spindle fibers of the muscles or golgi tendon bodies of the tendons, and the sensory cortex of the parietal lobe of the brain, appears to be a very accurate gauge of coherence or incoherence within the body.[159,160] When I ask a person to say his (or her) name while holding their arm up as I gently push down on it with about 2 pounds of pressure, they easily hold their arm up because saying their name is familiar. They have said their name so many times that it is hardwired into their brain. Theoretically, they could say their name, drive a car, and look at a street sign without any problem.

If, however, I ask the person to say, "My name is Pinocchio" and hold their arm up, they would have a difficult time holding it up against my downward pressure. It seems that since there is no hardwiring for the name Pinocchio, the brain is actively searching for some connection to Pinocchio and the message to hold the arm up is decreased. If I ask a person to think of a stressor in their life, the arm will go down with my pressure. I believe this happens because situations and things that are stressful for us, are stressful because we don't understand them. In attempting to figure them out, the brain is not only in stress mode, but is looking for connections that will assist understanding, and the message to the arm to stay up is decreased, thus it goes down when pressed upon.

For years, I have been demonstrating how one person who is feeling stressed can cause everyone else around them to become stressed as well, even if the others were thinking positively. In one such experiment, I asked a woman to think of a frustrating, stressful experience, and when I muscle tested her I could easily push her arm down. I asked her to continue holding the stress and then asked everyone else in the experiment to think positively. When these individuals were muscle checked, their arms stayed up. However, when I asked them to hold hands with the stressed person, or the next person in line that was connected through hand holding to the stressed person, their arms went down even if they were thinking positively.

So why didn't "thinking positively" change the stress reaction in the test subjects? Interestingly, thinking gets in the way of heart/brain coherence by taking us away from the present moment and each other. Even when we are thinking positively, we will access past reference memories for what is positive, in so doing, we leave the present. Researchers at Princeton University discovered that thinking actually decreases blood flow to the heart and inhibits its normal functioning.[161]

I then expanded the experiment, asking the stressed subject to continue to hold their stress while I asked everyone else to go into a simple, cross-lateral movement called *Hook Ups*, focus on their breathing and become totally present for a minute. Amazingly, when they held the hand of the woman who was stressed, their arms stayed up, and more amazingly, so did the arm of the person who was stressed. When I asked her what she noticed, she said she was unable to hold the stressed state, though she tried very hard, and that she felt much more relaxed, in control, and could see some solutions for her problem.

I used the *Hook Ups* movement from Brain Gym®[162] because it seems to be the most integrative and fast-acting intervention during times of stress. From my neurophysiology training, it makes sense to me that standing up in *Hook Ups*, with crossed legs, the complex intertwining of the hands and arms and the tongue on the roof of the mouth would demand balance and stimulate large areas of the neocortex in both hemispheres of the brain. Since the whole body is engaged and focused on breathing and becoming present this seemed to make it easy to come to coherence.[163] This same kind of integrative action with conscious focus would seem to also occur with yoga, tai chi, qigong, and meditation.

In the experiment, the stressed subject had entrained with the coherence around her, and it seemed she then had full access to all parts of her brain. These little experiments were astonishing to me, and affirming of the research done by Jacobo Grinberg-Zylberbaum, a neurophysiologist. In research with pairs of participants using EKGs and EEGs, he found that the participant with the most coherent brain wave pattern set the tempo and tended to influence the incoherent member of the pair in the study. He also noted that synchrony occurred between both hemispheres of the brain equally in both participants, showing a high level of coherence.[164]

Figure 3.9 Hook Ups

I have now shared this experience in hundreds of workshops worldwide with the same results. It is heartening to know that something as simple as an integrated cross-lateral movement like *Hook Ups* can bring us to coherence so rapidly and affect the coherence of the people around us.

When people are really suffering and can't pull themselves back into coherence, I stand close to them in *Hook Ups* (within their heart field), and focus on my breathing. Amazingly, I've noticed that within moments, they come back to that natural coherent state and relax. I've had many teachers tell me their students suggest doing "a heart connect" (my term for *Hook Ups*) when things get out of control in the classroom. When we are incoherent and out of control, we alienate other people, and isolate ourselves from the love and appreciation we all need. Children know this more keenly than we may think they do.

Simple, cross-lateral movements that assist us to become coherent, can be used everywhere: home, office, school, during a sports or art event, in a traffic jam — everywhere. If the incoherent person is resistant, our coherence sets up a safety net for them so they can relax and be more authentically themselves. I've learned that when all the kids in the classroom are "bouncing off the walls," I'd better check my level of coherence. I am often in an incoherent state, multi-tasking, not being present, and the students are just mirroring me. It's a great time for me to take a one minute "heart connect" to pull myself together again. Miraculously, the students will usually do the "heart connect" with me, and we all become more focused. This is far more effective than yelling, scolding or penalizing. Children seem to realize the benefits of becoming coherent and do it on their own when they start to feel out of control.

When stress is chronic, incoherent brain wave patterns become the homeostatic state for people, the pattern they are most at home with. If they are put into a coherent situation, it often feels foreign to them, so they may "stir things up" until there is incoherence so they feel more at home. I see this all the time in classrooms where children, coming from incoherent, survival-oriented lives, don't know what to do within a coherent environment. These are the children we tend to label hyperactive, attention deficit or emotionally handicapped. I also see it in people who thrive on drama in their lives.

The good news is: the strongest, most natural state is coherence, and we will gravitate back to that state if given the chance. I believe that is why there are certain people I love to be around. I see them as enlightened masters, be they spiritual leaders, close friends and family who are child-like players on the planet, or many of the amazing children today. Just their presence brings me into coherence, where I can follow my inner knowing, guidance, intuition and be more authentically, passionately and joyfully myself with them.

The Problem With Thinking

I have a knack for generating stress in that time right before dawn when it's too cold to get out of bed and my wide awake brain seems to run out of control. Fearful, worrisome thoughts cascade in, ruining my morning peace. If I have the presence to breathe, rest in *Hook Ups* and focus on the birds calling up the morning, I can stop the runaway thoughts; otherwise I enter the day incoherently.

When I first read that thinking inhibits coherence, I had a knee jerk reaction to defend the status quo. Aren't we supposed to think? Isn't that the responsible, rational thing to do, to figure things out so I feel safe in knowing what's coming next, to orchestrate events and plan all my actions? In the times when I'm truly creative, however, I'm not thinking about or even trying to be creative. I'm just in the moment, and the most remarkable ideas come to me, my world and events fall perfectly into place and I easily move from task to task consciously with what needs to be done in that moment.

The same thing occurs when I am fully present with a friend or even a stranger, listening, without thinking about what to say, or my grocery list. They become my teachers, opening up their unique corner of the universe to me. Something they say can trigger multiple pieces of a puzzle to fall into place. Voila! I experience the Ah-Ha, the exhilaration of seeing something in a new, more complex way, more clearly than I had ever seen it before and I feel I've been given a great gift.

Two cardiologists, Michael Cooper and Michael Agent, did an interesting experiment with a group of men who had very elevated cholesterol levels (ranging between 300-500). These men had been cardiac patients, some with severe problems. Besides keeping diet, exercise and body weight constant, these high risk men were trained to sit quietly for 15 minutes a day and clear their minds. They were told that if a fearful or worrisome thought came into their head, to just let it pass and come back to the present. Almost immediately, this caused their cholesterol levels to drop by one third. This kind of a drop is unheard of except with one specific drug now on the market. And this highly effective technique is cheaper and safer than any drug.[165]

According to Mihalyi Czikszentmihalyi creativity emerges from a playful, naïve place when there is no worry about failure, no self-consciousness, and no sense of time. He terms this being in the flow, a form of "in the moment stream of consciousness" that allows us to learn, to have new ideas and feelings about what we experience, thus assuring the "Ah-Ha" realizations and creativity in our lives.[166]

If we are totally in the present, relaxed and allowing our thoughts to just flow, ideas, understanding, and appropriate actions occur naturally. The resulting coherence not only affects those around us, but also appears to affect inanimate objects. In a study done at Princeton University, volunteers were asked to consciously attempt to alter the output of numbers from a random numbers generator. A random numbers generator is simply a computer that prints out numbers randomly over a period of time. The study showed that if the volunteers concentrated on and thought hard about changing the output of numbers, this lessened their influence on the output of numbers. On the other hand, if volunteers set a simple intention to change the output of numbers and then just relaxed, their influence on altering the computer was greater, and the numbers generated showed statistically significant tendencies toward more order and less randomness.[167]

In traditional Chinese medicine, the heart and mind are considered to be the same, thus one word heart/mind is used for both aspects. The Chinese feel that excessive thinking or excessive emotional strain detrimentally affects the heart/mind. The notion of "not thinking too much nourishes the heart" is heavily influenced by Taoist ideas of nourishing life by calming the mind and preventing distracting thoughts. I wonder if Taoist sages would say that rampant consumerism, multi-tasking and the strong intellectualism of our culture harasses the heart?

The heart runs the show, acting as though it has a mind of its own, profoundly affecting perception, intelligence and our interaction with others.[168] As mirrors for those around us, our greatest gift is coherence. As parents, educators, and friends, we miss the boat by focusing on an agenda, or driving ourselves beyond our limits, when the heart energy is not straightened out first.

The Yum Solution

STOP

- Stop the runaway thoughts on the past and possible futures.

- Be aware of where you are at this moment with no distractions.

- Be present, with who you are and who others are at this moment.

- Do Hook Ups and take long, slow breaths from your belly.

LOOK

- Look at your world with child eyes, experiencing the constant newness.

- Look at yourself honestly as a valuable, unique being.

- Look at others or the situation as the perfect learning experience

LISTEN.

- Listen to the rich sounds of nature.

- Listen from your heart to the tone of another's voice and words

- Listen to your intuition and your gut feelings.

TOUCH

- Reconnect through touch, which is our strongest anchor and bridge.

- Hug yourself and others with the hug of the beloved.

- Touch with your eyes, meeting another's eyes with total love.

- In a difficult situation extend your hand, and turn with the other person to look at the situation before you instead of between you

MOVE.

- Take a relaxed walk, swim or bike-ride, being aware of the feel, the smells, and the sights.

- Relax your shoulders and open your heart.

- Do integrated movements, yoga, tai chi, or dance to your favorite music.

- Move your mouth in song, laughter or gratitude for yourself and others.

YUM

- With pleasure, recognize and bless who you are, what you have in your life and the people and situations you have manifested to assist your growth.[169]

We don't need expensive technologies, therapies or designer drugs to come home to the heart. It only takes a moment of true presence and coherence to change the incoherence, not only in ourselves, but also in those around us. This forces us to more responsibly trust ourselves for the solutions, giving us back the power to structure our lives as we choose.

4

The Unified Field Of Information

"We delude ourselves with the thought that we know much more about matter than about a 'metaphysical' mind or spirit and so we overestimate material causation and believe that it alone affords us a true explanation of life. But matter is just as inscrutable as mind."[170] —*Carl Jung*

Perhaps the metaphysical mind or spirit that Carl Jung refers to in the quote above is a unified information field of vibration, which we are all part of, entangled in, and can draw upon and effect. The English physicist, David Bohm theorized that the universe must be fundamentally indivisible, a "flowing wholeness" of moving interference patterns that literally bear the mark of all the other waves of light, energy, and matter they've been in direct or indirect contact with, encoding an image of the whole within which the observer cannot be essentially separated from the observed.[171]

In previous chapters we've looked at the electric fields our bodies create through vibrations of our heart and nervous system and explored several studies suggesting that we both receive and emit these subtle vibrations when in contact with one another. Now we'll turn our attention to studies that suggest we influence one another in more elusive ways, even across long distances and without direct contact. Some scientists are examining the possibility that the vast sea of vibrations we are all part of is responsive to and affected by mind and the mind's intentions. It was the hard science findings of quantum physics that first ignited this venture into the integral nature of mind and the material world.

Peering Into Reality

Early in the 20th century scientists began to vigorously explore the tiny world of the atom. They confronted discoveries that came smack up against their conventional view of reality. Things were quite different in the subatomic world. It was discovered that subatomic particles, such as electrons, were energy packets that could only be observed in certain energy states and not in between these states. In our ordinary experience, we perceive that existence is linear and continuous. We walk through the back door of our house, down a path and into the garage. The way subatomic particles behave is analogous to first being in the house and then in the garage without having walked in-between.

Werner Heisenberg discovered that when subatomic particles were measured you could not know everything about them; for instance, you could not know both the speed and the location of the particle at the same time. Any physical measurement to find the value of either the speed or the location will always disturb the particle in such a way as to leave the value of the other uncertain.[172] In the large-scale world of ordinary reality, we can drive a car down the road and know our speed and where we are, but subatomic particles, presumably the fundamental stuff that cars and people are made of, are indeterminate.

The inability to fully measure subatomic particles as real objects moving through time and space is only one of the puzzling aspects that the quantum explorers discovered. Light (and eventually matter) was discovered to have a dual nature. It could be observed as a particle of energy called a photon and also as a smeared-out wave of energy. The famous double slit experiments were performed to investigate this seeming duality.

In the double slit experiments, a light source was placed in front of a wall with two tiny slits in it that would allow light through. Behind this was a target screen that would record where the light had struck. The light going through the double slits showed a smeared-out light pattern on the target screen indicating that light traveled as waves that bumped up against one another creating a pattern of interference. When experimenters shot single photons so that only one photon at a time went through the open double slits, they expected to see single shot patterns recorded on the target, the way particular objects like bullets and arrows make impact. However, a wave interference pattern showed up instead.

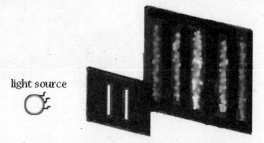

light source

singly shot photons making wave interference pattern

Figure 4.1 Double slit interference pattern

When the experiments were repeated with only one slit open, individually fired photons impacted the target as single shots or particles. However, when the second slit was opened again, the photons seemed to travel as waves and created a smeared-out wave interference pattern on the target. So, one photon at a time, one slit open created a bullet shot pattern; one photon at a time, two slits open created a wave interference pattern. Scientists wondered what was going on. How does one photon at a time create an interference pattern? What is it interfering with? How do the photons "know" how many slits are open? These were puzzling results.

Experimenters wanted to see what the photons were actually doing, so they installed photon detectors at the slits to watch the photons in the act of going through them. The results of these trials were even stranger than the earlier ones. In addition to the observation that photons seemed to "know" how many slits were open, the photons also seemed to "know" whether they were being observed or not. When the scientists were watching the slits they never detected a photon going through both slits at once, it would only go through one slit and impact the target as a particle. When the scientists were not watching, the singly shot photons would make a wave interference pattern. Whether there was an observer (i.e. a mind involved) or not changed the results of the experiment. Prior to this, scientists assumed there was an objective reality operating by laws of nature that were beyond and outside the influence of human observation. These experiments radically called this assumption into question. Later, double slit experiments were conducted with electrons and even atoms. These particles with mass behaved the same way.

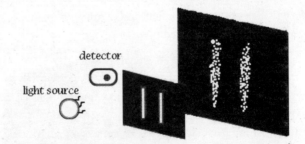

detector

light source

singly shot photons with detector making bullet shot pattern

Figure 4.2 Double slit with detector

What's Up With These Photons?

These experiments caused quite a stir in scientific circles and many minds wrestled with the peculiar results to interpret the underlying causes of such findings. One famous interpretation that many scientists adopted is the Copenhagen Interpretation. It is named after the place where Niels Bohr had set up an institute for the study of quantum mechanics. Many of the brilliant early discoveries in the field came from this group from Copenhagen, made up of Niels Bohr, Werner Heisenberg and other gifted scientists.

According to the Copenhagen interpretation, subatomic particles or photons of light don't exist in one state or another, but in all possible states at once called a superposition that can only be described statistically. And only when we attempt to measure or observe this probable state does it become a particle. This is called the collapse of a probability wave, which seems to imply that observers are necessary to bring particles into existence. Was there no fundamental existence to the material world without an observer to create it? Did observation collapse the probability waves of energy into matter? This was the unavoidable question for everyone who peered into the quantum world. Everyone did agree, though, that quantum mechanics worked beautifully for predicting and expressing the behavior of subatomic particles.

Albert Einstein and other physicists questioned the Copenhagen Interpretation. Einstein maintained that the results of these experiments must be incomplete. He once said, "I would like to think that the moon is there even if I am not looking at it." Together with Podolsky and Rosen he proposed a thought experiment, which is referred to as the EPR paradox. To put it very simply, their thought experiment described a situation where you could know a property of one particle by measuring another related particle. Thus, they maintained that if a physical property of a particle, such as its position or momentum, could be determined with absolute certainty before measuring it (observing it), then that property must be based on a physical reality.[173]

The seeming necessity for an observer to make particles real, wasn't the only mystery posed by the proliferating quantum explorations. At the same time the EPR paradox was being proposed, Erwin Schroedinger, who later won a Nobel Prize, first predicted quantum entanglement and non-locality for photons of light and fundamental particles. Unlike ordinary objects, the quantum particles' properties were not fixed. A property value for one particle of the pair depended on the kind of measurement performed on the other particle. What happened to one particle influenced the other instantaneously (faster than the speed of light); no matter how far apart (non-local) they were, they were entangled. John Bell's Inequalities Theorem mathematically proved this "non-locality" of quantum particles was accurate. Reality at the most elementary level of subatomic particles truly was indeterminate, insubstantial, and "non-local."

Then, in 1982, there was actual experimental proof of non-locality. Alain Aspect and a team of researchers at the University of Paris discovered that entangled subatomic particles do influence one another instantaneously no matter how far apart they are separated. If the spin of particle A in an entangled pair is changed, particle B's spin instantaneously changes also, no matter how far apart they are. The particles "know" what the other is doing and behave correspondingly. The Alain Aspect experiment demonstrated that there *was* non-local, superluminal (faster than the speed of light) communication.[174,175] Now, the experimental violation of Bells Inequalities can be demonstrated in undergraduate physics labs. It appears that an object's very existence depends directly upon its relationship to other objects in an entangled way.[176]

Many physicists, still unable to accept non-locality, instantaneous information transfer, and the possibility that there really is no objective material reality, have tried to explain away Alain Aspect's findings, but none have been able to disprove him. Other scientists, inspired by the whole quantum quandary, have put forth radically new interpretations of reality — pictures that bring into view an underlying realm beyond matter, beyond linear time and space, beyond the duality of mind and matter.

David Bohm, for example, saw the universe as an undivided wholeness continuously unfolding. Things we see in the apparent reality as separate objects, to Bohm, were merely explicate expressions of the underlying implicate order. Despite appearances, there really weren't separate things, just a flowing wholeness of ordered information much like a hologram.[177,178]

From extensive experimentation and research, Dr. William Tiller proposes that besides direct space/time with its electrical components of atoms and molecules making up the material world, there are other levels of substance existing at the same time, with the physical world being the coarsest and spirit being the finest level of substance. He proposes a reciprocal level of substance that is within and beyond our physical body. This reciprocal domain exists as a smeared-out, dynamic sea of magnetic information waves subtly impacting and connecting us vibrationally to everything else instantly as an entangled, non-local unified field of information.[179] To explain his conception of reality Dr. Tiller has invented the Duplex Reference Frame, consisting of two four-dimensional reciprocal spaces, one of the two is direct space/time (our familiar physical world), and the other is magnetic information waves (the reciprocal information field). He proposes that physical space/time is held in place by three reference domains: emotions, mind and spirit. Within the emotion domain, there are what he calls deltrons, that he defines as carriers of our emotions, intentions, desires, mind and spirit. These can be activated by consciousness to act as a coupler between direct space/time and reciprocal space. This coupling has the potential to create our physical reality out of reciprocal space — particles out of information waves. His elegant proposal incorporates quantum mechanics while expanding the field to address some unexplained phenomena, such as the observer effect, the creation of our material universe, psychoenergetic events, homeopathy and placebos to name a few.[180] Interestingly, his model with its deltrons that couple direct space/time with the reciprocal information field is reminiscent of the ancient Buddhist conception of the three worlds of desire, form and formlessness.

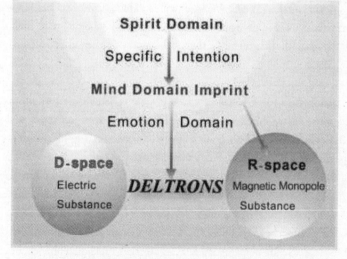

Figure 4.3 William Tiller's Duplex Reference Frame

Physicist Amit Goswami says the puzzles and weird findings of quantum physics are quite comprehensible once we abandon the idea that there is an objective, material reality outside of consciousness. Coming from an Eastern philosophical background he has no difficulty proposing that consciousness and not matter is the precursor and the medium of the physical world. To him, the quantum mechanical findings that observers are necessary for collapsing probabilities makes it absolutely clear that consciousness is more fundamental than matter.[181]

Because of our current paradigm, our senses have only been trained to an electromagnetic field frame of reference that includes atoms, molecules and the physical world. Though the subconscious picks up over 40,000 bits of information/second, it only feeds the conscious brain what it has a reference frame for. Thus we tend to only open to ideas and concepts that are already established and may miss other possibilities. Even with our electromagnetic frame of reference, we limit our senses as described in Figure 3.5 and miss much of the electromagnetic spectrum shown in Figure 3.4.

> "The only way to discover the limits of the possible is to go beyond them to the impossible" — Arthur C. Clarke[182]

Are Our Minds Entangled?

What does this new paradigm of reality mean for us as human beings doing our best to live passionately and beneficially in the world? Here's a proposal for consideration. We are not isolated, powerless beings with no real influence on the greater universe. Evidence is mounting that we are indeed entangled within the unified field, and our thoughts and actions do influence the whole, thus giving us some responsibility for the way things are.

Amit Goswami demonstrated that the phenomenon of *quantum entanglement* occurs between people as well as subatomic particles. He ran some experiments in which pairs of people were asked to meditate together for a period of time to establish "entanglement." They were then separated over a large distance (often over 2,000 miles) and hooked up to EEG machines. One of the pair of meditators was rigged with an apparatus that would flash a red light in his eyes. Whenever the light flashed in the 'target' meditator's eyes, the EEG pattern would change, and at exactly the same moment, the distant meditator's EEG pattern would also change in exactly the same way.[183] There is no way that the conventional view of reality can explain such results.

Entanglement in reciprocal space or the non-local, unified information field may explain why embryos and fetuses know whether they are wanted or not, and how very young children are so attuned to their parents' emotions, whether coherent or incoherent. Their understanding of the world may come first from reciprocal space, the realm of information, before it is recognized in material space/time.

When my daughter Breeze was three and four years old, out of the blue she would say, "Mommy, the phone is ringing, and it's Mary (or someone else)." THEN the phone would ring, and it would be Mary (or whomever she had said). Her sensitive system was somehow picking up energy patterns before they became a reality for me.

Scientific research shows that people who are closely bonded easily entrain with each other, picking up one another's thoughts even at a distance.[184] My Mother and I seemed to have had this kind of closely connected bond. She often could sense when I was going through an emotional trauma in my life. I could be 1,000 miles away and out of regular communication with her, yet when a trauma hit, she would call me at exactly the time I needed her, and ask me what was wrong because she had sensed I was upset. My own family is not unique in this regard. Larry Dossey, M.D. and researcher, also noted this phenomenon, which apparently occurs quite often between people who are emotionally close.[185]

When our minds are elsewhere, where are they? Whenever we use our imaginations, we are leaving our current established reality behind for a time to explore other possibilities, and what of our intuition that instantly keys into our knowing. It is like hooking into the internet with all its possibilities, and with what we find there, we can choose to change our software, our reality and even our physical structure.

We are antenna/receivers of the vibratory fields around and within us, analogous to the way televisions and radios pick up electromagnetic vibrations from the air. Our feelings, especially our sense of connectedness or dis-connectedness with others, are picked up via our "antennas" We know when people don't like us, are judging us, or are afraid of us, and also when we are fully loved and accepted, just as dogs and other domestic pets do. We call it instinct or intuition – inner knowing. We are also transmitters, influencing the information field with our intentions and attitudes.

What Are We Communicating?

Jesse, a 17-year-old middle school student I worked with, was not only rebellious, he, at times, was violent with classmates and teachers and came from a highly abusive home. I knew none of this about him because, with my hectic schedule, I hadn't taken the time to read his chart. I liked him, and when he indicated that we should work on his reading and that he was interested in motorcycles, we got on well. I loved motorcycles, too, having owned a Norton in the 1960's. Using Brain Gym and Superlearning techniques, and motorcycle magazines from the library, we worked together on his reading skills.

His reading improved greatly, even within the first few weeks, and I thought he might be a good example to share with the teachers when I was asked to do an in-service training for them at the school, especially after learning of his background. I asked Jesse to help me show the teachers some of the Brain Gym exercises and how his improved reading would show up as a positive muscle check.

Before I brought him into the in-service, I asked the teachers to view him as they had a month earlier, as a problem student, often violent and abusive in class. When he then read for the teachers, he did so haltingly, and when I muscle checked him, his arm went down, indicating stress in his body. He was confused and upset by the results.

I suggested he go into the hall, take a breath, drink some water, and then come back in to read again. While he was out of the room, I asked the teachers to have compassion and empathy for this beautiful young man who had come from an abusive situation and was attempting to do his best. I reminded them that he had greatly improved in both his outlook and his cognitive skills. When he read the second time, it was perfect and his arm stayed up when I muscle checked him. I believe the perception and attitude of the teachers had made a difference in his ability to succeed and how he saw himself.

Since then, I have read many studies in which teachers have been told in advance that the students they will be teaching are considered brilliant or way above average. In all cases, the students scored above average on all their tests, though later it was disclosed that the students were picked at random, and most of them had been labeled ADHD (Attention Deficit Hyperactive Disorder), dyslexic and even Asperger's (a mild form of autism). It seems that we are in danger of making the people around us into what we think they are, rather than seeing who they really are as pure potential.

I am now more consciously aware that every thought governing my actions is not caged and housed only in my head. Each is actually a missile, launched from my whole being into the non-local information field that affects at some level everything around me. I am especially aware of being "picked up" by unborn and young children before they learn to tune me out, picked up by their elaborate sensing apparatus and stepped down into every cell of their body. Picked up at some level are the vibrations of my thoughts, emotions, and judgments by not only children, but also everyone with whom I come in contact.

My perceptions have been conditioned for more than sixty years by the belief systems of my parents, culture, society, school, religion, gender, and race. My every experience shaped the elaborate synthesis of my sensual world into a contextual reality in consensus with my culture. Early on, I formulated a belief system of separateness, linearity, and myself as a body, connected only through experience to my family, society and the world. With a deeper understanding of my true nature I can change and expand what I am, but these children, unborn or newly born, are still unformed, unbounded, open to all vibrational patterns. They are alert to everything I project, sensitive to the survival value of each input, pulling together their reality in conjunction with my limited worldview. I must be very careful in the presence of these sensitive young people, careful not to limit their possibilities or stop their exploration due to my own fears and beliefs. I must be authentic, coherent, integrated, and also unbounded around them so they will not be caged by my dogma. These wonderful beings have the potential to show me an expanded, brighter world, one again full of all the vibrations I have blocked out.

The immense potential of the non-local, unified field makes me rethink every aspect of my reality. I no longer see the world, or myself, as a flat two-dimensional canvas. I've moved beyond a three-dimensional, linear, brain-oriented system, compelled by reasoning to view my world as matter, where I miss the possibility of being my mature wisdom and child wonder at the same time.[186]

For thousands of years Eastern cultures have tended to be more aware of reciprocal space. A. Shearer, a yogic scholar may be referring to reciprocal space in his expression: "Deep within the mind, beyond the faintest flicker of thought, it (our true nature) is experienced as an undying and omnipresent vastness. It is absolute consciousness. The nature of life is to grow toward an ever more perfect and joyous expression of itself. Each living being has a nervous system, no matter how rudimentary. This acts as a localized reflector of the all-pervading consciousness, just as a mirror reflects light."[187]

Field Consciousness And Inanimate Objects

In 1991, I did an in-service for teachers at the Ananda School in Nevada City, California. The principal of the school mentioned that she hated computers and that they always gave her trouble when she used them. The vice-principal was a real computer geek and loved the computer.

I thought it might be fun to do an experiment. I had both of them type out the same phrase on the same computer, each on a separate piece of paper. I coded the papers so that only I would know which was which. In order to stay out of the experiment, I trained 2 students to do muscle testing and go out in the community and have people look at one paper, muscle check and then look at the other paper. When people looked at the principal's paper, their arms went down over 90% of the time, and when they looked at the vice-principal's paper their arms stayed up well over 90% of the time. Somehow, the attitudes of the principal and vice principal toward the computer had influenced the output of the machine and/or the people who looked at the printouts. If indeed the unified field of information is entangled with everything, it is not surprising that my thoughts would also affect my relationship with the machines I come in contact with in my life. This little test may come across as far-fetched, but statistically significant mind effects on machines have been shown in study after study.

A more controlled study with inanimate objects (computers) was done by psychologist Roger Nelson at Princeton University's PEAR laboratory and replicated by psychologist Dick Bierman at the University of Amsterdam. The experiment was set up to find out if collective consciousness (people mentally focused on the same thing) could affect the pattern of a programmed computer called a random event generator (REG) as it generated 400 random bits (either 0's or 1's) every six seconds. Each 400 bits was called a sample. Each REG was programmed to collect samples for an hour before an event, during the event and for an hour after the event. The before and after data were considered the control samples. The number of 1's (ones) produced in 400 random bits was used to measure the degree of statistical randomness in the electronic circuit every six seconds.

They then measured three events: a Holotrophic Breath workshop (Breathing with music for nine hours with 12 people); the March 27, 1995, Academy Awards Ceremony (televised to an estimated one billion people in 120 countries); and the O.J. Simpson verdict on October 3, 1995 (to an estimated half-billion people worldwide via TV or Radio). In every case a most remarkable thing happened: in the Holotrophic Breath workshop, as the coherent attention of the group increased over the nine hours, the odds against randomness rose to about one thousand to one by the end of the workshop. In other words, the REG was putting out 1,000 times more of one digit than of the other. It had been affected somehow by the consciousness of the people and was now ordered instead of random.

With the Academy Awards, the researcher had one REG 20 meters away from where he watched the broadcast and another 12 miles away at his laboratory. Both readings showed an unexpected degree of order during the periods of high audience interest — again, the odds against randomness being as high as 700 to 1. In the O.J. Simpson verdict, the researchers used five REGs (one at Princeton, one in Amsterdam and three in the laboratories in Nevada). Precisely when the court reporter read the verdict, all five REGs suddenly peaked to their highest point in the two hours of recorded data, giving odds against randomness at approximately 800 to 1.[188]

By 2006, Roger Nelson and Dean Radin had studied the effect of 205 top news events on the REGs. A pattern emerged showing that the degree of order in the machine's output seemed to match the emotional intensity of the events, especially the tragic events.[189] In thirty-seven REGs worldwide, the greatest variance in the order of the machines away from randomness during all the years of study, took place during the events of 9/11. Human minds across the world had reacted with horror and disbelief and the machines with order during the key moments in the drama (shortly before the first tower was struck).[190] Interestingly, the machines became increasingly ordered a few hours before the first tower was hit.[191] It seems to me that the collective unconscious was keying into the incoherence of the perpetrators via the non-local field. This appeared to be a "giant psychokinetic effect created by six billion minds set to react in unified horror."[192] Psychokinesis is a word used to describe the mind reaching out across space to affect the behavior of matter in whatever form. Intensely felt experiences appear to be infectious across the entangled vibrational field, even affecting inanimate objects.

The Media and The Field

The implications of this are profound if we consider that our media is orchestrating how we view reality, which in turn affects our collective information field. We are influenced by all of our media, but TV and the news are especially potent. By the mid 1970's, when Breeze was born, 99% of homes in America had at least one TV running six hours per day in an average household and eight hours per day in households with children. By 1978 in the U.S., children before the age of five had watched 5,000 – 6,000 hours of TV per year.[193]

In October 2003, the Henry J. Kaiser Family Foundation released the results of a survey of 1,065 parents with children ages six months to six years. The survey showed that 43% of the children age two and younger watched an average of two hours of TV per day and that 26% of these infants had a TV in their bedrooms.[194] Preschool three-year-olds watched an average of 3.6 hours per day and over 28 hours per week.[195] By age thirteen, children will have seen well over 18,000 simulated murders and 200,000 acts of violence on TV.[196]

Through TV, we are ingesting images that have been edited, cut, rearranged, sped up, slowed down, and sensationalized in hundreds of ways. Instead of direct experience, we are substituting a secondary mediated version full of con fusion, fear and violence.[197,198] Our powers of discernment, discrimination and understanding of the world can become compromised. This incoherence determines our take on reality and affects our input into the unified field.

I personally experienced the distortion of a news story in 1993 when I was flying into Cape Town South Africa to give a workshop. Chris Hani, Nelson Mandela's right hand man, had just been killed, and this was just a month before the elections. On the plane, news reports were announcing that Cape Town was burning and there was mass rioting and violence. The person that picked me up had also heard the news and was fearful of driving across Cape Town to the venue. We were expected there in less than an hour so we decided to just go for it. We saw no violence, no fires, not even smoke on the horizon.

I feel that of all the violence presented by the media, the news is often the most violent — and certainly not a true indication of reality. With the media choosing isolated, sensational topics to present, viewers are left with feelings of helplessness and fear about the enormity of the situation and its effect on their lives. Keeping people in constant fear, terrorists need do nothing — fear can destroy a culture, its economic system, and freedom faster than anything else.

David Orme-Johnson states it this way: "Stressed individuals create an atmosphere of stress in collective consciousness that reciprocally affects the thinking and actions of every individual in that system. Crime, drug abuse, armed conflict, and other problems of society are more than just the problem of individual criminals, drug users, and conflicting factions in society. Such problems are more fundamentally symptoms of stress in the collective consciousness."[199] Considering our power to affect the unified information field, I feel our greatest defense and hope for ourselves and the world is to remain coherent. One way for me to stay coherent is to not invest too much time watching TV, and although I don't usually read the daily newspaper, I seem to get the news I need from other sources by remaining present.

Besides defending ourselves in these dangerous times by remaining consciously coherent, fascinating research is showing that through intention we may be able to change the tenor of the collective field. Maharishi Mahesh Yogi conducted many studies using meditation with the intention to lower the crime rate of various cities. In all the studies, it appeared that when one percent of the population of the city meditated (became coherent), the rate of violent crime fell and continued to fall.[200] Lynn McTaggart, in her book, *The Intention Experiment*, looks at the power of intention within small coherent groups to decrease global violence, positively affect weather patterns, stop natural catastrophes, and affect the global consciousness for the highest good.[201] The good news is that as we become more coherent and recognize our power to access reciprocal space, we may be able to affect the projected outcomes of global warming, wars and conflicts, and economic futures for the highest good of all.

Intention And Attention

"The thing always happens that you really believe in and the belief in a thing makes it happen." — Frank Lloyd Wright

The malleability of our system and the choices we make to intentionally focus energy in certain ways may explain how we can change our physical, mental, spiritual and emotional reality throughout our lives. According to Ilya Prigogine, a Russian scientist and Nobel Prize winner, as living systems we are able to maintain our material existence because we are in essence a flexible, open energy system that remains far from equilibrium.[202] As we saw earlier, the subatomic packets of vibrating energy waves that make up physical matter and living things are not something solid and stable. They exist in a malleable state of pure potential.[203] Even single units of light, as demonstrated by the double slit experiments, travel as a smeared-out wave with a large sphere of influence.[204]

In other words, we are open systems; dynamic, flexible, constantly changing while having a larger sphere of influence on our world than we might think. "Our observation of every component in our world may help to determine its final state, suggesting that we are likely to be influencing everything we see around us."[205] What we truly put our attention on is processed internally, causing us to change our nerve networks, rework our memory, and actually change our brain and belief system.[206] Just as we can change neural networks in the brain through peak and focused sensory/motor experiences, we may have the flexibility and potential to change our material structure depending upon the energy focused upon parts of that structure.

The Power of Belief

The placebo effect gives us an interesting example of just how malleable we are. Focusing attention and intention on becoming well profoundly influences the body's ability to heal itself. We tend to put a great deal of faith in certain people and ideologies when we think they understand the truth. Because we view them as authorities, what they say or do can determine our beliefs and intentions. In a study on pain, people who were told they were taking a powerful pain-blocker (they were given sugar) actually produced their own high levels of endorphins, their bodies' own pain-blockers.[207] And patients given "sham" acupuncture treatments for pain showed intense neural activity in brain areas that regulate pain perception, monitor external events and stop negative emotions such as anxiety.[208]

Even more astounding is a study done with terminal heart patients. Some of the patients were told they would receive a new laser surgery that was highly effective, and others were told they would be given a drug that grows new blood vessels. In the first case, a catheter was inserted in an artery and slowly pushed up to the heart with the surgeons going through all the motions of making the patients believe they were using a satellite-guided laser to drill holes in the heart muscle. However, the laser was never switched on. The other patients received sham injections of salt water instead of growth factor protein.

With all of these patients, sophisticated nuclear profusion scans showed improvement in blood flow to the heart and heart function. They had fewer angina attacks, and were able to exercise longer during a stress test on a treadmill. Amazingly, these people who received no active treatment were still doing well two years later.[209] These experiments illustrate why it is so important to monitor how we respond to people who respect and trust us. If they buy into our beliefs, thinking as we do, it can profoundly affect their mental, physical, emotional and spiritual reality.

"With our thoughts we make our world." — Buddha

There may also be another explanation for the placebo effect. In the past 30 years, the placebo effect has increased dramatically from near 0 in the 1980's to 70 – 80% by 1999. In one analysis of 19 anti-depressant drug trials, the "placebo effect" accounted for 75% of the anti-depressant effects on the experimental subjects.[210] Other trials show even higher rates of the "placebo affect." William Tiller suggests that there has been an increased connectedness, via duplex-space coupling, between the drugs and the placebo, so that the placebo actually takes on the vibration of the drug and can mirror the drugs' action. In his intention experiments, he discovered that his (UED) unimprinted electrical device (which was to act as the control) would pick up the vibrational field of the (IIED) intention imprinted electrical device if it wasn't covered with aluminum foil and placed in a Faraday chamber that blocked vibration transfer. This coupling might explain the potent properties of homeopathic remedies that exist in such a highly diluted state that not even an atom of the original remedy exists in the preparation and yet the homeopathic solution works. Homeopathic remedies are diluted with intention.[211] This idea may also apply to distance healing, or all healing for that matter.

Energy Healing

Qigong is an ancient Chinese healing practice with centuries of recorded results. Qigong provides clear and direct evidence of the energetic basis of life, as well as the mind's power to direct this energy. Recently, Shui-Yin Lo a physicist and qigong practitioner, together with a group of scientists and medical doctors conducted an experiment to test the effectiveness of qigong distant healing on a small sample of subjects. In the test, subjects were hooked up to an EEG machine, a brain imaging device called a SPECT and an infrared device that measures temperature distribution along the skin. Then, a qigong master, using focused intention, transmitted the qi energy to the subjects. He never was in physical contact with them; the qi was transmitted to them from a distance. To eliminate the placebo effect, the subjects didn't know when the qigong master was merely simulating treatment or actually administering the qi. The EEG, SPECT and infrared data from these trials consistently showed that the qi energy produced positive biological effects on the subjects. Before treatment the data patterns were disordered; after treatment they became more orderly showing highly activated cortical activity indicative of a high state of awareness. Dr. Shui-Yin Lo of the Quantum Health Research Institute says that qi energy is a mixture of low frequency electromagnetic waves and subsonic sound waves. He feels, with more sensitive machines, we will one day be able to detect and fully examine this qi energy.[212]

The Quantum Touch organization believes all people have the innate ability to heal themselves and facilitate the healing of others. Quantum-Touch practitioners feel that their techniques focus and amplify the life force energy (their term for qi, or prana in Sanskrit). When the practitioner holds a high vibrational field of life-force energy around an affected area, healing is facilitated through resonance and entrainment. Everything vibrates. Two things that vibrate at different frequencies have a tendency to synchronize their vibrations when together. Most often, the slower vibration will rise to match the faster frequency that promotes healing. Interestingly, Quantum Touch practitioners define the life force energy as love. As quoted on their web page, "When you learn to direct the life force energy, the possibilities are truly extraordinary; our love has more impact than we can imagine."[213] William Tiller would say that the emotional intention of love would become the "deltron" coupling reciprocal space to direct space/time to bring coherence to the physical structure for healing.

A Personal Experiment with Intention

To understand the effect of intention, I was again inspired to do my own experiment. I was told that many martial artists actually impact their opponent from across the room, simply with their intention. I convinced and trained some 16 year olds at Supercamp in Vermont to muscle check several burly football players standing approximately 20 feet across the room from me. I focused my intention on one of the football players, and with my hand extended toward him, drew a line down his central meridian, from his lower lip to his pubic bone. The central meridian is an energy meridian from Traditional Chinese Medicine that naturally runs from the pubic bone up to the lower lip. His arm went down when muscle checked even though he seriously attempted to hold it up.

Then, with focused intention, I drew a line up the central meridian (the natural electromagnetic flow direction) of his body and his arm stayed up. I even had him close his eyes so he wouldn't know which way I was running his meridian, and the muscle check was accurate every time.

I have watched martial artists wave one hand up the front of their own bodies while extending the other hand toward their opponent and intentionally drawing the energy downward. It seems that much of martial arts training is about improving focused coherent intention, the mastery of which supplies amazing amounts of energy and power, even at a distance. Our intentions appear to determine our reality, giving us the ability to coherently and passionately live our lives as an adventure or become stuck in fear.[214]

Interestingly, Schwartz and Connor found that directed intention manifests itself as both electrostatic and magnetic energy, again tying into Duplex-Space (direct and reciprocal space) and is like playing the piano, you need to learn how to do it, and some people do it better than others.[215] Breathing, heartbeats and movements of body parts produce electrostatic energy on EEG amplifiers. In studies using the Elmer Green room, a room that restricts external electromagnetic fields from entering, participants were asked to focus their attention to see what effects would register on EEG amplifiers. When meditators or healers focused their attention, the energy output coming from the center of their bodies (just below the navel called the dan tien in Chinese), would rise from pre-test voltages of 10-15 millivolts to as much as 190 volts.[216,217] Larry Dossey, MD, calls the energy that passes between the healer and the healed, the Nonlocal Gap.[218]

To explain the preceding phenomena, William Tiller states that all bodily processes and all processes in nature are driven by differences in thermodynamic free energy. He proposes that the acupuncture meridian/ chakra systems are already in a partially coupled state with reciprocal space because they constitute an electromagnetic symmetry system in our bodies that produce higher thermodynamic free energy per unit volume than other systems. And that our intentions and desires pump the qi or prana through this symmetry system, supplying us with expanded capabilities. As we activate this system via meditation, qigong, tai-chi, yoga, integrated movement, or coherence in all we do, we develop a rich infrastructure in this system, allowing us to become more adept at healing ourselves and influencing those around us. Simply the love, compassion and devotion of a person can raise the electromagnetic symmetry level of another, significantly empowering them to fulfill their intentions.[219,220] It seems that this symmetry system is somehow closely aligned to heart coherence.

Scientists have discovered that beside the use of electrostatic and magnetic aspects, such as resonance and brain waves to assert intention, both meditators and healers create coherent biophoton (light) emissions, and coherence among all the regions of the brain, thus aiding focus and healing.[221,222] Once again, I'm reminded of the Hawaiian wisdom that we are bowls of light, able to create, co-create and heal as we maintain coherence and focus our attention/intention.

The people we consider to be true healers, like Mother Theresa, appear to have several characteristics in common:

- They see the person as his or her own healer, honoring that person's wisdom.

- They become a conduit, turning the healing over to a greater source.

- They ask for the highest good of the person to be healed.

- They remain very coherent and focused.

- They accept, without judgment, all that happens.[223]

- They found that assisting the healing of someone else also healed themselves.[224]

I value my work with Brain Gym® balance techniques because I see constant miracles happen in people of all ages as they choose to change their existent beliefs and reality. Every session is like a treasure hunt as they gain a sense of their power to choose what is emotionally important for them in the form of a clear, focused intention. Then, using a large menu of possibilities, through noticing their bodies' reactions, they discover the movements, emotional activation, meridian/chakra systems or whatever else they need to bring their intentions into reality. I watch in amazement as people become coherent, open to their own knowing, and more able to bring into reality their intentions and desires. I have seen their emotions, mind and physical structure change in relationship to their intentions. William Tiller believes that focused intention begins at the level of spirit, which imprints patterns on the mind. These patterns are then emitted and activate deltrons in the emotion domain that imprint information on reciprocal space. If there is sufficient deltron coupling, information is transferred from reciprocal space to direct space/time and the process of physical reality will manifest some magnitude of that specific, original intention.[225]

Interestingly, it always seems that my clients' intentions have to do with some issue I am also working on at the time. I feel like "the teacher has arrived," and by being privy to their exploration, I too can change my homeostasis. We are like two children, coming to play in the field of possibilities; seeing the world as whole and feeling part of it, impacted by it and impacting it over and over again, always new and always an adventure.

Positron Emission Tomography (PET) scans of the brain show that if we are enthusiastic and coherent, the whole brain lights up as it looks for known information to connect new learning to. As the activity becomes learned, the brain is rewired and becomes more efficient regarding this activity, so it is once again ready and open for the next idea and adventure. This is the natural coherent state, bringing electrical structure out of vibrational interference patterns.

Sharing Coherence with the Inanimate World

In 1994, Masaru Emoto, a Japanese researcher using an MRA (Magnetic Resonance Analyzer), found that people's thoughts and written words could influence the crystal configuration of water as it freezes. He was influenced by studies explained in The Secret Life of Plants, and simple school research projects where cooked rice was spoken to both negatively and positively and exhibited totally different outcomes. He began by taking pictures of distilled water before placing the water between two speakers and playing a piece of music at normal volume. He left the water overnight, then froze the water to 5 degrees below zero C and took a picture (magnified 200-500x's) of the ice crystals that formed. With heavy metal music, no crystals formed, but with pieces like Bach's Air for the G String beautiful crystals formed. He stated: "The vibrations of music and words transmitted through the air affects water more than any other element."[226]

He didn't stop at actual sounds, though. Again, using distilled water, he affixed typed words and sayings to the vials of water. Some messages were positive others were negative, such as: "Love and Appreciation" vs. "You're a Fool," "Soul" vs "Demon," "Beautiful" vs. "Ugly." Then he froze the water and took magnified pictures of the resultant crystal formations. With the negative statements, no crystals formed, yet with the positive statements, beautiful crystals formed. He even froze and photographed water immediately following the Great Hanshin-Awaji earthquake and three months later. At the time of the earthquake, the frozen water showed no good crystal structure, but three months later, beautiful crystals formed and he felt this had to do with the love, cooperation, community spirit, and help that people had given to each other after the tragedy. This ties back to the belief of Quantum Touch practitioners, as well as many spiritual beliefs, that love is a healing force.

Our brains are 90% water, men's bodies are 75% water and women's bodies are 55% water, thus we are mostly water. With this in mind, Masaru Emoto's findings could imply that we might be able to change the molecular structure of the water in our bodies, simply through our thoughts and beliefs.[227] When we hold a focused thought/intention about others or ourselves, we have the potential to alter the very molecular structure within our bodies and that of others.[228]

William Tiller and his associates have shown us the power of trained coherent intentions on inanimate forms, as well. In experiments, a specific intention for a particular outcome (like raising or lowering the pH of water by a factor of 10) was focused onto a simple electronic device using the pooled intentions of four highly qualified meditators. This device, along with a control device, was covered with aluminum foil, placed in a Faraday Chamber (to inhibit extraneous electromagnetic influence) and shipped to a laboratory more than 1,000 miles away. Because the focused intention was so coherent, the electronic device overwhelmingly acted in the way the meditators intended by changing the pH of water within a few days. Their carefully designed and replicated psychoenergetic science research over the past few decades has shown the same quantifiable results. They feel the key is the robust belief and training of the meditators who are tying into the unified information field with their intentions.[229]

> *"Minds deal with eternity, brains deal only with temporality."*
> — *Buckminster Fuller*

In his book, *Conscious Acts of Creation*, William Tiller goes a step further to make a bold claim: "Human consciousness contributes to the creation and direction of the universe."[230] He, and researchers like him, are expanding our reality by showing us that consciousness: 1) can receive local and non-local information without sensory input, 2) can affect the functioning of inanimate objects, and 3) can affect the biochemical reactions of living organisms, thereby affecting the health and wellness of others and ourselves via the coherence or incoherence of vibrations emanating from us (our thoughts and perceptions).

Candace Pert made the statement that *"we condition our environment* with our thoughts and intentions." William Tiller discovered that his experiments using focused conscious intention were somehow conditioning the space where the experiments were carried out, so that the space appeared to have undergone some long-term thermodynamic transformation. According to Tiller, "The energy from intention appeared to 'charge' the environment and create a domino effect of 'order' that assisted the outcome of the experiments. The space appeared to self-organize into a higher state of coherence with each intention experiment."[231,232,233]

Sacred places where we go to dream, pray, do healing rituals, connect with antiquity, or even sleep, care for others, or seek guidance may all be power spots because they are highly conditioned, either by us, or by all the people who have been there.[234,235,236] My place in Montana is such a space for me. In among the towering Tamarack and Douglas Fir trees with the flowing stream, rich earth smells, lack of distractions from electricity or a busy community with lots of commitments, ideas seem to flow and I find myself enthusiastic to capture them. My mind seems to go to the space of *quantum tunneling* that Amit Goswami speaks of.[237] In this state of flow, my nervous system becomes a super conductor and I can drop my perceptual lenses of what is real and explore the field of possibilities, perhaps at times touching the primary light beyond the reflected light, as Plato and the Sufis remind me that I am.

With evidence of a unified information field existing in reciprocal space, we may indeed be children of the universe as well as master creators of our reality.

5

Vibration Into Matter – The Life Force

"We are magnificent manifestations of the life force." — *Virginia Satir*[238]

There are many mysteries about the occurrence and development of life. One that has mystified developmental biologists for decades is the mechanism of cellular differentiation that occurs in the developing embryo at about eight days following conception.[239,240] The fertilized egg (which in itself is a mystery) begins to divide into a hollow ball of cells called the blastocyst. Each cell has identical DNA, half from the mother and half from the father. Then suddenly following implantation into the uterine lining, the cells begin to migrate within the blastocyst and differentiate. Some of the cells become Ectoderm making up our nervous system, skin and hair. Some become Mesoderm making up our muscles, blood vessels, and internal organs. The rest become Endoderm forming our gut, respiratory and reproductive organs. Each cell perfectly migrates to its position, shutting off those parts of its DNA sequence that are not needed, and only expressing the genes and producing the proteins that perfectly suit the type of cell it has become. DNA is the master code for our proteins and in the past it has been assumed that DNA instructs cell differentiation in the developing organism, but it has been found to have no mechanism for directing cells in such a mammoth migration.

William Tiller speculates that coming into material existence as well as the cell differentiation process exists as much in reciprocal space as in direct space/time. According to Tiller, deltrons can travel at velocities greater than, less than and equal to the speed of light, and interact with both electrical particles in direct space/time and magnetic information waves in reciprocal space. He postulates that deltrons, as denizens of the emotion domain, carry a consciousness charge that is a necessary ingredient for the formation of deBroglie particle/pilot wave complexes, which are the essential building blocks for electric atom/molecule formation and quantum mechanics. Somehow the "would-be" human has the intention, life force, or desire, to come into material existence. This life force/intention (deltrons) would couple reciprocal space and direct space/time, collapsing the probability wave into the formation of particles, out of which life and cellular differentiation begins.[241,242,243]

In alignment with Tiller, Ernst Runair Holland, neurophysiologist, experimenting with intention states, "Our intimate thoughts, dreams, desires are the result of electromagnetic field action on the brain and nervous system, which gives rise to matter."

In the 1940's Harold Burr, a neuro-anatomist at Yale University, studied the shape of energy fields, the electro-magnetic fields generated by living plants and animals, using conventional voltmeters that supplied data at micro-voltage levels. He discovered, while studying the developing electrical axis in salamanders, (an electrical field aligning with the brain and spinal cord), that this axis originates in salamander eggs, well before the egg is fertilized or differentiates. Also, the electromagnetic field around the developing embryonic salamander was roughly shaped like that of the adult salamander instead of the fairly amorphous embryo. Burr also experimented with the electrical fields around developing seedlings of many different plant species, but his results were not as conclusive as those experienced with salamander eggs.[244]

At the same time in Russia, Semyon Kirlian developed Kirlian photography (electrography, or bioelectrography) to study electrical fields of the body.[245] His photographs showed the electromagnetic discharge patterns surrounding and produced from living organisms in the presence of a high frequency, high voltage, and low amperage electrical field. These discharge patterns were captured on photographic film inserted between the object and the electrode. With this technology, Kirlian was able to translate Burr's work with seedlings into a visual electrical corona. Amazingly, the electrical field of the seedlings resembled the adult plant rather than the little two-leafed seedling. From these studies, Burr theorized there was a growth template, a map, generated by the organism's individual electromagnetic field.[246] In the last twenty years, fascinating work by Konstantin G. Korotkov has elaborated on Kirlian's and Burr's work. Using the GDV (Gas Discharge Visualization) Bioelectrography, which he developed, he can show the electromagnetic discharge patterns around a human body, elaborating areas with less and more discharge that correlate with different states of being like health or disease, relaxed or tense, etc..[247]

English biochemist Rupert Sheldrake proposed the idea of a "morphogenic field," a vibrational template responsible for organizing vibrations into material systems.[248] Fritz Albert Popp sees the process of incarnating as a reconstruction beam (our intentions or desires) illuminating our vibrational template into ordered material structure.[249,250]

The electro-magnetic, bioenergetic or light field, surrounding the physical body, with its higher vibrational frequency, has been termed the etheric body.[251] Research suggests that within its energetic map, the etheric body carries spatial information on how the physical body of the developing embryo will grow, and guides repair following damage or disease in adult organisms.[252] It seems probable to me that the etheric field holds the blueprint for our structure, and how the DNA will encode for specific proteins that comprise each unique area of our bodies.[253]

"The physical body is so energetically connected and dependent upon the etheric body for cellular guidance that the physical body cannot exist without the etheric body." — Richard Gerber[254]

It is the premise of Donald Ingebar, a physiologist at Harvard University, studying tensegrity in muscles that one can't influence the energetic system without also influencing the structural system, and vice versa.[255]

Sound — The Cosmic Motor

"In the beginning was the word…" — Gospel According to Saint John

In order to see a clear demonstration of vibration emerging as form we need look no further than the power of sound. According to Paramahansa Yogananda, a great yogic teacher, the sound Aum (OM) is believed to be the cosmic vibration out of which all was manifest.[256] Rudolf Steiner, in describing human evolution as spirit coming into physical form says: "This organism, consisting of the astral and etheric bodies was like a delicate, wonderful musical instrument, from the strings of which the mysteries of the universe reverberated."[257]

Astronomers discovered that sound vibrations coming from the Big Bang have orchestrated the patterns within galaxy clusters and the huge voids of space.[258] These sound vibrations orchestrated a specific 3D pattern with a nearly periodic spacing between galaxies of about 390 million light years.[259] As in the galaxies, sound vibrations, these very slow vibrations, may provide the patterns that form the structure of our cells, and ultimately our physical structure.

In 1800, German acoustical physicist Ernst Chladni experimented with sand on vibrating metal plates. Chladni clamped a metal plate onto a pedestal stand, sprinkled sand onto the surface and then drew a violin bow vertically along the rim of the plate. The diameter, density, rigidity and thickness of the plate determined its frequency and the pattern the sand grains would make on its surface. Different, intricate patterns would form with different frequencies.[260]

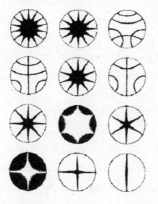

Figure 5.1 Chladni shapes from vibration of tones

Over 150 years later Dr. Hans Jenny, a Swiss Scientist, further studied the influence of sound vibrations on matter, which he called the study of cymatics.[261] Cymatics shows how tones affect and change the shape of both organic and inorganic matter. Jenny put sand, liquids, moss powders (lycopodium), or metal filings on steel discs, drumheads or rubber diaphragms. He then photographed the intricate designs that took shape in these materials when a specific vibration was transmitted from oscillating crystals, or a violin.[262]

According to the pitch of the note, the drumhead, disc or diaphragm would vibrate and the sand or liquids, etc. would collect in areas that were not vibrating, forming beautiful symmetrical patterns.[263] High notes vibrate rapidly while low notes vibrate slowly. Whatever the vibrational source, there is a tendency for any material object in proximity to vibrate in sympathy (at the same frequency) or in some harmonic derivative of the frequency. The intensity of the source vibration determines the level of molecular excitement on the disc, drumhead or diaphragm as the patterns are formed.

Using a tonoscope (similar to an oscilloscope), Jenny was able to produce pictures of the sound "oh" which formed a perfect circle. Then he chanted OM into the tonoscope, which formed a circle within which were concentric diamonds and triangles from the harmonics produced during the "mmmmmm" sound. The formed image was almost identical to the Tantric Buddhist Yantra, a mandala for the sacred vibration of creation.[264]

Using cymatics, Dr. Peter Guy Manners discovered that specific vibrations cause water droplets to change shape, just as Masaru Emoto discovered years later. With higher frequencies the droplet shape developed a more elaborate latticework pattern than with low frequencies. When he used five frequencies together, especially the higher frequencies, he was able to get a three-dimensional structure in malleable plastic that resembled the specific enfolding of embryonic structures. He was the first to suggest that sound vibration causes matter to take shape and orchestrates the structure of the cell. Sanskrit is said to be a perfect language because the cymatic patterns formed by any specific sound are the same shape as the Sanskrit letters representing the sound.[265] "As the sound, so the shape and form."[266,267] Even the beautiful patterns seen in spider webs, snowflakes, and flowers are believed to take their shape from the sound vibrations they are exposed to in nature.[268]

Our Bodies As Cymatic Systems

"As is well known, sound has great power over inorganic matter. By means of sound it is possible to cause geometric figures to form on sand and also to cause objects to be shattered. How much more powerful, then, must be the impact of this force on the vibrating, living substance of our sensitive bodies?"
— *Roberto Assagiolio, Psychoanalyst*

Sound is the slowest vibration, traveling on parallel wavelengths with color, which exists forty octaves higher. Sound profoundly influences us in utero, throughout our life, and is the last sensation we experience at death. The influence of sound begins even before the rhythm of the mother's heartbeat establishes the first beat pattern for the embryonic brain to synchronize with. We know that embryos respond to sound as early as twenty-three days after conception, and maybe even earlier. Fetuses at three months, which is prior to the development of the cochlea and auditory nerve, respond within five seconds to frequencies higher or lower than the range of the ear. This suggests that sound vibration is conducted through their skin and bones.[269,270] Attention and response to sound continues through the development of speech, from the early sounds of the mother's voice in utero, to the baby listening to and mimicking the sounds, and finally to the elegance of self-generated speech and song.

Sound has the capacity to energize us, make us more responsive to other sensory input; connect us to our society through music and rhythm; and assist us in understanding patterns in art, language, and mathematics. Sound helps to orchestrate our thought patterns and facilitates us sharing those thoughts through expressive language and music. We've seen that sound affects the structural organization of galaxies, snowflakes, and possibly embryos, as well. As the slowest vibration, it could well be the materialization from reciprocal space via deltron coupling, onto the energetic template of our etheric map.

"Living tissues are extremely responsive to coherent energy. Coherent sound patterns help to structure the physical system." — Donald Ingebar[271]

Sound And The Environment

The earth has the greatest effect of any force on our physiology, so it would make sense that the cells of our body align with it. The earth's electromagnetic field pattern, the Schumann resonance, is named after the German physicist Winfried Otto Schumann, who in 1952 mathematically predicted its existence.[272,273] But the story begins with Nikola Tesla in 1905 who first documented the existence of an ionosphere, a layer above earth's surface that could trap electromagnetic waves from the earth. He used his findings as the basis for his proposed wireless energy transmission scheme, which unfortunately was way ahead of its time. Only within the past 20 years has wireless communications transmission become a worldwide phenomenon.[274]

As the liquid iron at earth's core swirls around, it sets up an electromagnetic dynamo that powers a magnetic field that can be sensed at earth's surface.[275,276] The earth's electromagnetic field is negatively charged while the ionosphere layer (55 kilometers above the earth) is positively charged. The prevailing electrical tension between the two forms a resonant cavity where extremely low frequency (ELF) electromagnetic impulses are generated, activated mainly by lightning strikes. There are between 50 – 1,000 lightning events per second globally.[277] These electromagnetic impulses spread out laterally all around the earth and set up a resonance pattern of approximately 7.8 Hertz (Hz) or cycles-per-second with harmonic frequencies of 14.3, 20.8, 27.3, 33.8 Hz. etc.[278] Not surprisingly, each of our cells and organs have a specific resonant frequency of 7.8 – 8 Hz also.[279,280]

Herbert Konig, Schumann's student and successor at Munich University, using EEGs, demonstrated a correlation between Schumann Resonance and brain rhythms, especially alpha brain waves (with a frequency between 7.8 and 12 Hz) that assist learning.[281]

Dr. Wolfgang Ludwig, a German Physician, in his book *Informative Medizin* discusses the research of E. Jacobi from the University of Dusseldorf who discovered that the absence of Schumann waves on test subjects caused serious health problems.[282] In a study done at the Max Planck Institute for Behavioral Physiology in Erling-Andechs, volunteer students lived for four weeks in an underground bunker that completely screened out magnetic fields. These students experienced emotional distress, migraine headaches and altered circadian rhythms. With brief exposure to 7.8 Hz waves, their health returned. Similar complaints were reported by the first astronauts and cosmonauts who, while out in space, were no longer exposed to the Schumann waves. Now spacecrafts are equipped with devices that generate the Schumann resonance.[283] All the chemical and electrical reactions and processes of our bodies follow patterns imposed by sound vibration from our environment. Some researchers point out the importance of this electromagnetic wave as a background frequency that influences biological functions within living organisms, calling it the tuning fork for life.[284]

We in the U.S. and Canada can easily match a B flat pitch because it's the pitch of our 60 Hz electrical system. In Europe, people easily match the G sharp pitch, which corresponds to their 50 Hz electricity.[285] Once my jazz musician husband forgot his electronic tuner, so he tuned up to the "B" of the vacuum as workers cleaned the conference hall for his performance.

Astronomers studying the Perseus cluster of galaxies, 250 million light-years from earth, discovered that a super-massive black hole fills the galaxies and is emitting sound waves 30,000 light-years across as a cosmic hum in B flat, 57 octaves lower than middle C.[286] As I sit on the front porch of my farm-home in Hawaii, the avocado trees are full of new buds and flowers, and bees. When I use the piano to check the main sound produced by the bees, it is a B flat. So the bees are resonating with the universe or at least the electrical wires strung among the trees.

Because we are so sensitive to vibrations, unbalanced, incoherent sound has the potential to create disharmony or dis-ease within our vibrational field. A two-month old infant will already turn toward coherent sound vibrations and away from incoherent vibration. When I was pregnant with Breeze, ultrasound had just become popular for hearing the fetal heart beat. We often think of sound, especially if we can't hear it, as harmless, but Jim and I had concerns about the use of ultrasound on the delicate developing structures of our unborn child. In searching the literature, we found studies from Japan that showed a greater risk of problems in newborns after prenatal ultrasound. Ultrasound technology bounces ultra-high frequency sound waves against the developing embryo and fetus in order to obtain a picture.

In the laboratory, ultrasound wave experiments have been shown to damage chromosomes, retard normal development in cells, and produce internal cellular heat that damages cells.[287,288] Further studies show lower birth weight babies, delayed speech in humans and decreased locomotor, exploratory activity and brain function in mice.[289,290,291] Two very large studies found that ultrasound does not reduce the number of infant or maternal deaths, or lead to better care of the newborn.[292] As vibrational beings, all vibrations affect us.

Our delicate, dynamic, open-ended vibrational system appears to reflect the cosmic systems and energy of the universe and remain in balance with the coherence of our environment. In understanding our ability to create our reality from these dynamic vibrational fields, William Tiller suggests we look at the magnetic information waves of reciprocal space that formed during the inflationary period of what is presently called the Big Bang as the template for forming the electromagnetic physical universe.

With our understanding of reciprocal space, magnetic information waves and deltrons, must not humans, and all life forms, be capable of utilizing the entire available information field as the playground to come into physical being? And further, understanding that we have the potential to bring our dreams and intentions out of high energy magnetic waves into the lower energy patterns of matter and order we recognize as life and live deeply the remarkable drive and malleability of the human spirit.

6

Order and Chaos

In every culture, there is a creation story that begins with a primordial state of nothingness or chaos out of which all things and beings spring forth, and to which they return. In these ancient myths, there is always tension between chaos and order, and unpredictability to the flow from one to the other. In one Chinese creation story, the masculine Yang, a ray of pure light, jumps from chaos to build the sky, and the more reflective, receptive, feminine Yin comes from chaos to form the earth. Together Yin and Yang create everything, but they retain the qualities of chaos from which they spring allowing for continual change and re-balancing. Thus, in Chinese medicine, balance between Yin and Yang is important, with too much Yin or too much Yang bringing about chaos, change, and possibly disease within the system.[293]

The idea of a turbulent chaos as the primordial seed for life and matter pervaded human thought until Aristotle offered the proposition that order is actually the natural state, occurring at every level of a hierarchy, from simple to more complex systems, from the order of simple worms to the order of complex humans. Then, with the rise of Western science, and the views of preeminent scientists such as, Galileo, Descartes and Newton, the role of chaos was mostly forgotten. The work of these men contributed to a conception of the universe as an ordered, linear, mathematical and mechanical system. Newton and Descartes claimed that everything was ordered; and like a clockwork, even the most complex system could be understood once the ordered pattern was discovered.

In the mid-nineteenth century this mechanistic view was somewhat undermined by the recognition that the clockwork universe was prone to "rust." The formulation of the Second law of Thermodynamics and its introduction of entropy established a scientific drift toward disorder as fundamental to the universe. Like the rusting away of an old automobile, through entropy, ordered materials revert from order back to their original random atoms. The disorder of entropy, however, didn't have the creative power ascribed to chaos in the old creation stories.

Today, chaos as a causative factor in the universe has been fully reinstated to scientific legitimacy; in fact, the twentieth century saw the emergence of a new field of scientific inquiry called chaos theory. Insights from many fields led scientists toward this new perspective. Evolution theory, introduced by Darwin and simultaneously by Wallace, provided undeniable evidence that new biological forms and variations on forms were dependent on the tension and chaos of environmental factors and genetic mutations.

Newton's laws of differentials indicated that small changes produce small effects and large changes produce large effects. However, twentieth century scientists and engineers noted that small changes could have disproportionately large impact, such as a windstorm in the Sahara Desert causing worldwide weather changes, or the idea that a butterfly flaps its wings in South America and causes a hurricane off the coast of Florida.[294]

The complexity of life forms, abrupt forms of chaos like high winds, earthquakes, explosions, and sudden breaks in engineering materials represented disordered, non-linear, chaos-generated situations. In the 1970s mathematical advances and high-speed computers were able to access nonlinear equations and prove that small changes could have large effects resulting in chaos. As questions kept arising regarding the complexity, and unpredictability that occurred in the real world as a rule rather than the exception, it became clear that exact prediction regarding order is theoretically and practically impossible.

Henri Poincare, a nineteenth century French mathematician, theoretical physicist and philosopher, studying the relationships of planetary movement discovered that even a small change or perturbation in the orbit of one planet could be magnified through feedback and cause chaos. His "perturbation theory" suggested that chaos or the potential for chaos was inherent in and the essence of nonlinear systems, which include almost everything.[295] In the 1920's Max Planck discovered that energy is not a continuum but comes in small packets or quanta, which are dynamically sharing energy in a rather chaotic manner. Einstein's Theory of Relativity, first published in the 1930's is nonlinear and includes feedback loops where one change will cause another, which feeds back to affect the first. Feedback loops show up everywhere in nature, as in predator-prey relationships, or in amplifying a trait like height in a giraffe.

In 1977, Ilya Prigogine, a Russian physicist/chemist received the Nobel Prize for his Dissipative Systems Theory also known as chaos theory.

He theorized that if a system is non-linear, existing far-from-equilibrium and is open, constantly exchanging energy with the outside environment, it can maintain its identity, and, when perturbed, can change and recreate itself.[296] As a biologist, I had always questioned the law of entropy regarding living systems. If entropy was true, and all systems lose order, how do living systems constantly create and recreate dynamic, ever-changing, yet ordered systems, and hold these systems together? Prigogine's theory was an Ah Ha for me, explaining how we maintained a living form against entropy for a lifetime. We, as open systems are constantly exchanging energy with the outside world. We eat food for energy; our inhaled oxygen then breaks the chemical bonds in our food, releasing the energy to be used in all our bodily functions, including movement, and learning. Since we do not function purely out of instinct, as most insects do, our behavior is mostly non-linear, constantly changing as the environment and experience demand. Also, our body chemistry and blood flow, when functioning properly, is continually fluctuating far from equilibrium to maintain balance within our bodies. Then, any small change of focused energy (a perturbation) can further destabilize our system, causing chaos to arise, which has the potential to reestablish a different or more complex state of order.

Our skin, our largest dissipative system, can be used as an example of chaos to new order. When high-energy ultraviolet light from the sun's rays is focused on our skin, it causes the atoms within the skin to become agitated, increasing their chaotic nature, releasing more energy, and we get a sunburn. If this focused perturbation continues, the chaos within the cell can actually cause genetic changes to occur. The nucleus of the cell enlarges, the cell gains the ability to reproduce faster, and thus it comes to a new state of order or homeostasis that we call skin cancer. This is an example of chaos yielding what we perceive as negative effects upon the body, but chaos also underlies creation, greater orders of complexity and understanding.

Lynn Margulis, a Boston University Microbiologist, suggested that on early earth, one-celled organisms, perturbed by the release of toxic oxygen from cyanobacteria, symbiologically joined together to survive. These, now multi-cellular organisms exhibited more complexity, and were thus more able to survive in their environment. Their survival and rise to complexity occurred, not from competition or survival of the fittest, but out of chaos through cooperation and communication. These self-organizing systems continued, via environmental perturbation, chaos and the establishment of new order to become more and more complex, providing us with the vast diversity of living organisms on earth today.[297]

Since cooperation and communication can establish a higher order of complexity in the microbial world, it seems to me that this should be our main theme as we move into the times ahead. Shouldn't we be looking to cooperation and communication as the means toward understanding, creativity, global coherence, and survival, no matter what occurs in the environment, and maybe also because of what occurs in the environment? Continually replenished by the dynamic, teeming, chaotic soup of energy and information, there's really nothing to stop us from self-organizing into a higher order of organization and cooperation — vibration into not just matter, but full potentiality.

Upgrading Our Idea of Potential

My training as a scientist runs deep and I still find myself wanting to find the exact pattern, the specific reason for a phenomenon, the exact unchanging order within form that makes it simple and easy to explain, always! Yet, in the over 50 years that I have been fascinated with biology, I have seen it change vastly. What was a fact in the 1960's became nonsense in the 1980's. Most neuroscientists have begun saying, "at the moment, we may understand 10% of the brain, but probably ten years from now we will be saying exactly the same thing." I've truly come to learn that there are no facts, just vibrational energy packets of unpredictable, possible, orders of ideas swarming around.

Throughout history, the science of the time has been incomplete and it remains so today. Looking backward we can see, for instance, that classical physicists, who clarified so much of the world for us, left many things undiscovered, the quantum world, for one, reciprocal space and deltrons for another, and the chaos of complex systems for yet another. The classical view, that matter is fundamental, that we can reduce it to its parts, study it objectively, and learn immutable laws of the universe is still very much with us, and still has some utility. However, given the last hundred years of scientific discovery, we know the "materialist/reductionist" view is not the end of the story. Reducing matter to its smallest parts has only increased the mystery of what this universe is and what we are.

I feel we're at a point in time when science can greatly benefit by including subjective experience to more deeply understand the totality of causation and, especially, our human potential. Science, by tradition, rules out anecdotal evidence as a valid avenue for exploring the truth. I feel this is a mistake, because without such human testimony, science will not have much of relevance to say about us, and to what degree we as observers are bringing about the material world. Reductionist science, in exploring the quantum realm, has hinted at a role for consciousness, yet it invalidates the fruits of consciousness (subjective experience) as reliable evidence. Where does scientific objectivity leave us as responsible human beings, with deep questions that are not so amenable to answers from test tubes or even brain imaging devices? I, myself, have had fully awake, perceptually sensed experiences that fall outside the realm of what science considers possible, and I am not alone.

My Ordered Universe Flies Apart

In my senior year of college, if anyone had told me I would be learning, traveling and teaching in over 30 countries, I would have been delighted and astonished. And yet, I had an experience then that allowed me to glimpse that potential for myself. On a beautiful late summer afternoon in 1965, I was sharing an outing with a friend at Maroon Bells, a wilderness area near Aspen, Colorado named after two mountain peaks there. As I sat on our blanket near the lake, under the aspens, he napped next to me. The stillness and brilliance of the sky, lake, and mountains seen through the lacework of aspen leaves suspended from white branches filled me with a deep calm and peace.

Suddenly I was flying away from the sheltered glen, and when I looked back, I saw myself sitting there, peacefully. Amazingly I wasn't alarmed, just curious and a word I had heard somewhere entered my consciousness — transcendence. With a sense of exhilaration I watched the Maroon Bells and aspens recede under me, and held by what looked like a silver thread to my body, I ascended. Many images flooded my awareness, people and faces, all speaking different languages, and yet I seemed to understand them. I could feel their feelings, as I experienced a sense of limitlessness. There was such peace and connection with each new face, and language. When I read Jill Taylor's account of her stroke, it resonated with my experience.

Suddenly I was pulled back, jerked back, as my friend shook me. Awakening from his nap, he saw me sitting there peacefully with my eyes open and called my name. When I didn't respond he shook me, and I was suddenly back in my body, on the blanket by the lake. The feeling of expansion, of people, of experiences was so deep that I can still feel what I felt then, over 40 years ago. Many years later, I read about out-of-body experiences and realized that may have been what I experienced. It certainly could have been precognition of what would later be such an important part of my life.

There may be millions of people on the planet who have had this or similarly expansive conscious experiences. Because of the fear of ridicule, few people publicly acknowledge them. We risk our reputations and careers if we talk about such things. Why this ridicule? I believe it stems from the pervasive materialistic view our culture maintains. Yet, such experiences are clues to our potential as human beings. Having such an experience certainly expanded my own sense of potential, wonder, and trust in life. It made me more comfortable with chaos, ambiguity and simply not knowing what to expect. This more open sense of potential has helped me on many occasions.

Going to Africa

At 2:00 am on a November morning in 1988, in our living room in Kona, Hawaii, the presenter of a course I was sponsoring, a participant (high school special education teacher from Kauai), and Breeze and I were still awake and playing with "divining rods." I had never experienced them before and was curious about them. They basically consisted of two metal coat hangers, bent at a 90-degree angle with one side being at least twice the length of the other side. The idea was to grasp the short side loosely in a closed fist so that the long end could swivel freely. The two long ends needed to be parallel to each other and it was important not to move either your hands or the rods as you asked questions. If the rods stayed parallel and together, the answer to the question was considered to be "NO." If they moved apart, the answer was "YES."

I held the rods and asked about what courses I should teach in the Fall because I needed to get a schedule to the University. I included with each question, the phrase, "Is it for my highest good" . . . "to teach College Biology? ...to teach Anatomy and Physiology? ...to teach Ecology?", etc. The divining rods didn't move. I had run out of questions and figured this was a hoax when my daughter Breeze suggested I ask about Africa.

Our friends, Martha and Cal had worked in Africa and both Breeze and I had been mesmerized by their stories. Africa seemed to draw us like a magnet and both Breeze and I had been dreaming about Africa. So I asked,

"Is it for our highest good to go to Africa?" and to my amazement, the rods swung apart. I ended up asking the same question over and over, getting the same response — and even going back to asking about the university courses with the same "NO" responses. My scientific background had left me highly skeptical about most things, and divining rods lay outside the limited perimeters of science I had been exposed to, so I needed lots of reinforcement.

I had experienced a lot of miracles in my life, especially since coming to Hawaii, and so I had come to trust most of life's surprises. That following week, instead of handing in a Fall schedule to the University, I let them know that my daughter and I would be teaching in Africa.

In June, 1989, we left Hawaii behind to summer in Montana. In September, Breeze went to Colorado to be with her father and attend High School Redirection, a school that would accept her abroad-study as she traveled with me from January to May. I stayed in the mountains working on my first book and teaching a couple of classes a month. Alone in my secluded cabin in the woods, I began to question what I was doing and what I had left behind in Hawaii. It didn't help that my mother was very worried that I was bringing 15-year-old Breeze to a country (Kenya) that was in the middle of a civil war.

I was in the habit of taking long walks, which generally helped to put my thoughts in order, but one morning my thoughts were a-scramble with questions. I didn't have anything solid set up in Africa and I wondered how we were going to make it financially. I had a little nest egg, saved for years, but we needed all of that for our flight. We would be teaching for 18 days in Russia, during April, and end with a course in Zurich before coming home the first of May. I knew there would be no funds in Russia, though I hoped we would be taken care of with food and lodging. I knew I would get some money from the Switzerland course, but was totally unsure of the amount.

Walking on an overgrown logging road above the cabin, every fear flooded my mind; the brain chatter was intense and agitated when a voice boomed through me, saying, "SHUT UP!" I immediately asked out loud: "Am I doing the right thing?" Loudly, the voice inside my body boomed, "SHUT UP!" Then more quietly I heard, "Sit Down." I instantly found a log under a brightly colored aspen and sat. Again I asked, "Am I doing the right thing?" and the voice answered: "BE STILL."

So for the first time in over a week, I sat on a log in the warm autumn breeze among the trees, and was still. I began to breathe deeply again and noticed the birds, and the wisps of clouds in the intense blue of space. I felt the moss covered rocks, and tasted end of the season wild strawberries. The peace and beauty filled me and brought me into the present again. Gratitude for my freedom, this wondrous space and the possible adventures that lay ahead engulfed me and for half an hour I was calm.

Then the questions came and I softly asked, "Are we to go to Africa?" "Do they know we are coming?" And the answer came with such love and warmth that it still, as I write this, brings tears to my eyes: "Yes."

I sailed down the mountain that day, lighter and excited by the journey ahead. In the months that followed, the head of a school in Bloemfontain, South Africa called and asked if I would do a teacher training for them. He had heard of my work at a meeting he attended in New York and was interested in having his teachers experience it. He apologized that he couldn't pay us, but that he would take us to a game park and provide food and housing while in Bloemfontain. We accepted. I also got a call from a couple in England who had been working with the Botswana Insurance Company in Haborone. They wanted us to do a one-day seminar and said they could pay us a small amount. Of course we said yes. I miraculously met Karl Nel, an Art Professor from Witts University in Johannesburg, who offered to have us stay with his family when we were in South Africa, which we also accepted. We also got a rather cryptic message from a couple in Lesotho asking if we would come and share our work with them, to which we also replied yes. So Breeze, with her school curriculum in her backpack and I, with excitement, curiosity, and some foreboding, flew to Africa on January 1, 1990.

Welcoming Chaos

It seems that we, as humans, long for an unperturbed life, where everything is predictable, we know what to expect, we have all the answers, every desire and need is met, and we are always happy, calm and in control. Yet, is this really true? Because, it also seems that we seek and activate the chaos, the perturbation that moves us to a higher level of understanding and complexity. Why? Chaos, it seems, keeps us from becoming stuck, dogmatically positioned and inflexible while providing us an exciting, passionate life journey, full of challenges, wonder and the growth we have chosen by coming into this material reality.

Other than the aforementioned teaching situations, we were scheduled for three months in Africa, mostly in Kenya, where our friend

Martha agreed to pave the way for us. As fate would have it, just a week before leaving, Martha let us know that the government had stopped her trip to Kenya because of the civil strife. So suddenly we were on our own! Martha had friends in Nairobi who promised to take care of us, but this was not without some interesting political complications. We landed in Nairobi with its luscious warm air, flower smells, palm trees, soft spoken language, people with skin ranging from golden to deep night black, women with glorious smiles and elaborately printed fabrics they wrapped around their bodies and hair in intricate patterns. A Masai, wearing red ochre in his long dread locks, a short animal skin cover, and huge earrings dangling from extended earlobes, strode elegantly down a street next to a man in a business suit — both talking adamantly. The marketplace had beautiful handmade animal skin bags, fabrics in rich, brilliantly colored patterns that spoke "Africa," musical instruments, and tropical fruits. I felt the tingle of newness, the excitement of a different world opening up its spectacle to me. I felt no fear, no fatigue, just sheer excitement and eagerness to take it all in, smell it, feel it, hear it, be it!

Civil war in Kenya meant there were no books in the schools from grade school through university, no laboratory equipment, and the professors were getting minimal pay or none at all. Students and professors alike were doing their best to adjust and learn and teach in more organic ways. Aside from all the beauty, there was always the threat of violence, palpable and chaotic at the edge of our new reality.

Breeze and I taught together for the Adult Literacy Council, and met with several educators, taking in a overview of this highly complex country. Besides teaching with me during the whole trip, Breeze was also doing her own independent study, keeping intricate notes that she weekly sent back to her teacher at High School Redirection. Nairobi provided her a rich palette of experiences for the beginning of our amazing journey.

After a week with caring people, much confusion and great beauty we flew onto Johannesburg. Other than two planned teaching situations, each a couple days long, we had no set plan, yet in that three-month period of time in South Africa, Lesotho and Botswana, our world expanded. We met fascinating people, listened intently to their stories, experienced new landscapes and opened our minds to vast new learning. Day after day, we rode the wild rapids of chaos to order and back to chaos.

From our initial planned gigs in Bloemfontaine and Botswana, we ended up doing 79 presentations, accepting any invitations that came our way. Though we were not paid, we were housed, fed well, treated to amazing experiences, given authentic handmade African gifts and loved deeply at every turn. We were forced to open to and receive whatever was offered and became as little children, ready to explore the new. There were moments of trepidation, as I would ask myself "What have I done"? But the fears melted as the adventure took hold and the moment became all that existed. And each night, as we found our beds in new places under the African sky, Breeze and I would say to each other, "Can you believe what we experienced today?"

Figure 6.1 Picture of the author in Lesotho with the village children

In April we returned to Nairobi for a week on our way to Russia. Our 18 days in Russia would fill a book by themselves, and again each day was filled with much chaos, inspiration, and extraordinary learning. Our last stop was in Zurich, Switzerland to teach a course for two days to around seventy-five people. At the end of the course, Rosemarie Sonderregger, the head of the institute, handed me a check for the class. The amount was the exact amount I had taken out of the bank (all my savings) to take this amazing trip.

This was a huge lesson in the power of our intention, our passion to experience the world, and trust. I often hear stories of synchronicity and miracles from friends and people I have met around the world. Apparently, the chaos these miracles are birthed from, are an important part of our existence. It seems that when we are doing what assists our growth, the miracles, the chaos, and often, the ease propel us forward. Many positive life transformations begin with events that may at first appear fiercely chaotic, or challenging.

Every human life is different, based upon the dynamic tension we exist in, between order and chaos. It is the spring from wholeness to duality that produces the drama, the chaos and the return to wholeness as the lessons are learned and balance is reestablished. The chaos that forces us into an unstable state, out of our comfortable homeostasis, has the potential to empower us to be more consciously aware and connected to all that is. If we live in an open-ended state of interpretation and reinterpretation, within our authentic nature, we will experience the vast potentiality of human life. Then the goal of our theories, as scientists, and conscious human beings will be to coherently assimilate the chaos into order to convey our "understanding in this moment", realizing that our understanding is incomplete, and relishing the growth that leads to new "understanding in this moment" and then do it again and again for the adventure of it.

If we can accept unpredictability, so inherent in our world, reveling in the uncertainties, interrelationships, and mutual dependence that demand communication and cooperation, it becomes a richer playground. Under this new banner of possibilities, our ideas and observations can't be scrutinized like some juried art show. But they can be accepted as un-dreamt of realities and un-thought of adventures, again seeing through the eyes of our childlike nature, the unknown world for what it truly is.

Whenever we learn something new that is important and interesting to us, our neural networks are changed to reestablish a different and usually more complex state of order, of understanding. I am excited to live in these "dangerous times" where chaos exists in every domain, from the epidemic of autistic children, to the depressed economy, to global warming and fascinating climate changes, to nuclear threat. If we truly understand our power as coherent beings, this can be an auspicious time of change to a higher order of complexity, understanding, and passionate living from our hearts.

7

Passion, Emotion and Coherent Connection

"We as humans are here to experience emotions and to use our bodies as vehicles to achieve emotional wisdom." — Marlo Morgan[299]

In the preceding chapters, we've expanded the paradigm of what human beings are and what our potential is for transformation. We are dynamic, highly malleable, open systems within a unified field of information. We are the playing field and we are the players. We can choose our actions, navigate chaos with resilience, and we can learn from both success and failure. For the remainder of this book we'll be looking at how to play in the field to bring about our greatest growth in consciousness, creativity, and joy. We'll begin with examining our emotions.

The emotions that coursed through Breeze and I on our first trip to Africa were often different from each other's, yet very deeply felt. Our experiences were so new, so immediate, that we lived in our emotions, and in so doing, became our authentic natures, out of which came the miracles we experienced. As conscious beings, emotions (energy in motion) are the templates that define our experiences in life and motivate us to fully tap into our power as creators of our reality. Emotions fuel our intentions, our relationships, our creativity and actions. As William Tiller says, emotions are powerful deltrons that assist us to bring our material reality out of reciprocal space. They are like a double-edged sword, able to bring about cooperation, harmony and peace, or conversely, conflict, stress and violence. The determining difference is whether we maintain coherence or slide into incoherence. And the determining difference between coherence and incoherence is conscious awareness.

The Feeling of Reality

Emotions orchestrate every part of our reality, structuring our intelligence, our ability to do high-level formal reasoning, our language and the drive to create new and interesting ideas and things.[300] Our diverse emotions release hormonal patterns that motivate our bodies and minds to take action, and experience the world as conscious, sentient beings. Emotions allow us to understand and more deeply connect with others through empathy and compassion while providing us with passion for living the mystery of life. "What we feel about an experience creates our reality, our model of the world."[301]

Emotions play an important part in determining how we filter our world, thus determining what information we will retain as our reality. As we experience our world, the incoming sensory information goes through the thalamus and then the primary neural path runs directly to the amygdala and cerebellum[302] that act as the portals for emotion regulation, bypassing conscious awareness, so we can instantly act or react if need be.

The secondary path is slower, going from the thalamus to the information rich neocortex that allows us to consciously identify and respond appropriately to the stimuli. Over time, mirror neurons scattered throughout the brain allow us to mirror the actions and emotions of those around us, and the amygdala creates a map that details the emotional significance of everything in our environment. Messages from the amygdala then activate the frontal lobes that regulate the resulting behavior and the autonomic nervous system, which prepares our body for action.[303]

The amygdala's consolidation of emotionally laden memories is vital in deciding what matters. The amygdala enhances and directs our perception and attention regarding emotions such as pleasure, fear, disgust; and it confers emotional significance to a wide range of experiences. The amygdala gives life meaning, and along with other subcortical organs, it defines who we are. Our identities arise from the unique array of desires, associations, fears, and expectations housed in our subconscious.[304]

In the early stages of emotional development children are acutely aware of the emotions of people closest to them within their environment, and physically mirror and mimic them. Because the child must anchor new learning on the body, emotions show up as full body expressions (crying, shouting, jumping for joy, giggling). As the child's mirror neurons mature in an emotionally rich environment, the bodily reactions become more subtle and the child learns how to responsibly express emotions and trust her intuitive knowing, her gut/heart feelings.[305] The preceding scenario is that of a child growing up in a safe and coherent environment with a rich emotional palette of human interaction to learn from. Emotionally rich models are able to authentically and responsibly express their full range of emotions, in a safe way for themselves and others.

Emotions are a key element of experience, thus making us fully conscious and available to learn, remember and grow in understanding and mastery. Emotions can be expressed as laughter, tears, screams, swaying, stomping, jumping, dancing, backing away, holding one's self or reaching out, and most often will be devoid of words. Talking about our emotions relegates them to the linear, language brain away from the whole body experience. Bruce Lipton, a cellular biologist, who is bridging science and spirit, maintains that we developed language to cover up our emotions.[306]

The right frontal insula of the brain lights up when we feel strong physical sensations and all the quintessential human emotions (sad, joyful, scared, mad) that arise from those sensations. Thus it gives rise to the map of "the emotional me" and "the emotional now". The more we are aware of our body's sensations, the more emotionally attuned we are, and able to mirror the emotions of others, experience empathy and live passionately. People who experience whole-body paralysis and are unable to experience physical sensations complain of lack of passion and emotion.[307]

Children physically experience emotions beautifully, if allowed. Their emotions are whole-bodied, magnanimous and very real. When they are joyful, their enthusiasm is infectious. When they are sad or scared, they cry, and, if acknowledged, within moments are off playing again. When they are mad we call it a temper-tantrum, but if left alone to fully experience their anger (we don't need to tie into their emotions, in fact it can either inhibit or prolong them if we do), within a short time they have forgiven and forgotten. They will grieve a loss and move forward, which allows them to stay healthy.

Antonio Damasio, MD, Ph.D, and head of the department of neurology at the University of Iowa College of Medicine, delineates three kinds of emotions. The first are the primary or instinctive emotions such as fear, anger, disgust, surprise, sadness and joy. These survival emotions keep us safe and healthy. Fear and anger give us the courage to stand up to threatening situations, while disgust protects us from eating something poisonous. Isolation and abandonment seem to elicit the greatest fear in possibly all sentient beings. It seems that we all need connection, and without it pathologies and even death ensue. Both sadness and joy can and do occur with changes in relationship, job, home, and health. Change is our only constant and our emotions physically assist us to process and move forward through the change.

The second kind is social emotions. Damasio says these include sympathy, embarrassment, shame, guilt, pride, envy, jealousy, gratitude, admiration, attraction, contempt, and indignation, as well as empathy, compassion and altruism. These emotions allow us the interplay with others that can either keep us stuck in drama or allow our souls to grow with understanding and altruism.

The third category is feelings that stem from self-reflection. Damasio defines feelings as sensations that arise as the brain analyzes and interprets emotions coming from the body's condition. "I feel sick," or "this feels wonderful," or "I am so sad," or "that color makes me happy," are examples of feelings. While all other sentient beings experience emotions, Damasio believes that only humans think about, manipulate and even feign feelings as actors and some politicians do.[308]

In order for our children to have enriched lives, we must share our true feelings with them. When we are sad or scared, our children know it in their bodies. If we affirm our emotions to them and allow them to comfort us, that affirmation anchors their trust in their intuitive knowing. The same is true when we feel joy, to really express it, welcoming that expression in our children as they join with us.

Breeze seemed to always know when I was scared or sad and would ask, "What's wrong Mommy?" When I felt that I had to protect her and make her life always happy, I would answer, "Nothing is wrong." This was confusing to her because from her mirror neurons and vibrational sensing she was feeling that I was sad, and since I wasn't acknowledging that, she lost faith in her intuitive knowing. If instead I shared with her that I was sad (no need to share the whole story, just the emotion), it gave her the confidence to trust her knowing. It also gave her an understanding of the emotion "sad" so she could name it when she felt the same way. This key step in development allows children to trust their mirror of your emotions, and gifts them with an enriched, passionate life and the ability to connect deeply, empathetically and compassionately with others and the world.

The Power of Empathy

"Coherence is personal power through increasing one's integrity, understanding and capacity for compassion"[309] — *David Hawkins*

Empathy is one of the most important emotions for us to develop within the structure of a loving home, neighborhood, society and global community. Empathy is the ability to internalize the emotional state of others and even understand that another person's experience and feelings may differ from one's own, and that those experiences and feelings are important for that person's growth. Empathy with others also provides us with the mirror to become aware of our own feelings and connect more intimately with ourselves through others.

Empathy is learned through mirroring those around us. Mirror neurons fire when a person performs an action, expresses an emotion and when he or she observes someone else engaged in the same action or emotion. When our mirror neurons are activated, we can know and feel what another person is feeling just by looking at his or her face. Because our brains fire in synchrony with other people's actions or emotions, we are directly sharing the experience of others. This is key to who and what we are, how our brains and minds evolve and how they develop from childhood.

Neurons in the prefrontal cortex, especially the insula and anterior cingulate may act as mirror neurons since they fire in relationship to the "I care" or "I don't like this" aspect of pain, (rather than the "where, when, what type" of pain aspect). Recent studies with animals bolster the evidence that other mammals exhibit something akin to empathy, thus showing that empathy arises from basic neural mechanisms that human evolution has simply elaborated on.[310] Mirror neurons must have played a great part in the evolution of empathy, imitation, imagination and social understanding. If we experience compassion and empathy in our environment, we embody those traits through the mirroring process.[311,312,313,314]

The more people receive empathy, the more "whole," coherent and empathic they become. Empathetic parents use firm discipline when their children hurt others, and emphasize the rights and welfare of others. Their children are more likely to show high levels of pro-social and reparative behaviors throughout their lives.[315]

"These good acts give us pleasure, but how happens it that they give us pleasure?
Because nature hath implanted in our breasts a love of others, a sense of duty
to them, a moral instinct, in short, which prompts us irresistibly to feel
and to succor their distresses." — Thomas Jefferson, 1814

In the first year, empathy is gained through bonding, in which the parent and infant share and mirror emotions, cooperate, and take turns with each other. Babies show comforting behavior by crying at another's pain and by patting and hugging that person. By the second year, the child learns to regulate his emotions and doesn't become overwhelmed by another person's suffering. Comforting becomes more appropriate to the situation, more frequent and differentiated.[316] Research has shown that more empathetic children perform better on SAT, IQ and school achievement tests, and get along better with peers than children who have not developed empathy.[317]

There is much concern about the current epidemic of autism, which affects 0.5% of American children. Speculations as to the causes of autism include stress, genetics, vaccines, environmental risk factors and temporal lobe epilepsy. I feel these children are the "canaries in the mine" for us. I believe that these highly sensitive children are locked in survival mode, beginning even before birth. They are more sensitive to threat stimuli like changing lights, loud sounds, and sudden movements in this survival state, and their thalamus will only take in sensory information that has to do with survival. Thus they become unable to activate and mature their mirror neuron systems for the non-survival, social/emotional cues of the people around them. For an autistic child, the stimulation of looking at a human face with all its changing expressive emotions is too much when the child is focused on threat stimuli.

The mirror neurons in autistic children have been found to be dormant and inactive rather than missing. Autistic children can experience fear, rage and pleasure, but lack genuine empathy for other people, are oblivious to subtle social cues and unable to mime other people's actions. Simply, their ability to connect in joy, empathy and compassion has not been developed.[318] The good news is that the pro-social, interactive floor-time play developed by Stanley Greenspan and others appears to activate and mature these mirror neurons, greatly assisting these children to grow healthy emotional landscapes.[319,320] Also, even though autistic people score low on IQ tests, they score much higher on challenging, nonverbal tests that tap a person's ability to infer rules and to think abstractly about geometric patterns. Autistic people are also able to shift flexibly back and forth between focusing on details of a scene and its overall configuration, a trait not common in non-autistic people. We often sell short the unique features of these highly sensitive people.[321]

Emotions And Health

Authentically expressing our emotions is essential for keeping us healthy. When we are able to responsibly express our emotions and create a safe place for ourselves and others, the survival response is not triggered in the body, and the body remains healthy. If we suppress or are unable to express our emotions, the survival response is triggered which can cause devastating disease or major psychological problems. In a major study, it was found that people who suppress their emotions (especially frustration, fear or sorrow) were more pessimistic, more prone to depression, less self-confident, less able to meet mental challenges, had fewer and less meaningful friendships, and a much greater chance of dying early.[322]

One of the very telling activities I do in my courses is ask participants to physically feel, throughout their whole body, one of four emotions (sad, glad, mad, or scared) and then do a muscle check to demonstrate the quality of the emotional state. Often, the emotion is being processed in their heads. They are thinking about the emotion rather than truly experiencing it in the body, and the muscle test indicates stress, even when they are focusing on gladness. It appears they have armored their bodies not to fully feel the emotion. It would make sense that if you can't feel mad or sad, you can't feel joy or delight. When we don't feel our emotions as a whole body experience, it is like being wrapped in cotton, not fully living.

I have found that when a person is authentically experiencing the emotion with his or her whole body, their muscle check will be strong, even with sadness. In this state, I feel the body is doing what is natural in order to process its world, so the survival reaction in the body is not triggered. Julia Cameron notes in her book, *The Artists Way: The Spiritual Path to Higher Creativity*, "The quality of life is in proportion, always, to the capacity for delight." Children are easily delighted until they are taught to suppress and armor themselves against emotions and self-disclosure. I believe that because this is an unnatural process the body experiences stress and all that goes with it.

It seems important that we fully experience our personal emotions about a situation in order to process and learn from it. Through Elizabeth Kubler-Ross's work, we have known that we must go through all the stages of grieving when there has been a loss, in order to come out the other side in a healthy way.[323] With the loss of someone close to us, the grieving period will typically take 18 months or more. Friends and family of a grieving person can support them by allowing and encouraging them to experience the process. If the person in grief is a child or teenager, don't minimize their need to mourn and be a good mirror when you are mourning, by doing so openly. Teens may not acknowledge the pain they feel, so suggest ways to memorialize the loss, such as a ritual or a memory box.

Managing Emotions

In traditional Chinese teachings, emotions are considered the driving energy of the body, necessary for life, while spirit and social training control their manifestations.[324] Managing emotions in a healthy way requires a clear perspective that does not include victimization. As Shakespeare's Hamlet says: "There is nothing either good or bad, but thinking makes it so." If, in our own lives, we take responsibility for being masters, calling forth the lessons that will best evolve our beings, then we see each situation as another gift for growth. If we also see others as masters, doing the same thing, we can distance ourselves enough to have empathy, but not get tied into their journey and stress about it.

I had a beautiful lesson in empathetic, compassionate detachment while observing a teacher named Patrick at the Forest Kindergarten in Kirchzarten, Germany. A three-year-old boy wasn't watching his step as he walked across a very low (2 foot high) bridge and fell. The boy began to cry and I wanted to run to him, but Patrick looked at him and said he wasn't hurt and to allow him the time to realize his mistake without jumping in to help. Patrick then knelt down and opened his arms. The child ran into his compassionate embrace and within moments was off playing again.

So often, when a person is crying, we will touch or hug them. This is most likely because we are either uncomfortable with their emotional expression or conditioned to enable others. In either case, it tends to interfere with their processing of the emotion, and the full experience to grow from it. As a reformed enabler, I look back on how I jumped in too often when Breeze was faced with challenges, and "saved her." We, as parents, don't want our children to go through the pain and trials of life, and yet, that is how we learned, — through experience. I also see this enabling scenario with my husband. When I am faced with a challenge I just want him to hold me, while I go through the emotions, and listen until I am able to look at it clearly enough to come up with my own solutions. However, this highly empathetic man feels he must "ride in on his white horse and save me." He is then frustrated when I don't take his advice.

Men and women process stress differently. A study at UCLA found that when women are stressed their oxytocin rises, buffering the fight or flight response. Women befriend and bond with other women, sharing their stories and emotions in a loving but detached way, which produces a calming effect, rather than the stress reaction.[325] Men tend to feel they must be strong, not show emotions and seldom seek the bonding or empathy of others. This may be one of the reasons men die earlier than women in our culture.

I ask people in my workshops to just remain present, stand in *Hook Ups* from Brain Gym® and focus on their breathing to support people as they process their emotions, only touching them if they ask to be held or touched. People always have the option of asking for assistance if they need it while emoting. This way we don't interfere with their important emotional processing.

Australian Aborigines have a saying: "Support another with few actions and fewer words." They believe that emotional detachment, such as observation free of judgment is healthy, and life enhancing. They feel we are all responsible for our energy and the discipline of our emotions. Though everyone experiences negative states, to linger in them and not learn from them is to be irresponsible, immature and unwise.[326] When we see others in pain, or facing fierce challenges in their lives, empathy and compassion assist us to link with that part of our own humanity. But we can never know the actual function of those challenges or pain for that person. When we label someone less fortunate, we miss seeing his or her mastery and connectedness to the whole.

When we tie into this empowered, responsible perspective, the prefrontal cortex is more active, allowing us insight.[327,328] Tibetan monks, during meditation, are able to access a gamma wave state in their brains (frequencies between 25 and 45 hertz), which increases awareness and modulates emotions. Through this increased awareness, they are able to take in and altruistically understand the larger field of consciousness beyond suffering, without judgment or becoming personally enmeshed. In so doing, they gain insight and easily rid themselves of negativity.[329]

Zen Master Dennis Genpo Merzel, with his *Big Mind, Big Heart* work affirms the practice of letting go of dualistic thinking, right vs. wrong, good vs. bad, and coming from the mind of oneness and being.[330] Genpo Roshi teaches that every emotion is a unique source of wisdom for us, and we can discover its wisdom through awareness: by identifying as the emotion, speaking as it, and honoring it. Owning and acknowledging emotions through the *Big Mind* work, each emotion can develop from immature to mature in its expression. Using the symbol of a triangle to represent our whole being, Genpo Roshi describes the left base of the triangle as our human side that seeks, wants, and has emotions. The right base of the triangle represents the being part of us that is "no self," at peace, and free from judgment or wanting. The Apex of the triangle represents the full human being where the human emotions and the objective awareness of being are fully integrated. Our perspective may move back and forth from the human side to the being side, but we are always both, always the whole triangle. We can observe ourselves as complete in each moment, living fully our journey.

"Forgiveness is the ability to make peace with your own life by no longer arguing and objecting to the way it unfolds." —Fred Luskin[331]

We really only suffer when we want things to be different than they are. Neuro-imaging research shows that forgiveness is good for our physical, emotional and mental well-being. When we choose to forgive a person or situation, areas of our brain associated with empathy are activated. According to the research, forgiveness does not necessarily mean reconciliation, or forgetting, or condoning an unkind action or situation. Forgiving does mean acknowledging it, maybe even grieving it, and accepting it for what it is, a step towards deeper understanding and an opportunity to proactively take the steps necessary to assure that the unkindness stops with us.[332] It seems that seeing each situation, the ones we like and the ones we don't like as a gift for our evolution, allows us to fully experience our emotions and move forward.[333] This appears to be the most natural process and allows us to live passionate lives, full of energy and understanding that advances altruism and connects us more fully to others and ourselves.

Immature, extreme, and harmful emotions seem to be on the rise today. I believe these extreme emotions come from "stuffed"(suppressed) emotions that eventually erupt, usually with no direct connection to the immediate situation, thus they make no sense. Emotions are suppressed because the natural expression of those emotions may not have been encouraged or acknowledged, and are often judged. When emotions and memories are suppressed, there is a dampening of activity in the prefrontal cortex and a greater chance of depression.

Depression — Sign Of Our Times

"Loneliness and depression are the diseases of the West" — Mother Theresa

A 2005 survey done by the National Institute of Mental Health showed that forty million adult Americans exhibit anxiety disorders. This constitutes 18.1% of the adult population. Of those, 14.8 million, 6.7% are clinically depressed.[334] And approximately 3.4 million young people under age 18 experience serious depression each year. At its current rate depression is projected to be the number one disease in the U.S. and number two in the world by the year 2020.[335]

In our society, which touts cool headed intellectualism, there appears to be no socially acceptable emotional action we can express for sadness, fear, loneliness, or joy for that matter, so we tend to "armor" ourselves.[336] When we "tough it out" we are suppressing our feelings or actions by tightening the muscles that would normally express them. Tension shows up in tight jaws (inhibiting verbal expression), shoulder problems (inhibiting the fight reaction), and low back problems (inhibiting the flee reaction).

People learn early to construct their "armor" if their emotions are not allowed an outlet. The chronic tension of "armoring" limits mobility and the ability to feel, thus, we drift out of touch with our bodies, and our inner and physical natures. Lack of regular exercise and rigid muscles impede the flow of energy throughout the body, so the system becomes depressed.[337] Depression becomes the body's way of withdrawing to conserve energy and minimize risk.

When emotions and memories are suppressed, the left pre-frontal cortex with its ability to focus on the positive side decreases its function, as does the amygdala, leading to depression. In depressed people, the ventral anterior cingulate that connects the left pre-frontal cortex to the hypothalamus and orchestrates the hormonal response that assures survival is 40% smaller, so depressed people do nothing, they just give up.[338,339,340] Simple exercise, especially walking, if done in groups or with family and friends, has been found to be as effective as taking anti-depressant drugs, and is far less addictive.[341] Music that lifts the spirit is also highly effective as an antidepressant.

Close to 10% of men and women in America are now being medicated for depression.[342] This startling fact raises serious questions regarding diagnosis and whether pharmaceutical companies are more interested in making profits from health than contributing to it. A New York University study done in 2007, showed that about one in four people treated for depression are in fact just dealing with the aftermath of recent emotional blows from loss and/or a sudden life change. These emotional blows could more effectively be helped through exercise and a closely connected community.[343,344]

Some of the tribal Africans groups I encountered in South Africa, Botswana and Lestho have a solid family/clan structure that assures everyone is taken care of and a sense of belonging. These people live by "UBUNTU" which means, "Because I am, we are, and because we are, I am." Depression is unknown in the intact tribal areas I visited. Dean Ornish MD, author of many books on lifestyle, claims that nothing more powerfully affects our health than love, connection and community.[345] Yet we remain ruggedly individualistic in our Western culture, which can easily lead to a sense of isolation, loneliness, and depression. Thus we are at least three to five times more likely to get sick and die prematurely, not only from heart disease, but from all causes, than cultures who have strong cooperative communities and honor emotional expression.

Recently, researchers found that a short serotonin transporter gene can produce a highly vigilant emotional brain that predisposes a person toward depression, but this gene only boosts depression risk in the presence of a number of significant stressful events.[346] Depression is most frequent when people have gone through a trauma, loss, or major life change and constantly rethink the event, worrying about it and anticipating further difficulties. Anxiety is the root of almost all emotional disorders: post-traumatic stress disorder, generalized anxiety disorder, obsessive-compulsive disorder, schizophrenia and depression. Because there are more neural pathways from the amygdala to the cortex than from the cortex to the amygdala, our anxieties often control our thoughts.[347] Breeze pointed out to me, that perhaps depressed people watch horror movies because they can physically go through the anxiety and actually experience the emotions, rather then just thinking about them and continually mulling them over.

Within weeks of depressive stress, the hippocampus wears out as the spines on its neurons wither and the cells die, hindering its ability to tell the hypothalamus to stop delivering more stress hormones, thus stress rises.[348] The communication breakdown between the prefrontal cortex and the amygdala distorts emotional responses and the social decisions one makes.[349] In violent men and schizophrenics the hippocampus and amygdala are smaller by as much as 19%.[350]

Depressed people tend to have few social contacts and become negative about the people around them, making relationships difficult. They don't feel like they fit in and have little curiosity about other people or new ideas, so they become antisocial and isolated. The isolation leads to low self-esteem, a lost sense of value, and even self-abuse.[351] People are only mean when they've forgotten their own value.

Isolation has become a way of life for many children and adults in our society. TV and computers become focal areas for the family, decreasing first hand interactive communication or real play and touch. Parents are busy earning a living, often leaving latchkey kids, who are missing out on the full quota of family warmth and connection, and we experience the consequences in the form of violence. As adults, isolation and our longing for self-value and connection often take the form of obsessive consumerism, necessitating that we work more and leave our families more. Thus the cycle of isolation continues.

Real Life Depression

I hadn't really thought much about depression until I met Catherine Carrigan. She had survived years of depression, suicide attempts, hopping from one drug therapy to another and from one therapist to the next. She ended up in one of my courses because she had discovered that she could stop her depression through integrated movements and wanted to know more. Her experience sparked my interest, and I began reading the studies, studies that tied right back into our culture's stress addiction.[352]

Everyone has their own take on depression. I saw it from the outside as Breeze went through a brief bout of it years ago, and wrote about it in *Awakening the Child Heart*. Now Breeze has challenged me to write about my own experience with depression, and how it looks from the inside.

My years of being on the road, traveling in many countries, hauling heavy luggage full of books, teaching 10 hour days, and in my time off assisting in the building of our home and spending endless hours on the farm weeding, planting and pruning were taking their toll on my body. I had even commented that if I didn't slow down, my body would stop me, and sure enough, in the fall of 2006 it did. I came home to my husband Ahti and Hawaii crippled with a severe spondylothesis scoleosis and herniated disc, unable to lean over or even move much without massive pain.

First I was angry with this once strong but now fragile body that had always worked at my command. I was frustrated with my inability to pull the weeds that had their way with the farm while I was gone, or ride in a car for more than fifteen minutes, or move with grace and flexibility, or even be present enough to enjoy my close friends. I have always been a driven, doing person and my world had turned inside out. Standing up and lying down were the only two positions that afforded some relief from the pain. It got to a point where there were only moments of freedom from the burning, shooting pains in my back and legs.

I hid away, not wanting to see anyone, even my loving and supportive husband. I would sleep long hours, eat very little and sleep again. I couldn't understand much of what I read, and had no interest in writing. My once quick mind worked slowly and seemed so empty. The word that constantly hung over me was "Lazy." I judged myself harshly at every turn. The powerful self help tools I had acquired over the years were forgotten as I spiraled downward. I felt so helpless and hopeless as each new therapy failed to make much of a difference. All this culminated in a deepening sense of depression where the phrase "non-thinking, non-emotive with underlying anxiety" from Scott Walker's NET (Neuro-emotional Technique) Chiropractic work applied fully.

Ahti introduced me to Eckhart Tolle's books, which I read piecemeal, but which struck a chord. I began seeing my back problems and pain as my shaman's journey, a gift that was essential for the evolution of my soul. Stillness and conscious being became my teachers. I realized that depression occurs when we forget what and who we truly are: masters, not victims. I made a storyboard, a picture representation of where I was choosing to go, with a fluid dancer in the center encircled with light, a reminder of my power. My emotions began to flow freely as I cried often, began to laugh and even experienced bliss at times. I took walks, remembering the importance of cross lateral movement, walking through the pain, knowing it was helping to relieve the pressure on my lower back while taking in the abundant, ever-changing landscape around our Hawaiian farm. I could even play my violin (standing up) for several hours without much pain, which filled me with joy.

Ahti and tenacious friends invaded my seclusion and invited me into life while my loving physical therapists and an osteopath taught me to be empathetic with my body and listen deeply to its messages. Breeze, now a social worker on the mainland with minimal time off, took her earned vacation time to be with me, assisting me through love and a profound Brain Gym balance to come back to my power, my authenticity, and understand this great gift that had been given to me.

The months grew into a meditation on just being present and listening to the startlingly beautiful world around me. I moved past the deep depression, practicing to be more coherent and present in each moment while listening to and honoring all that my body was sharing with me. The final step was major back surgery, and learning to trust the medical profession, not just alternative therapies, and that I didn't have to do it all myself. The healing had to do with changing my perspective, and how I live my life. Now and then I look at my storyboard and realize the miracle. I can dance all night in my light, flexible body without pain.

The Depressed Angry Heart

If depression is not addressed, violence can become one of the outcomes. In March of 1999, America was stunned by the incident at Columbine High School in Colorado as two boys, good students, each from high socio-economic, two-parent families, killed 13 and wounded many other students, then killed themselves. In a special report on Troubled Kids in *TIME Magazine*, May 31, 1999 the word depression kept coming up. Of the nine boys spotlighted in the article, five were considered depressed and three were on Ritalin, Prozac or Luvox. All of these boys were known to spend long hours on the internet, playing video games and listening to dark music. Their favorite video games were: *Doom, Mortal Kombat, Quake* and their music came from Marilyn Manson, Nirvana, and Tupac Shakur. The incoherent content of the video games and music surely had an effect on these young men desperately attempting to connect with something meaningful that expressed what they were feeling.

Breeze suggested that the anger expressed in the music mirrored the hopeless, helpless sadness they could relate to, but were unable to express themselves. They weren't alone in their pain. The internet also provided them some connection, where they could interact with other people, create a virtual persona, and somehow be part of a community. But the interactions were secondhand, with no touch or movement to ground the connection. Gangs symbolize a form of reaching out for connection in community. Without a community, or other people to relate to, we don't have a sense of being real.

The Power Of Connection

We know that the more social contacts people have, the happier, more optimistic and healthier they are.[353,354] Our strongest ties are those relationships characterized by frequent contact, deep feelings of affection and obligation, and a broad base of understanding. Strong ties tend to buffer people from life's stresses and lead to better social and psychological safety.[355] Knowing that we are in constant communication with one another and continually influencing one another through the invisible vibrational fields issuing from our hearts and brains should certainly allow us to feel more connected. When these fields are coherent there is a natural sense of safety, belonging and peace, and we feel in harmony with one another. We are able to express ourselves fully, passionately, and emotionally.

Our amazing technology can leave us overwhelmed by volumes of email, blogs, and other internet activities, while dramatically infringing on our peace and quality of life. The flicker of the computer screen increases our levels of adrenaline and cortisol, and vastly decreases our dopamine levels.[356] We spend large chunks of time daily checking the internet while missing the first hand experience of being with the flesh and blood people just a few steps away. And then we wonder why we are lonely!

Our emotional connections nurture and allow us to remember our worth. We must invite people into life, through our modeling of coherence and passion, or they will choose depression, violence and/or death without connection to others or themselves. We have no time to leave our precious children, elderly, friends, family and even strangers out of our lives and in the hands of an incoherent technology-based world, devoid of authentic human emotions and connections. It seems that a million worlds of separation vanish when we embrace another being.

What can we as parents do? Take the time to truly be present with our children, without judgments about their music or outlets to community. Get involved personally, go with our children to concerts, play the video games with them, and then ask, honestly, out of curiosity, why is this music or video game important for them? Listen, listen, listen to this precious being your love created, and then model coherence for them. Honor and mirror back to them their emotions with empathy, for example, "I hear that you are feeling very isolated and angry." Ask them about their choices and how those choices assist their lives, helping them to feel less stressed, angry or isolated. Listen without judgment and again mirror back their choices "you have chosen to . . . , which assists you with . . . ."

Accept teens as exploring, wise individuals, seeking what they need most, a solid sense of themselves. Make them partners in your life, working and playing along-side you. Give them options to be of value such as working with younger children, the elderly or animals. Keep offering them healthy outlets as they develop greater responsibility, things that demand constructive action, and a sense of accomplishment. Adolescence is an especially sensitive time when the need for intimacy and the desire to be of value through constructive action is paramount. As we trust our kids to learn how to handle themselves, we give them back their power.[357,358]

In all cases, the young men/killers mentioned were physically inactive. Take the time to move, play, and walk in nature with your child, friends or family on a daily basis for all of your sakes. Seriously limit TV and computer time for your children and yourself so you share more. Be creative and have reflective time alone. Our children need our presence, not our presents. It may be time to simplify our lives, needing less "stuff" and more connection.

To manage the depression cycle, we may have to first remember who and what we are — masters of our lives, not victims and then honestly address the underlying causes. And then, stop the runaway thought patterns by focusing on the present, choose to see everything as a learning opportunity; and get the body moving and the emotions flowing through sound, music and play. All of these measures assist the spines on the neurons of our hippocampus to re-grow, and new replacement cells to develop.[359,360] Touch increases production of oxytocin, our bonding chemical, and is a great healer. Social workers, like Breeze, are prescribing Therapy Pets for disenfranchised children, depressed suicidal individuals, and elderly patients who lack touch and companionship. The close alliance with a pet re-ignites the flame of connectedness and concern for another that is so very healing.

Mature emotions allow us compassion, altruism, empathy, and love.[361] They also assist us in developing intuitive discrimination of what is being authentically expressed or not in our community and world, thus making us more able to respond and assist for the highest good of all. To me, being in control means acknowledging, emotionally expressing in a responsible (responding) way, all the aspects of who I am. It is expressing the richness of me by being genuine and passionate in my life.

A Sleep Of Prisoners

Dark and cold we may be, but this
Is no winter now. The frozen misery
Of centuries breaks, cracks, begins to move;
The thunder is the thunder of the floes,
The thaw, the flood, the upstart Spring.
Thank God our time is now when wrong
Comes up to face us everywhere,
Never to leave us till we take
The longest stride of soul we ever took.
Affairs are now soul size.
The enterprise
Is exploration into God.
Where are you making for? It takes
So many thousand years to wake,
But will you wake for pity's sake!

— Christopher Fry[362]

In Sufism and many other mystical practices, God is equated with Oneness, our wholeness as entangled vibrational patterns. Perhaps Christopher Fry also had that image in mind when he wrote this poem, so full of emotion, potential, and connection back to Oneness.

8

Communication and Higher Order Dialogue

Seeing our world through the potentiality, non-locality and entanglement of quantum physics, and reciprocal space, communication is both the fruit of our oneness — our wholeness, and a means to cultivate that unity. As mentioned in chapter six, Lynn Margulis contends that early evolution was spurred *not by* competition, but by the communication and cooperation that enabled single-celled organisms to amalgamate into higher-level species. The evolution needed now to come to a higher order may again be based on our ability to communicate and cooperate with nature as well as with one another, but how evolved are we in that regard? There are many questions to explore about how we communicate, and how we cooperate.

Humans see themselves as the pinnacle of intelligence and communication. The verbal languages we speak allow us to talk about things that are not immediate and tangibly present. Human beings can communicate about the past, the present, the future and the conditions, feelings and mental assessments we remember or project onto these three divisions of time. Communication between other creatures is mostly bound to the present and mostly non-conceptual. Our intricate voices and complex languages are great gifts. However, is complex speech the only criteria for deep communication, sentience and intelligence? What about communication through light (i.e. between our cells, fire-flies, dinoflagellates), or chemicals (pheromones in most species) or touch, or gesturing, or intuitive sensing? Every one of us has, no doubt, experienced how language can just as easily obscure communication as foster it. What constitutes real communication, what makes us aware that real communication has taken place? I feel it might be enlightening to examine communication and cooperation in other organisms as well as humans.

I remember an experiment we did in graduate school that made me question the idea of whom and what was intelligent. I was experimenting with a group of vorticella, a single-celled organism with a long stalk that opened into a cup-like structure with cilia (hair-like appendages.) The cilia enable the vorticella to move through the water, and also, as they rotate, they form a vortex of water that brings microscopic food into the cup structure. I was measuring desensitization time by tapping the slide and timing how long it took them to recoil as they were trapped under the cover slip of my microscope slide. At first they would recoil instantly, but after each succeeding tap, the recoil slowed down. After I had tapped the slide a dozen times, suddenly, as a unit, they all pulled in their stalks and swam out from under the cover slip to the edge of the slide where I couldn't observe them further. Their decision to make a move was somehow communicated instantaneously among themselves. It was so deliberate, I had the distinct feeling they were communicating "this is enough, we are not performing for her anymore; we are out of here!"

Bonnie Bassler, molecular biologist at Princeton University, discovered that bacteria, one celled organisms like the vorticella, communicate constantly with each other via enzymes. They communicate by what she calls "quorum sensing" to collectively stage attacks, evade immune systems and protect themselves with a slimy covering. The first bacteria she studied, communicated via this "quorum sensing" to collectively bio-luminesce, which assisted the symbiotic relationship they had with the bobtail squid, that used the bacteria as a light source for their nocturnal hunts. Fascinating!!!. She also discovered that these single-celled organisms are multilingual, with a second enzyme, an inter-species enzyme, to communicate with bacteria different than themselves. With this collective communication, bacteria have been able to carry out tasks they couldn't do by themselves.[363,364] This communication and cooperation fits beautifully with Lynn Margulis' idea of multicellularity, that lead to more and more complex systems.

Cleve Backster, a polygraph tester for eighteen years, on an exploratory whim, hooked a polygraph to the leaf of a plant and discovered that the plant's polygraph showed the same response to threat as a human's polygraph. Equally amazing, all Backster had done to communicate this threat to the plant was think about burning one of its leaves. Had the plant "picked-up" his violent thought?

He later found that leaves, even detached, have response capability. That began years of intense research both with plants and brine shrimp, discovering over and over again, non-local, non-verbal communications in non-human organisms. He did not release his research to the public until he had applied the scientific method with intense experimentation.[365]

He then experimented with human white blood cells, which have the amazing ability to sense where they are needed in the body. They navigate through the blood stream to the affected location and then through the walls of the blood vessels to protect that area of our body. That communication between the white blood cells and the rest of the body is stunning in itself, but Backster also found there was an invisible communication link between the blood cells and the humans they came from.[366] He continues to study biocommunication, which closely correlates with quantum physics and non-locality that allows consciousness and the phenomenal world to share an invisible web.[367]

I have often wondered how and why the schools of fish I encounter when swimming know when to instantly change direction as a unit. And how and why do flocks of birds move in synchrony, suddenly rising from a lake or the avocado trees on our farm? What communication cues them? How do my cats know when I am returning home, and meet me at the road even though my schedule varies greatly? And how do they know when I am sick, and come to lie directly on an area of my body that needs their rhythmic purring, warmth and pressure?

Researchers, studying a variety of animals are finding they exhibit what we consider sentient intelligence. Octopus, squid, cuttlefish, manta rays, sharks, gold fish, reptiles and birds have demonstrated advanced abilities in mimicking the behavior of others. Many animals can find their way in complicated spatial environments, solve complex problems (such as unscrewing the cap of a jar to get to the contents within — seen in octopus), manufacture and use tools, and even remember specific past events, and anticipate future events.[368]

The forebrains of fish and amphibians receive the full array of sensory information we do. Even the common ancestor of cartilaginous and bony fish, as well as land vertebrates, may have possessed a hippocampus-like structure involved in processing emotions and spatial cognition. Reptiles and birds possess a structure in the brain called the DVR (Dorsal Ventricular Ridge) that is involved in similar processing, i.e.: executive planning and reasoning, learning and memory, perception, fine-motor control and language.

In birds, there is even a specialized area, like the frontal lobes of mammals for executive control of behavior. In recent years, researchers have documented stunning cognitive abilities in parrots, crows, ravens, jays and jackdaws. Tools made by New Caledonian crows have more sophisticated features than those made by chimpanzees. The crows can craft a diverse variety of tools, add improvements, and teach other members of the flock to copy their good designs accurately.[369]

Irene Pepperberg of Purdue University studied Alex and his pals, a group of African Gray Parrots. The parrots became famous for their ability to name 50 different objects, ask for and only accept what they asked for, know different colors and shapes, know the meaning of "same", "different", and "and". They also demonstrated an understanding of complex relationships, exhibited perfect memory, could learn intricate communication systems, and were very curious and very social.[370,371]

Listening to the frogs and crickets at night, and the insect sounds and uniquely complex bird calls during the day, I feel the world is awash with communication and we just need to tap in to become "animal whisperers."

Empathic Communication

William Benda M.D., a doctor of Integrative Medicine at the University of Arizona, and Rondi Lightmark, co-author of *Beyond Obedience: Training with Awareness for You and Your Dad*, claim that animals are by nature "people whisperers". In their work with people and animals, they see that animals have the capacity, either innately or intentionally to sustain and restore us in ways that we've forgotten or never imagined. They cite an Australian study that found cholesterol, triglycerides and blood pressure to be higher in non-pet owners and estimated there would be a $145 million annual savings in medical visits, pharmaceutical savings and hospitalization if susceptible people had pets.[372]

Interestingly, cats purr at 25 Hz or 50 Hz, the most effective frequencies for promoting bone growth and repair. At these frequencies, the production of natural anti-inflammatory chemicals in the body is increased, joint pain and swelling improves, and bone fractures heal faster. Cats purr when they are content, under stress, caged, severely injured or giving birth. An old saying that's popular among veterinarians is: "If you put a cat and a bunch of broken bones in the same room, the bones will heal."[373] Some people even claim they can stop a migraine headache by lying with their head next to a purring cat. My cats will show up out of nowhere when I am working with children and adults. I see them as holding a coherent space, raising the electromagnetic symmetry levels of the space for these people and for myself to heal old wounds and grow. In studies with patients hospitalized with myocardial infarctions, or unstable angina, only 5.7% of pet owners died within a year compared to 28.2% of non-pet owners.[374]

Just communing with a pet decreases stress hormones and increases emotional stability. Consciously taking care of an animal and keeping it healthy and happy provides a sense of self worth in the caregiver. It is often easier for people to love a pet than another human being. All of my pets, even my Siamese cats, tended to be fully present with unconditional love and acceptance for me. I have found them to be great models and teachers, if I will only follow their lead.

Figure 8.1 Breeze with her cat Tildy

Since empathy is such an important part of how we see ourselves as humans, researchers have become interested in whether other animals also exhibit empathy as a part of communication and cooperation, and the answer is definitely yes.[375] Even mice show empathy, joining the call of pain and activating the mirror neurons within their own brains, when seeing a cage-mate experiencing pain.[376] Empathy requires emotional involvement, mirroring another's pain or joy, with the cognition of that pain and joy coming later.[377]

Just hearing the emotional outbursts, observing the actions or facial expression of another activates the same brain areas. Often we will unconsciously cry or laugh, or mimic physical actions (crossing our legs) when someone we are with expresses those emotions or takes those actions.[378] Studies show that this may act as "social glue," setting up feelings of friendliness, of being together, a sense of unity with each other. Empathy is a deeply transmitted, deeply received non-verbal communication that appears to be deeply engrained, even in place on the first day of life in humans and other animals. When performing a task with another person, there appears to be an "integration effect" where we not only pay attention to what we are doing, but also to what they are doing so that the task is handled as a single person.[379]

Activating our mimicry circuitry is important for facilitating altruistic and compassionate behaviors because we don't have to experience something directly in order to feel what another being is feeling. As we become more sensitive observers and more knowledgeable about the organisms around us, we may find that empathy, communication and cooperation apply to all forms of life on our planet, even the planet itself.

"Humans appear to be uniquely endowed with a capacity that enables large-scale cooperation among unrelated individuals and supports stable relationships that rely on reciprocity."[380] — *Marc Hauser*

Knowing what we do about empathy and the connection exhibited by the few other organisms we have studied, perhaps we should take Hauser's statement and add: "All organisms, from one-celled to humans, are endowed......"

Language — Expressing Our Essence

When certain esoteric people talk about our voice, they use the term *"will."* For them it is the spiritual expression of our inner thoughts, beliefs and actual essence. I find myself saying, "communication is the last frontier," perhaps because we have compromised our will and been unable to truly express our essence amid the distractions of our current technological and social order. In the new paradigm, as we step into our full power, we may be able to more readily trust our intuition regarding the communication around us and speak less, but more coherently, honestly, and openly.

Humans possess an extraordinary capacity for linguistic expression speaking at least 6,800 tongues worldwide.[381] The diversity and complexity of speech is a testament to our vast creative nature, the ability to express our true essence through sound, vibrating our environment and the beings around us. Don Campbell compares sounding our own voice to massaging and vibrating our bodies from the inside out,[382] and David White, an Irish poet, calls speech "astonishing intimacy." The most intimate thing we can do, he says, is to amplify the vibration of our thoughts, ideas and emotions into an audible vibration in our vocal cords and resonant mouth chamber, and then send that vibration out across the air waves to vibrate the tympanic membrane, inner ear, and finally the whole body and spirit of another person.[383] Our bodies, which are living bio-oscillators, are the most complex instruments on the planet, and vibrating them with our own voice should be an integral part of our daily life.[384]

Every single culture in the world uses hand gestures when they speak. The brain area involved in hand motions is the first area to light up in a PET scan when someone is speaking. The second, smaller area has to do with vocalization. Humans use the same area of the brain for spoken language as modern apes use to interpret hand signals via mirror neurons.[385] Hands, as an extension of our intimate being, both receive and transmit energy and speak a universal language. It is said that our upright posture, which gives us the freedom to use our hands to communicate with those around us, was essential to the evolution of language.

To get a sense of how important our hand gestures are, try this simple experiment. Sit opposite another person with both of you sitting on your hands. Now explain your favorite dessert or exciting vacation while the other person simply listens for a short time (one to two minutes). Then change roles. How easy was it to verbally communicate to the other person, and how easy was it to listen with attention? You may have noticed that when your hands were out of commission, other parts of your body wanted to move (head, feet, etc.). Language is a whole-body phenomenon incorporating our intricate facial expressions, elaborate hand gestures, emotions and sounds. Using sign language with children who are having difficulties with verbal language has been highly successful in initiating and supporting verbal language development.

Insects, fish, amphibians, whales, dolphins, songbirds, humans and other vocal organisms have developed neural circuits that specialize in both the perception and production of sounds. Grasshoppers "sing" at 7,000 to 100,000 Hz and hear between 100 to 15,000 Hz, while green frogs both sing and receive sound from 80 to 10,000 Hz, and dogs bark at between 482 to 1080 Hz, yet hear the vast range of sound from 15 to 80,000 Hz. The human spectrum for vocalization lies between 85 to 1100 Hz yet we can hear from 15 to well over 20,000 HZ. Below 15 Hz is considered infrasound and above 20,000 Hz is ultrasound. We can experience both in our bodies through bone and skin conduction, though we can't actually hear them with our ears. Human speech lies between 125 Hz and 8,000Hz.[386]

With each sound there is a fundamental tone, above which are the harmonics and overtones that give us the full analog (range, depth and color) of sound. If you have had the joy of listening to chanting in a cathedral, you know what analog sound feels like in your body with all the rich tones and overtones melting into one another, vibrating your bones and filling every cell with sound.

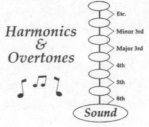

Figure 8.2 Fundamental sounds and overtones/harmonics

In the following analog sonogram of English and American spoken phrases you can easily see the rich array of harmonics and overtones in speech that make spoken language and the human voice so complex. Even the upper levels of vibration, above 20,000 Hz, above the range of hearing, affect our understanding of language. These upper harmonics help to delineate the fast sounds of language like "ch, sh, tha" that articulate the words.

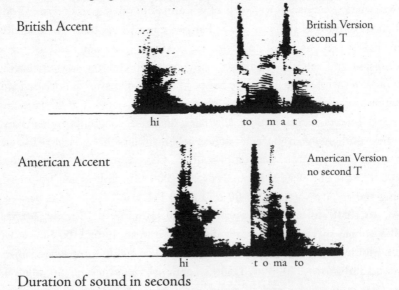

Figure 8.3 Sonogram of English and American spoken phrases[387]

We are dependent on what we hear to develop our vocalization. Our perception of how to vocalize comes from imitating/mirroring our parents and others around us. In order for children to learn language, they must have the full spectrum of the language, including the harmonics and overtones that lie above and below the range of hearing. The human voice contains these sounds. CD's, most audiotapes, computer-generated sound, TV, and many instruments today are electronic and digitized. Digitizing compresses the sound, taking out overtones or harmonics above 20kHz, causing many of the beneficial high frequency sounds to be lost. Low soundproof ceilings, carpeting and cushioned furniture in our homes and offices also muffle those important high, energetic frequencies.[388] Many musicians prefer listening to the old vinyl records, because they still present sound as a full analog with all the rich harmonics and overtones.

The human infant first babbles, but as it hears the vocal patterns over and over again, it adjusts its vocal output to correctly mimic the patterns. I hate to admit it, but some of the first clear sounds, besides "ma-ma" and "da-da" that Breeze uttered were imitations of the resident chicken that became her constant companion because of the trail of Cheerios she dropped on her first vertical jaunts into the world. To hear and feel the sound vibrations of others and mirror them must be the most natural way to learn.

Our ability to speak is written on our DNA. Researchers have discovered that the FOXP2 genes on our DNA, if damaged or mutated, hinder the regions of the brain responsible for motor control and language processing. Large quantities of FOXP2 proteins produced from our genes are found in a cortico-basal ganglia loop essential for learning languages. This loop consists of the basal ganglion (organizing motor functions) that connects to the thalamus (filters sensory information) and the vocal centers in the neocortex (Wernicke's area allows us to understand speech, and Broca's facilitates production of speech) of the brain.[389]

"Both music and language are about long, highly organized streams of sound."
— *Robert Jourdain*[390]

One of my greatest joys in life was reading to Breeze, the rich diversity of stories and creative images in children's literature. I loved to add accents and a lot of emotion to the characters. "Read it again" was always her retort when I finished, as her mind longed to get every detail and nuance to fill in her understanding.

After many readings she would mimic me whenever we returned to the story. I'm sure it was influential in her later ease with spoken accents in her story telling and acting. I felt a loss when she began silent reading for her own enjoyment, and still find myself reading kids' books in libraries and bookstores, just for the fun of it. We sometimes still read to each other, and I revel in the vivid images she brings to life.

Children hear the language, as parents and caregivers talk to them, first in the high-pitched Parentese that energizes the brain. The extended vowels and exaggerated tones of Parentese facilitate comprehension and teach infants basic grammar. This higher frequency speech has also been found to convey meaning between people who do not speak the same language.[391]

As we speak to children in increasingly complex sentences, they need to speak in response, mimicking and matching sounds and speech in order to understand it. Young children, still so tuned into vibrations, love to play with the language, saying words over and over to feel them in their mouth, to vibrate them throughout their bodies, and to get other people's attention with them.

In homes where there is a lot of parent-child communication, language development is much faster, with children using 131 words at 20 months and 295 words at 24 months.[392] With more TV and computer use in our homes, and working parents, family communication times have decreased. Below are results of a study comparing the number of words in the vocabulary of an average 14-year-old in 1950 and 1999. I wonder what current research would show us?

- 1950:   25,000 words;
- 1999   10,000 words [393]

Many (maybe most) teenagers today have a distinct "sitcom language," consisting of monosyllables and incomplete sentences. Typical phrases are: "It's like," "you know," "sort of," "don't go there," etc. Jane Healy points out that the way we speak is a reflection of the way we think.[394] Many Americans even watch TV during meals, which inhibits family discussion, so necessary for language development and human connection. As I was growing up, no matter what, the whole family would sit down to dinner together and discuss everything, from school to summer plans. As an open forum, it wasn't always calm and rational, but it did keep us connected as a family and allowed us to speak our thoughts and emotions as our parents added sage advice, stories from their lives, corrected our grammar and insisted on comprehensible communication.

Sensory addiction to constant and loud sounds can inhibit communication. I am hard pressed to find a restaurant today that does not have a TV blaring in the background. I also see people everywhere with iPod buds in their ears, turned up loud enough that I can hear what they are playing. Sound has become louder and louder, damaging the delicate structures of the inner ear and profoundly affecting our hearing. These loud noises not only damage our hearing, they decrease our ability to express ourselves. When people have a hearing loss, there is a greater sense of isolation, which can lead to depression.

Any damage to the hearing mechanism will result in inaccurate imitation of the sound and difficulties with language. Hearing loss in the range of 500 Hz. results in poor perception of the voiceless consonants (m, n or p, t & f). This prevents children from learning to mimic the language properly and may be a source of confusion about how to speak.[395]

Hearing loss between 500 – 1000 Hz makes it impossible for a true appreciation of music. A hearing loss between 1000 – 2000 Hz prevents one from singing in tune; and above 2000 Hz prevents hearing harmonics and other tonal qualities that make the voice pleasant and melodic.[396]

Dyslexia has been found to be primarily a hearing problem, and only secondarily a reading problem. Following are some of the steps researchers are finding that lead to dyslexia.

1. Maternal stress elevates adrenaline and cortisol in the mother and developing embryo and fetus.

2. Stress sustains the withdrawal and Moro reflex for a longer period of time, thus delaying development of the reflexes necessary for vestibular development.

3. Not enough exploratory movement or interactive language leads to an underdeveloped vestibular system, which leads to unstable balance, underdeveloped head-righting reflexes, poor spatial awareness and orientation, hearing difficulties and lack of eye teaming.[397]

4. A reduced immune system makes the baby susceptible to middle ear infections, asthma, allergies, epileptic seizures and winter diseases like influenza that affect hearing.[398]

5. Parents try to help the child's performance, which over-stimulates the child beyond its developmental level, causing dys-coordination and hearing difficulties, that the child must develop compensations to overcome, but which lead to

structural problems, mostly in the eyes, backs, rigid muscles and homolaterality.

6. Stress inhibits normal development of the right ear to left hemisphere preference for hearing and decoding language, resulting in hearing delays of 0.4 – 0.9 milliseconds, making it difficult to hear the fast sounds of language.[399]

7. The child has a hard time discriminating sounds, words, or sentences and categorizing sounds or occluding miscellaneous sounds.

8. Fatigue occurs due to the futile attempts to follow the language. Hearing, speech and reading difficulties occur.

9. If a child can't hear it, they have difficulty speaking it or sounding out the symbology to read it. Dyslexia is twice as prevalent in the U.S. where matching English sounds that make up a word to the symbols that represent it are dramatically at odds.[400]

10. This vulnerable situation can lead to behavioral problems including social withdrawal, ADHD, dyslexia and emotional handicaps.[401]

Some of the top research in dealing with and eliminating dyslexia and other learning disabilities comes from Denmark. Rather than pushing reading remediation, as we tend to do in the U.S., the Danes immediately begin to work on the vestibular system to increase the ability to hear and discriminate sounds. They get the child swinging, twirling, rolling, and using slow cross-lateral movements for balance. They also focus on singing, speaking, and improving the child's listening skills by putting them in a choir or other musical experience. Singing in a choir allows the child to hear himself in vibrational reference to others, and gain the full range of sound necessary to understand the pieces of language. Reading is the culminating activity of their work, rather than the only therapy. Thus, by the time students graduate from school, there is 100% literacy in two languages, and their society isn't left with learning disabled or dyslexic adults.[402]

People from other countries who effortlessly speak four or more languages, give us a beautiful model of how to connect and share an understanding of cultural diversity through communication in our ever-shrinking global family.

Coming Home To Our Voice — Our Will

What a gift our voice is. Our need to communicate is so deep that cell phones have become ubiquitous accessories, but unfortunately they tend to eliminate the intimacy of the true human voice, and the beholding of facial expressions, emotions and the body language of another person. In amazement I stood on the campus of my alma mater and watched as masses of students walked past on their way to classes — each with a cell phone in hand, making no eye-contact or verbal connection with the people they were walking alongside or passing by. Cell phones exemplify our longing to express ourselves, for connection, for oneness, but minimize the true intimacy we so long for.

In my workshops I ask people to sound like children playing, and very tentatively they make quiet high sounds. We have armored ourselves against making too much sound. The early edict "children should be seen and not heard," the struggle of teachers and parents wanting children to be quiet, the even earlier pacifiers to stop a baby from crying have subdued our voices. To really experience what it feels like for adults to sound like children, I have everyone in my workshops do "blithering cross-crawls" as introduced to me by Chris Brewer. First you shake a leg, then the other leg, then your arms as you cross the midline and cross-crawl. And then shake the head while you are shaking everything else. This releases the armor and when the participants are again asked to sound like children playing, the room fills with joyful sound, coming from the depth of their being.

Our American constitution is adamant about freedom of speech, yet many are like sleepwalkers, abiding by the status quo, never questioning, and never feeling powerful enough to share their intuitive wisdom. Since we are the models for our children, our voices and our will must be clear, coherent, connected to all potential; then theirs will be as well. Failure to express our voice, emotions, physical being to our children as passionate, curious, powerful, enthusiastic beings will leave them shut down and armored to their own essence and wisdom.

Some of the veterans that Breeze works with at the VA hospital claim to have life changing insights but then don't take the physical actions necessary to bring their intentions into reality. Their behavior is incongruent with their intentions. Unless we internalize and actively participate as responsible beings, expressing our will verbally and physically, we cannot access our full potential. Anthony Trowbridge says it is necessary to balance five different aspects to bring about our will. His brilliant diagram shows the five elements necessary for that balance: 1.survival, 2.motivation (emotion), 3.reason, (discrimination, duality), 4.insight (higher level understanding, creativity and altruism) and 5.physical action.

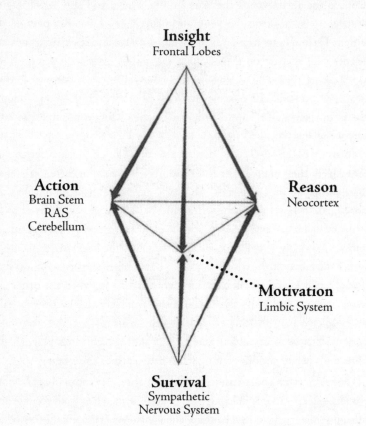

Insight
Frontal Lobes

Action
Brain Stem
RAS
Cerebellum

Reason
Neocortex

Motivation
Limbic System

Survival
Sympathetic
Nervous System

Figure 8.4 Anthony Trowbridge model of whole person balance [403]

We can use the above diagram to explore what happens when we don't come from a balanced perspective. If we take action from our emotions and survival needs, as would be the case in a barroom brawl, we are not in control. On the other hand, if we simply add reason without insight to the above-mentioned brawl, it can lead to aggressive rationalization, or violence for some reason, for instance, violence against those who are different from us, and in extreme cases, war.

Resistance to change occurs when we have an insight and the reason to back it up, but are caught up in survival, so we don't invest emotionally or take action. This occurs when we have a new idea, a new job prospect, or on a new relationship possibility, but survival fear kicks in with thoughts like, "you may fail, or you won't get your pension, or it might be painful", so no emotion or action ensues. Apathetic idealism (intellectualism) occurs when we have some insight, and reason things out, over and over without emotion, action or survival drive. I see this with theorists who go over and over an issue without committing to it emotionally or with action. Energetic ignorance occurs when we have an insight, tie into our emotions, and take action without understanding the reasoning behind it or the survival value. I experienced this when, as a young graduate student in Colorado, I was a lobbyist for the Open Space Council. I was a rabid environmentalist with a black and white perspective, and saw industry as the enemy of the environment, until I took the time to understand the research and care that went into many environmental impact statements. When we live and communicate from a balanced perspective, we create a space that is safe for ourselves and for others to deeply explore all of life.

In the emerging paradigm, our voices, our will, must again become the glue connecting us in cooperation with others that share the planet. We must be able to express our wisdom and have it honored. In small villages all over Africa there is a process that assures all are allowed their voice. No matter what the issue, the whole village is called together to discuss it. Everyone has their say and it may take days, and sometimes weeks to come to a unanimous decision. They feel strongly that everyone's wisdom must be included so they don't miss a single valuable perspective that their individual perceptions may block from their awareness.

Indigenous people all over the planet share an attitude of receptivity, respect and thanksgiving for a greater intelligence beyond personal consciousness, the language of which emerges from nature, and the land, where everything is in relation to everything else. Language for them is based on process and relationship. Their lives are rooted in the relationships of the current manifested world, and the implicit possibilities that exist in the heart, not just of humans, but animals, plants and inanimate objects — all of nature, "the very heart of the cosmos itself." They understand that knowledge is dynamic, alive and not held by any single individual, but part of a greater whole.

To the Blackfoot Indians of North America, reality can be explained as constantly moving events emerging out of a fluid, interconnected flux. This intuitive perspective shows their direct understanding and appreciation of reciprocal space and the quantum realm, which is also reflected in their language. The Australian Aborigines believe that knowledge is always seeking us, or seeking the right vehicle to carry the message, the wisdom, and this may more rightly be plants or animals.[404]

"One reason we do not generally recognize the primacy of the implicate order is that we have become so habituated to the explicate order and emphasized it so much in our thought and language that we tend strongly to feel that our primary experience is of that which is explicate and manifest." — David Bohm

David Bohm is well known for his theory of a highly interconnected, constantly evolving and holographic universe. In 1959 he read a book by Indian philosopher J. Krishnamurti and found parallels to his own theories in those of Eastern spirituality. Bohm instigated a meeting between Eastern spiritual leaders, including Krishnamurti, and a select group of physicists, including Einstein, to share insights and validate mutually held discoveries and beliefs.[405]

Krishnamurti shared with Bohm the idea that problems with communication and understanding between people are created because each person holds so tightly to their acquired beliefs that they don't truly listen to the other. He saw this in the debates between Niels Bohr and Albert Einstein where both continued to defend their perspectives without truly listening for the jewels in each other's ideas that would have brought about cooperation and a higher order of possibilities.

Maintaining an ongoing dialogue with and seeing the value of Krishnamurti's insights on communication, Bohm put together his insights about dialogue and presented them in his book, *On Dialogue*. [406] Bohm set about teaching people to suspend their beliefs in order to listen to others in a receptive way that became known as "Bohmian dialogue." He pointed out that with ordinary conversation, a relatively fixed position is maintained and each party attempts to convince the other of the rightness of his or her position. With a dialogue, both parties listen deeply to what is being said while suspending their own personal and cultural thoughts and beliefs. The core is to listen, and attempt to understand fully the other person's position without any expected result. During and after these dialogues, the participants reported having a sense of collective consciousness, which could be easily tapped into for creative solutions.

Influenced by Bohm's work, Leroy Little Bear, a Blackfoot elder and former dean of the Native American Program at Harvard, initiated a series of "science dialogues" that began in 1992 and continue to this day. Bohmian Dialogue, cooperative communication, may be one of the most important steps in moving through our current chaos, to creative solutions of a higher order of evolution.

Hearing And Listening

"The yearning to be listened to and understood is a yearning to escape our separateness and bridge the space that divides us. We reach out and try to overcome that separateness by revealing what's on our minds and in our hearts, hoping for understanding." — Michael Nichols[407]

Not only do Krishnamurti and David Bohm underline the need to deeply listen, according to otolaryngologist, Dr. Alfred Tomatis, listening involves the whole body.[408] Interestingly, the word "Listen" is the most used word in the Bible. The following symbol from the Chinese word for "to listen" involves not just the ear, but also the heart, eyes, and the rest of the body in undivided attention. The literal translation is: "Use the heart to listen and both the messages from the outside world as well as from within will come straight into the heart." It is a profound expression of the manifestation of life force through sound.

Chinese Symbol --- To Listen

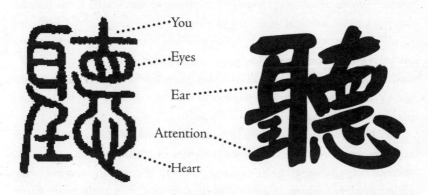

............You

............Eyes

Ear ....

Attention............

............Heart

Ancient   **Modern**

Figure 8.5 Chinese character for listening

My mother, through her example, taught me to always listen and keep the communication lines open. Perhaps it's the most "right thing" I did with my daughter Breeze, even though it was almost impossible at times not to jump in with judgments or solutions. Breeze told me everything, many things I didn't want to know. I learned to bite my tongue when she told me of her explorations with drugs, boys, tattoos, etc., because if I could listen until the end, I would always be struck by her discoveries and the wise choices she made in support of her highest good. We all have to explore our current worlds, and make our own mistakes, often to the dismay and fear of our loved ones.

I hear kids today saying, "Don't dis me". Dis indicates negation, lack, invalidation, deprivation. These developing humans are desperately asking us to listen to them, not to dis-miss, dis-card, dis-able, dis-regard them. In other words, "Don't disconnect from me, I want to be listened to." One of the most coherent and loving things we can do as parents and loved ones is to listen.

How Do I Listen?

How do I listen to others? As if everyone were my Master
speaking to me His Cherished Last Word. — Hafiz[409]

Besides listening to others, I am learning that listening to my own intuition/knowing is vital to being in the moment and coherent. Am I listening to the messages that tell me whether the situation is safe or not, whether my energy is ready for this experience or not, whether it is time for quiet or playfulness, and whether I can keep going or should quit? Listening to my own knowing may mean disappointing another in order to follow my body's needs, my passion or my attunement with the whole information field to guide my actions. When I truly listen, it seems that I take right action and open to experiences that will further my evolution, to live more deeply and passionately.

Our voice and our ability to listen with wonder to the communication of the diverse others that share our planet may be one of our greatest gifts. In so many ways listening can re-connect us with our true nature, our oneness and wholeness with the explicit and implicit world. Let us make music, sing, intimately communicate, laugh, and enjoy the intricate instruments we are, sharing our vibrational waves and receiving from the infinite field of information.

9

The Sound Of Music

"Music is a Moral Law. It gives soul to the universe,
wings to the mind, flight to the imagination,
a charm to sadness, gaiety and life to everything.
It is the essence of order, and lends to all that
is good, just and beautiful." — Plato

As Jim and I were singing in the car on our way to the Colorado raft trip where I would discover I was pregnant, Breeze was already feeling the vibrational patterns of our song in her watery environment through her developing skin and body.[410] Our song hung in a vibrational sea with the other sounds that were orchestrating her developing form. Sound is the template for not only our incarnation, but also how we experience the world before and after birth, and the music that guides and motivates us to truly live deeply and harmoniously.

As I look at Figure 9.1 of a two-month-old embryo, two features immediately stand out: the perfectly formed semicircular canals, inner ear structures that are key parts of the vestibular system for hearing, balance and proprioception, and the very large heart, elegant generator of our largest electro-magnetic field. The vestibular system, fully developed by five months after conception, is the vestibule or entryway into the brain. The vestibular nuclei, a group of neurons lying in the medulla oblongata and pons of the brain stem, connect sound, body orientation and balance impulses coming from the semicircular canals to the Reticular Activating System (RAS). The RAS, a group of nerves, carries impulses to the thalamus (consciousness center) and neocortex, "waking it up" and increasing its excitability and responsiveness to incoming sensory stimuli from the environment.

By four to five months in utero, the 8th (vestibulo-cochlear) cranial nerve pair, carrying auditory information from the ear to the brain is the first sensory nerve pair to develop. The high frequency of the mother's voice, heard through the amniotic fluid, is believed to energetically charge the brain of the fetus via its vestibular/RAS system.[411]

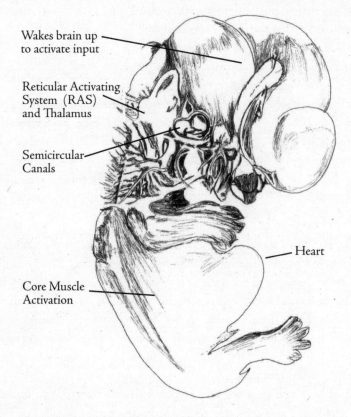

Wakes brain up
to activate input

Reticular Activating
System (RAS)
and Thalamus

Semicircular
Canals

Core Muscle
Activation

Heart

Figure 9.1 Vestibular System of two month old embryo

The semicircular canals and the cochlea (our sea-shell shaped organ for hearing) share a common chamber, fluid, and the 8th cranial nerve. Thus, hearing is influenced by information passing through the vestibular system, and the vestibular system is influenced by sound.[412]

The first area of the cochlea to develop in the fetus accommodates the higher frequency sounds, like that of the mother's voice. Higher sound frequencies, with their faster vibration and higher energy (as seen in cymatics), may cause more intricate patterns to arise in the brain. Both men and women instinctively talk to babies with a higher voice, called "Parentese" that energizes the baby's brain, making it more alert to all sensory input and able to take in specific patterns and rhythms, thus aiding learning.[413]

Dr. Alfred Tomatis, a French ear, nose and throat doctor asserted that the first function of the ear is to "charge" the brain and body with energy, nurturing the functions of thought, reflection, and creativity.[414] After a music fest, or singing and jamming with friends, it takes several hours before I can go to sleep. In fact, I have stayed up whole nights playing music without needing to sleep, and still felt energized.

All of our auditory impressions of the world come from the way in which the eardrum wiggles back and forth in response to how hard it is hit by vibrating air molecules (volume), and how fast the air molecules are vibrating (pitch). This wiggling of the eardrum vibrates three small bones in the middle ear, which wiggles another membrane (oval window), which vibrates the fluid in the cochlea. The fluid vibrating in the spiral cochlea hits up against specific cells with hair-like extensions (hair cells), which in turn push against nerves sending impulses to the brain. These undifferentiated impulses go to the cerebellum, the auditory cortex of the cerebrum and the thalamus. Immediately, input from the integration areas of the cortex, amygdala, hippocampus and cerebellum begin to compare and integrate the information, making inferences from known reality and giving us a conscious perception of our auditory world. Amazing!

Tomatis discovered that factory workers, who have had their upper range of hearing damaged from constant high frequency machinery sounds, exhibit depression, low muscle tone, and lower energy states. In examining the cochlear structure of some of the men who had died, he found the hair cells were broken and scarred.[415] This same kind of damage to the delicate hearing apparatus can occur prior to birth and can affect or even kill the developing embryo and fetus.[416,417]

Loud sounds damage the delicate structures of the inner ear and profoundly affect our hearing. Exposure to loud sounds is the cause of hearing loss in over 28 million people in the U.S. today. Six percent of fourth graders, nine percent of ninth graders, and sixty-one percent of college freshmen have measurable hearing loss. Due to the noise in our environment, an average twenty-five-year-old in the United States hears less well than the average sixty-year-old in traditional African societies.[418] We measure loudness of sound in decibels (dB), named after Alexander Graham Bell and the decimal system. Decibel readings are logarithmic and doubling the intensity (loudness) of a sound results in approximately a 3 dB increase in the sound. The ratio between the softest sound we can detect (0 dB, the softest whisper of the human voice) and the loudest sound we can hear without causing permanent damage (85 dB) is more than a million to one. Decibels are measured with an electronic instrument via a microphone and metering system representing units of 10x10 for each unit on the metering system (0dB – 10dB is 10x's louder, 10dB – 20dB is 100x's louder, 20dB – 30dB is 1,000x's louder, etc.) These hand-held devices are used to measure industrial and concert volume levels to assure they stay within safe perimeters to avoid permanent ear damage.

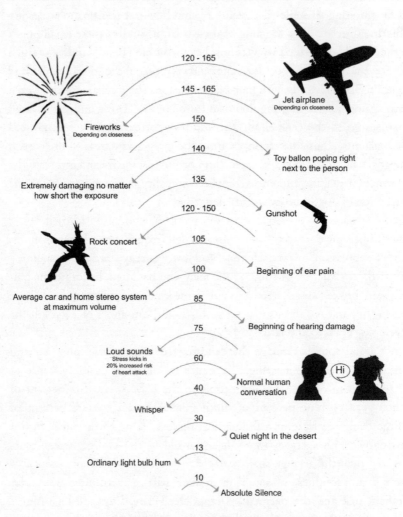

Figure 9.2 Common sounds in decibels

Sound And Balance

"Everything passes through the opening of the ear; we speak, read, sing and dance with our ears, we maintain a vertical posture, establish relational dynamics and laterality thanks to our ears." — A.A. Tomatis

Tomatis believed balance to be the second function of the ear, providing verticality through muscle tonus, which eventually assists both hand and verbal communication.[420] By five to six months in utero, the fetus can actually process sound, which stimulates muscle tone (especially of the core muscles), equilibrium, and flexibility.[421] Projections from the inner ear go directly to the cerebellum (for movement and emotional integration), which connects directly to the frontal lobes of the brain (our most advanced cognitive area). Connective fibers between the cerebellum and frontal lobes run in both directions.[422] Muscle tone occurs from constant neural activity between the cerebellum and the motor and sensory cortexes of the brain, causing some muscles to be relaxed while others are contracted. This allows the fetus to move with some coordination in utero, such as bringing the thumb to the mouth to suck.

"All human beings... and only human beings... have language and music.
They are hallmarks of what it means to be a human being."
— Donald A. Hodges[423]

The newborn hears and moves in rhythm to the mother's voice in the first minutes of life. There are no random movements; every movement of the newborn has meaning, with particular movements being linked to particular sounds.[424] For example, with a sudden loud sound the baby will throw out its arms and legs in a Moro reflex.[425] In response to his mother's voice, he will turn his ears, and thus his eyes toward her. Studies done using high-speed film show that newborns and infants have a complete and individual repertoire of body movements that precisely synchronize with syllables or sub-syllables of a speaker's voice.[426] This important matching of movement to words, or "entrainment," actually begins in utero at about 4½ months. When the mother says a certain phoneme (ah, oo, eh), the fetus will move a specific body part in alignment with the sound. Thus, they are already anchoring the various sounds on the muscles of their bodies, which leads to full development of the vestibular system and the ability to later understand the patterns in music and language successfully.[427,428]

Muscle tonus continues to elaborate as the baby explores its environment, via reflex movements stimulated again by sounds in the environment, such as lifting the head (tonic neck reflex) in order to hear with both ears. As the baby continues to move, reflex movements are integrated into chosen movements that are more and more coordinated, balanced and complex. Thus the child learns which muscles to use to sit up, roll over, crawl, stand up, walk, run and skip. The close connection between sound and muscle tonus, continues to bring us into form throughout our life and allows us to not only maintain our posture and balance, but actually create our body's ability to move in new, elegant, and amazing ways.[429,430] It is easy to ascertain how energetic and fully alive a person is by just looking at his posture. An unconstrained child literally jumps for joy, twirls, runs, and balances perfectly with her toned muscles while exuding great life force.

In working with depressed patients, Dr. Tomatis noticed that their postures communicated their state of depression; they slumped, dragged, and had a hard time sitting and standing up straight. As older people lose their hearing, especially the energetic high range vibrations, their muscles lose their tonus, and their posture, as well as their enthusiasm for life, changes radically. Think of several people in your life whom you are close to, one old and one young, and then walk like them for a minute or two. You may notice that just by experiencing their walking you can more compassionately understand their emotional state. I did this exercise, walking like my ninety-eight-year-old mother, and I could finally understand the pain and discomfort she must have felt when walking with her arthritic knees. The Native Americans wisely ask us to walk a mile in the shoes of another, in order to more deeply understand their reality before judging them.

Children naturally sound their instrument and activate muscle tonus when they are playing. There are wild shrieks, joyful laughter and even singing. Too often we ask children to be quiet, and in accommodating our wish, over time, they may armor themselves against making too much sound. I see this armoring in many adults when I ask them to sound like children at play. They stiffen up, barely open their mouths, and make a feeble attempt at sound. This armoring can affect our muscle tonus, balance and even ability to learn optimally.

The natural play of making sounds in babies and children is also important to us adults — throughout our lives. Our society's love of sports events, where we can really shout, or concerts where we can sing and dance to the music, allows us to activate our bodies and minds again. Just getting the people at Friendship Manor (a home for the elderly) to sing along to the songs of the 30's and 40's seemed to markedly increase their vitality and joy of living as well as their ability to walk with more balance. Sounding our instrument, in tune with the universe, our environmental resonant field, and each other anchors us back into the creative force that formed our structure, and keeps us sensorily awake to the tension between chaos and order that is life.

Rhythm And Steady Beat

Once I listened to an audiotape of in utero sounds recorded by Alfred Tomatis. The experience propelled me deeply into the world of the fetus, floating in surround sound, right next to the stomach, digestive tract, heart, and lungs. The dripping, churning sounds of digestion are fairly innocuous, but stomach rumblings are loud and may peak, though only briefly, at 85 – 95 decibels in this unborn world. Normal human speech lies at about 60 decibels.[431] The fetus, far from being inert in this noisy incubator, is very active and responsive to all kinds of stimuli both from the womb and the outside world.[432]

In listening to the tape, the most noticeable sound for me was the mother's rhythmic breathing, which sounded just like the ocean waves lapping gently on a Hawaiian beach. It's easy to understand why people place their towels right next to perfect strangers on a beach and don't feel their space has been invaded. They are back in the womb, secure with the rhythm of the surf, a remembrance of the soothing, breathing sounds in utero.

The other controlling sounds in utero are the loud beat of the heart, and the rhythmic flow of blood through the mother's blood vessels. Heartbeat is such a strong pattern that a human fetus will respond rhythmically to a tympanist during an orchestral performance within twenty-five weeks after conception.[433]

Heartbeat is a touchstone pattern for the developing embryo whose heart beats well before it has blood to pump, at forty-one days after conception.[434] The mother's heart rhythm, either coherent or incoherent, allows the embryo and fetus to discern whether the mother is safe or in danger. After birth, mothers instinctively nurse their babies on the left first, with the baby's right ear against the mother's heart, which will allow it to assess the safety or danger of the environment from the mother's coherent or incoherent heart pattern. The left ear is available to pick up the tone, melody, and emotional quality of the mother's voice and environment.[435]

If our mother's heart rhythm is coherent, it forms a framework for our ability to maintain a steady beat pattern throughout our lives. There is a very strong correlation between the heartbeat and the breath, such that for every inhalation there are three heartbeats and three for every exhalation. This waltz rhythm shows up in music throughout the world. The pattern stays fairly consistent, even when a person is running — when both the heartbeat and the breathing rate speed up. These early patterns provide us with a template for understanding patterns in general, so necessary for learning and remembering. They allow us to translate the patterns and symbols present in every experience of our lives, from the intricate patterns in nature, to the patterns in art, music, mathematics and language, and the emotional patterns in the people we explore the world with.

The embryo and fetus are constantly moving with the mother's heartbeat and body movement. Steady beat continues after birth as the baby rides on the mother's body or is rhythmically rocked in a caretaker's arms. Our affinity for steady beat is innately demonstrated by the rhythmic rocking we fall into when someone hands us a baby, or when we join a circle and hold hands. This same rocking occurs among the singers in our local community choir, and must somehow bond us to each other, to open the physical channels of communication as we move and sound in synchrony.

Steady beat is basic to our love for the beat within music — where the bass carries the rhythm that moves our body during a dance or annoys us at night as a teenager turns up the volume and cruises through our neighborhood during his courting ritual. Beat helps us organize our breathing, walking, dancing patterns and assists us to make patterns of our incoming sensory information in order to learn.[436]

Many of the world's musical rhythms stem from the coherent rhythm of the heart. Ancient instruments like the frame drum depicted on a wall painting in Catal Huyuk in Turkey from at least eight thousand years ago were undoubtedly built to mimic the heartbeat, as are drums today.[437] In horror movies, film producers use the heartbeat rhythm to entrain the audience's heart rhythms and then speed it up and make it incoherent during dramatic scenes to activate fear in the audience.

During maternal stress when coherent steady beat is missing, the fetal heart rate and breathing also become incoherent. Babies with irregular (incoherent) heartbeats face a forty-one-fold greater risk of SIDS (Sudden Infant Death Syndrome) in their first year than babies with a regular heartbeat.[438] Incoherent heartbeats and breathing can be seen in monkeys or orphaned children who have been isolated from their mothers right after birth and left without movement and touch. They rock back and forth in an attempt to reestablish the steady beat movement they missed.[439] Therapists now realize this self-stimulation is an attempt to tap into a coherent pattern that will facilitate their brain growth and learning process.

Many of today's youth and more than fifty percent of adults in the U.S. are deficient in steady beat competency (the ability to hold a steady beat for one minute) and, thus, are missing the foundation patterns for learning and languaging well. Phyllis Weikart, in testing large samples of high school students, found that in just ten years time, between 1981 – 1991, the ability of students to hold a steady beat decreased by half with boys doing far worse than girls.

From the figures, it is not surprising that there are six boys for every girl in special education programs that focus on reading difficulties. In 1998, when testing in elementary schools, Dr. Weikart found that less than ten percent of students had steady beat competency, which should be in place by two to three years of age for adequate linguistic development.[440] I wonder what it is now, ten years later, as music and movement programs are being dropped from school curriculums all across America.

According to Dr. Weikart, English is the only un-metered language, being a collection of sounds from different languages, making it all the more important to ground English with steady beat. When parents and caregivers rock infants and toddlers and pat or burp them in steady beat, the child's ability to sense and use beat begins. Simple rhymes like "Pat-a-Cake, Pat-a-Cake" are great for instilling steady beat in the child. It is best to take the baby's hands and slowly and gently clap them together during each phrase. Clap during "pat-a-cake" then clap again during the next "pat-a-cake," and then during "baker's" and next "man," etc. Do not clap on each syllable (pat – a – cake) as it will fracture the rhythm and set up incoherence in the brain.[441]

Nursery rhymes and children's songs are elegant ways to establish steady beat competency early. The child can rock, pat her knees (and other body parts), clap her hands, march, or dance with whole body participation while listening to the rhythms and songs, and "chime in" with the words and/or melody when it becomes familiar.[442] Once steady beat is an innate part of our body rhythm, we can advance to rhythm changes in music and language easily. I always start with rhythm and steady beat when sharing music in the local elementary schools, and often go back to the early nursery rhymes and simple children's songs. The children love it.

The Power Of Music

"As neither the enjoyment nor the capacity of producing musical notes are faculties of the least direct use to man in reference to his ordinary habits in life, they must be ranked amongst the most mysterious with which he is endowed." — Charles Darwin (1871)

In the Hawaiian culture, many of the family members sing, play the ukulele or guitar and dance the Hula. Children learn early to dance, mirroring the swaying rhythms, and embodying the patterns, again so close to the coherent heart rhythm. Hawaiian music and other indigenous music (Native American, Australian, African) have very strong heart rhythm patterns and are the best for me to intuitively dance to.

Traditional Chinese Medicine recognizes this heart – hearing connection writing: "The color of the Southern direction is red, it is related to the Heart which opens into the ears...."[443] Asians have a practice, called Tae-gyo, which begins the education of the baby by exposing expectant mothers to music that relaxes the embryo and fetus and has a pattern that assists learning development.[444] Babies come into the world already connected through sound.

Our bodies are cymatic (vibrational) representations of our thoughts, intentions, desires, language, our sense of self, and how we sing and dance our song in this lifetime. The human body is the most complex musical instrument on the planet, and our voice, with its vast potential for sounds is like none other. Music developed before language, and neurons for its reception and expression are ubiquitous throughout our brains, beginning in utero.

"Music is unusual among all human activities for both its ubiquity and its antiquity: no known human culture now or anytime in the recorded past lacked music." — Daniel Levitin[445]

Breeze started her out-of-womb life with a song. In the low light of the delivery room, just moments into the world and still attached to me via the placenta, Jim held her and sang to her. She listened to his tonal rainbow, full of his love and delight with her. As with all babies, Breeze was born with the ability to perceive and process basic musical sounds and patterns.[446] Jim and I sang often to her, the lullabies of our youth, rowdy college songs, and our favorite folk songs for fun and in an attempt to get her to sleep, or ease the wailing of teething bouts. Our singing consisted of musical patterns with rising and falling pitches called musical contours that eight to nine month old infants respond to, even if the same pattern is repeated in another key. The responses of infants to musical contour are the same as adults, showing that brain specialization for contour is present at a very early age.[447]

It is believed by researchers that infants are born with the ability and longing to compose music. By the age of nine, children can produce original compositions naturally, using the same processes as professional composers. This ability ties directly into a child's understanding of pattern within sounds and their innate creative processes. When children can retain sound patterns because of the coherence in their lives, it facilitates their ability to compose music and also to understand and create usable patterns in all areas of learning.[448,449,450]

*Figure 9.3 Babies are fascinated by music, especially
if allowed to make it themselves*

According to Robert Jordain, of all the animals on our planet, the human brain has discovered music — the ability to manipulate patterns of sound far more complex than any other animal's brain can manage. Our brains encode relationships between melody, passages, chords, and rhythms for the sensations of sound to arise. "We model patterns upon patterns upon patterns, right up to the movement of a symphony."[451] We have the ability in our mental iPod's to remember hundreds, if not thousands of tunes and lyrics, feel deeply the vast diversity of emotions in music, recognize dissonance or wrong notes, and tap our feet to musical rhythms so complicated that most computers couldn't do it.[452]

Though our musical prowess is astounding, I question Jordain's over-arching statement that excludes other animals when I listen to the complex whale songs while swimming in Kealakekua Bay. And recently I saw a documentary on Thailand elephants who, when placed near rhythm instruments (gongs, chimes, xylophones, drums) were able to produce distinct, interesting, harmonious and complex musical compositions. And what of the rhythmic dance of bees that communicate "sweet spots" near their hive, the complex songs of mockingbirds and the sonic songs of other creatures. Perhaps the neural complexity for music is more prevalent throughout nature than we are yet aware of.

"I would teach children music, physics, and philosophy,
but most importantly music, for in the patterns of music and all the arts
are the keys of learning." — Plato

The patterns in Mozart's music are excellent for steady beat patterning and, therefore, have been found to assist learning. College students who heard ten minutes of Mozart's *Sonata for Two Pianos in D major* (K.448) raised their IQ scores on tests of spatial-temporal reasoning, a skill related to math.[453,454] Other researchers have used this same sonata to improve the spatial-temporal reasoning of Alzheimer's patients and to reduce the number of seizures in epileptics. Parkinson's disease patients tend to stutter or stumble because they grossly misjudge time and have difficulty coordinating speech with movements. Music gives them the rhythm and tempo to organize their timing and function better.[455]

A more recent study discovered the power of sustained, complex rhythms, such as experienced in African and Latin music where different musical themes are laid upon each other in a coherent meld of sound and rhythm. These have an even greater impact than Mozart's sonata, as much as 20% more, on spatial-temporal reasoning skills.[456] Music that elicits a coherent heart rate variability pattern, whether complex or not, also assists in decreasing heart rate, blood pressure, and the amount of lactic acid in muscles during exercise or physical exertion, thus reducing muscle tension and increasing efficiency.[457]

The power of music to assist the brain in understanding patterns can be seen on SAT (Standardized Achievement Tests) scores for verbal and math skills. In 2005, students with music performance in their school curriculum scored 56 points higher on the verbal portion of the test and 39 points higher on the math portion compared with students who had no coursework or experience in the arts. Students with music study and music appreciation scored 60 points higher on the verbal and 39 points higher on the math portions of the test compared with students with no coursework in the arts. And students with four or more years of music education scored dramatically higher on SATs than those that had no music.[458] Of great interest to me was the research showing improvement of four grade levels of reading in "low readers" after just six months of instrumental music instruction.[459]

In elementary and middle school, music classes aren't just about learning to play an instrument. They're about working together, listening to each other, coordinating the hands and the fingers with a whole group. That's what music is about. It is not just about the concert at the end of the year."[460]

I experienced first hand the complex benefits of music for learning while playing cymbals in a community Fourth of July parade band. Our group, led by professional music teachers, was comprised of students, ages nine to sixty-plus. The younger members were just beginning the exploration of music and the older ones were reconnecting to musical roots they wish they had continued earlier in life. Incredibly, not only did we have to follow the bandleader, play complex instruments, read complex musical scores and make beautiful music together, we had to march in time and precise physical formation with all the other band members.

For me, someone who had always had difficulty with timing and hated metronomes, keeping the cymbal beat that alternated with my marching steps was a complete breakthrough — from chaos to order. Every part of my mind/body system was fully engaged.

At an English cathedral, and also at Cambridge, the Masters of Choristers found the reading age of all their choirboys improved by twelve months within six months of their joining the choir. Listening, vocalizing, learning to hear pitch and rhythm, as well as reading the written music enhanced all their learning skills.[461] Harmonic toning, as in singing or chanting, activates the whole cranium and increases respiratory rate and the flow of cerebral spinal fluid in the brain, thus optimizing brain function.[462]

Music in the curriculum was also found to assist social interactions. Students taking music classes worked better in groups and got along more with both peers and superiors alike. Their overall self-esteem was higher, and their chance of dropping out of school was much less. Music has the ability to cross racial, cultural, and economic barriers making everyone equal.

I am impressed with organizations like Musikgarten, Kindermusik, Music Together, Music with Mar and many more whose programs are excellent for integrating all the elements of sound, movement, touch, and music in the preschool years of life. These programs begin with whole families exploring sound when the children are very young, as early as one month old. They incorporate sound with real instruments and singing to energize and alert the body and mind. Families participate in integrative, cross-lateral movements and steady beat to assist the process of pattern finding in their children. The child gets lots of touch through play and massage and develops a lifelong love of music and rhythm, which makes pattern recognition and learning infinitely easier.[463]

Musical training, beginning at an early age, has an abundance of rewards. In brain studies of musicians versus non-musicians, music was shown to greatly assist fine motor development and significantly increase gray matter volume in both the left and right sensori-motor cortexes and the left basal ganglion that orchestrates movement. The research also showed a significantly higher EEG coherence, a more receptive and 25% larger auditory cortex, and greater cerebellum and corpus callosum differen tiation.[464,465,466,467] Music engages many areas of the brain, including areas for creativity, emotions, as well as those normally involved in cognition and language.

Music is more complicated than language, consisting of falling and rising patterns, the sequence of tones, the pattern of the melody, and the lyrics. These all determine what areas of the brain will fire. Coherent (consonant) chords activate an area of the right hemisphere, the nucleus accumbens that deals with feelings of pleasure and reward.[468] When music is so beautiful that it gives us "chills," the pleasure centers of the brain light up, just like they do when we eat chocolate or make love.[469] We enjoy music because it elicits emotions and feelings. People with Alzheimer's disease appreciate emotionally evocative music because it allows them to recall emotions, memories and scenes they seem to have lost.[470]

When we are listening to music, the following brain regions are activated instantaneously: the auditory cortex (where we first process sound), the frontal lobes processing musical structure and expectations, the limbic system involved in arousal, emotions and production of dopamine, and the nucleus accumbens, which also stimulates dopamine production. The emotions produced by coherent music, where dopamine is being actively produced, act as natural anti-depressants and are able to very effectively elevate mood in depressed people.[471]

Plato, and so many other wisdom seekers, knew that music should be an integral part of life and education, with children singing many times during the day, if only to sing their assignment back to the teacher. Learning to "play" a musical instrument, first by exploring rhythm and tone for the fun of it before introducing music, must occur at least weekly in the classroom.

Music must continue in the curriculum, as it does in most European schools and all Asian schools, until the child/young adult graduates. Besides energizing their whole system, keeping the brain focused and attentive to the cognitive patterns we wish students to learn in language and math, music allows for greater sensitivity to the vast vibrational fields that enrich life and make the whole planet more coherent and pleasurable. Chris Brewer has written the book, *Soundtracks for Learning: Using Music in the Classroom*, which I consider to be indispensable for classroom teachers.[472]

"The ability to appreciate music is a defining quality
of our humanity." — Oliver Sachs

I sit with all my instruments around me now very aware of how each has brought coherence to my life and helped to structure my learning. My own voice resonates my inner being to the world in emotional outbursts, language, and song. The drums and rattles, sophisticated versions of the first pots, pans, and measuring spoons I beat on as a child, mimic the familiar rhythm of my mother's heart beat. The piano is an elaborate version of my first xylophone that introduced me to varying pitches and an understanding of the elaborate harmonics, overtones, and patterns inherent in language. The violin with its rich woody vibrations energizes and releases the deepest emotions of my soul. The guitar allows me to blend my voice, rhythm, tones, patterns, and emotions with others.

Cecily, a neighbor, taught in an inner city middle school where children faced many challenges in their homes and also with learning. Knowing the importance of real sound for brain and learning development, Cecily was able to procure enough violins for each of her students to use during the school year. The violin with its high frequency vibrations stimulates the whole mind/body system. Over the year the students became an impressive group of violinists as well as good students with positive energy and self-confidence.

Natural acoustic instruments, made of wood, and metal have internal structures that cause molecules of air to vibrate, producing several frequencies of energy at the same time. Single reed instruments such as the clarinet, saxophone, or recorder also vibrate and energize the body as the mouthpiece rests against the upper teeth sympathetically vibrating all the bones in the head. So, even in an orchestra or concert band where clarinets traditionally sit right in front of trombones and trumpets, making it difficult for them to hear what they are playing, they can actually feel the sound through their teeth and head.[473]

There is a growing awareness of the need for music in all aspects of our life. Turn off the cell phone, the radio, the CD player and sing in the car. Play with song, energize yourself with your voice, or any available sounding structure, from the echo of a stairwell (or shower stall), to the metal pipes of bicycle stands, to rocks rubbed together or sticks with their tonal diversity, to any man-made contraption known as an instrument. As Ahti, my musician husband, and I travel throughout the world, I am always amazed at what he finds to make sound and music with — there is no limit.

In my workshops I have people do a *sound flower*. Standing in a close circle, using our full breath, we begin by toning (sounding) the vowels: "ah" as a low tone, "aa" as a mid tone, "ee" as a high tone. Then everyone plays with the shape of their mouth while toning so they can hear and feel in the bones of their head and larynx the harmonics and overtones. And finally for the sound flower, everyone begins on a tone and holds it out for their full breath. Immediately they take another breath and come in on the same tone or a different, and continue for a good 12 breaths. People usually close their eyes and just let the sound wash over them, sometimes dissonant but often coherent as they more sympathetically come into harmony and form a beautiful evolving flower of sound. To me, it feels like the deep resonance of Gregorian monks chanting in a cathedral. Children in classrooms also love to make *sound flowers*.

I re-discover the joy children have in singing as I share music in my local elementary schools. Each week I teach them a song (with movements of course), and a week later, when I return to the classroom, they joyfully sing it for me, even though they have not sung it since the week before. They all know that their bodies are the most complex instruments, so we get their instruments ready, we sing and sing and they love it, just like I did when I was their age, and still do.

Standing Up To Dance And Sing

Song, dance and music have nearly always occurred together and been a communal activity during tens of thousands of years of evolutionary history. In fact, according to new findings in paleontology, we may have developed bipedalism (upright posture) in order to sing and dance.[474] This connection between movement and music shows up in brain scans where the cerebellum and motor cortex are active when listening to or just imagining music, even if the person is not moving. Singing, playing music and dancing increases our dopamine levels, and assists us to express various feelings: sadness, joy, love, friendship, excitement, and fear.

I was blessed to experience an Aztec dance for Mother Earth recently. Forty or more dancers with feathered headdresses and elaborate costumes executed complex, beautiful and ritualistic dances to drum rhythms under the full moon. One of their members commented, "this is the way we pray". It seems that all indigenous people pray with dance and rhythm. I've experienced the expressive and strong dances of the Hawaiians, the rhythmic chants and dances of Native American tribes, the soul inspired dances of Australian Aborigines, all of which connect to spirit and their ancestors through dance and music.

Whenever people come together for any reason, birthdays, weddings, funerals, picnics, graduations, religious services, there is music. Some of the strongest bonds in our society are formed when people dance, sing and/or play music together, or dance to each other's music. Playing music together can be more intimate than any other activity. Taking turns and accommodating other people's music calls for a great amount of empathy and generosity. The contribution of each to the whole makes the music even grander. Our ancient forebears who learned to synchronize the movements of dance were those with the capacity to predict what others around them were going to do, and signal to others what they wanted to do next. These forms of communication may well have led to the formation of larger human communities.

Dance has always been a passion for me, even from childhood when I took ballet and creative dance at the age of five. I believe it helped me develop an understanding of rhythm and how my body naturally moves to the rhythms around me. Our innate nature is to dance to music, even at concerts. Children do it naturally, spinning, swaying, leaping, and generally participating when they feel like it at a concert. Levitin comments that the advent of musical concerts by a society's most skilled performers separated performers from listeners and participators. Rather than enjoy the child heart at play and join them, we train children to act "civilized." The natural tendency toward movement is thus so internalized; it is manifested in concert halls only as a mild swaying of heads.

> "We would have more fun if we moved freely in a concert rip out the seats and let us dance."[475] — Daniel J. Levitin

> "Music is the electrical soil in which the spirit lives, thinks and invents" — Ludwig von Beethoven

Our ability to make sense of and compose music depends on

experience, hearing, learning the grammar of notes, pitch, rhythm and playing the music that excites us. Once the grammar of music is learned, then the real creativity begins. Jazz and many other contemporary music forms, where players are following a chart of music at times, but then taking improvisational solos and coming up with something totally new, are highly creative.

As a classically trained violinist, I am very dependent on the charts (sheets of music) to guide what I do, especially if I am playing with someone else. My husband who plays all the woodwinds, as well as percussion, guitar, dobro, sitar, piano and many other instruments, approaches music differently. He is called to play with many bands, and without any practice or hours of rehearsal he "knocks their socks off" with his beautiful improvisations and sensitivity to playing backup for their solos and group harmonies. He is constantly composing and creating something new each moment, beautiful and compelling.

"Music being the most exalted of arts, the work of the composer of music is no less than the work of a saint. It is not only the knowledge of technicality, of harmony of theory that is sufficient: the composer needs tenderness of heart, open eyes to all beauty, the conception of what is beautiful, the true perception of sound and rhythm, and its expression in human nature." — Hazrat Inayat Khan[476]

When musicians are engaged in the highly spontaneous, creative activity of improvisation, the dorso-lateral prefrontal cortex area of the brain, that consciously monitors and judges one's performance, is totally shut down. Instead, the medial prefrontal cortex, a small subconscious area of the brain involved in organizing self-initiated creative thoughts and behaviors is highly active. This suppression of the inhibitory, self-monitoring brain area helps promote the free flow of novel ideas and impulses of full creativity. These same areas are active during dreaming or when we are in the flow, doing something creative (art, poetry, dance, music, writing) that takes us out of time and space. This may be the area of the brain that most directly connects into and amplifies the unified field of all possibilities. There is also increased activity in the emotional centers of the brain as well as sensorimotor areas for touch, seeing, hearing and movement.[477]

When I know my music by heart without the charts, even complex classical pieces by Telemann, or Bach, I find I can truly play them by heart. I feel the music running through my violin to my soul and I soar, fully experiencing the bliss of the music, lost in sound, embracing every movement of my bow upon the strings that sets my cymatic system vibrating with patterns. And it is only when I begin to think about the music, the notes, the timing, and where my fingers should go that suddenly it all falls apart.

Music becomes play, as strong consistent patterns are active throughout the entire brain, and body. This state of flow, being fully present in the moment, allows us to be creative and express our emotions. Music is a doorway into our true nature as well as the next step toward expression of our being through language and emotions.

10

Play: The Unscripted Present

"A child's world is fresh and new and beautiful, full of wonder and excitement.
It is our misfortune that for most of us that clear-eyed vision,
that true instinct for what is beautiful and awe-inspiring, is dimmed
and even lost before we reach adulthood." — Rachel Carson

The Essence Of Play

During play, we exist in a state of total coherence/pleasure, in the most natural learning state available to us. To truly understand coherence, play with a young child, and *let the child lead*. Release control, worry, the past and the future. Exist purely in the moment and notice how harmoniously connected you become with your intricate world, seeing with undeterred vision, curiosity and joy; stepping totally into your childlike nature.

Children are Zen Masters of play, optimally learning and setting in place the perfect mental/emotional structures for a flexible, dynamic and socially connected creative life. The blueprint for lifelong success lies in this childlike state where both children and adults are totally engrossed in the moment-to-moment wonder of the world. Our understanding of ourselves and of our interactions with others comes from this ego-less place of total connection.

Given a rich environment, we are all natural sponges, gently exploring each new moment, event or object with intense curiosity. Our whole system is finely calibrated to take in and attempt to make sense of each new experience. In this state we are perfect learners, living in the now, our eyes, ears, touch receptors fully engaged, sensuously scanning each detail, hue, smell, and sound. It may take all afternoon, but time is irrelevant.

A shift in paradigms, especially about learning, would essentially elevate the value we give to play, with its elements of imagination, full sensory/motor/emotional activation, and heart-centered interaction. Play is the platform to access all possibilities and our creativity as masters of our life. Growing up under the heavy yoke of the Puritan ethic, I reveled in every delicious moment of play I could grab, either alone or in joyous rough and tumble play with the wild assortment of neighborhood kids I grew up with. My Aunts' and Uncles' farms in Iowa became favorite summer playgrounds for me, rich with cousins, haymows, and baby animals. I jumped, rolled, and climbed my way through the heat of many Iowa Julys, my imagination, curiosity and joy of life aflame like the fireflies that studded the sultry nights. Play included family camping trips to the mountains of Utah where I explored for hours its streams and deep, enchanted forests.

According to current research, these growing up play experiences teach us flexibility, curiosity, how to create our dreams, and how to be in relationship with nature and other people. They shape our sense of adventure for all of life's experiences, both joyful and challenging, and the way we continue to see, explore and act on our world as adults.[478,479]

When I speak of play, my meaning is that of unstructured, sensuous, voluntary, spontaneous, connected, explorative, risk taking, unpredictable, lost-in-the-moment play that creates a sense of no-time. Play, for me is the way my spirit authentically expresses itself, and evolves in understanding. According to Stuart L. Brown, MD and psychiatrist, play is: "a spontaneous, non-stereotyped, intrinsically pleasurable activity, free of anxiety or other overpowering emotion, without a visible, clear-cut goal other than its own activity."[480] Johan Herizinga, in his book *Homo Ludens* (Man at Play) stipulates that real play is in fact freedom, without compulsion or constraint, with the spur-of-the moment spontaneity that most of us adults remember from childhood.[481]

During college I spent two semesters in animal behavior courses and double that in psychology courses. At that time, it was popular for scientists to emphasize the species survival value of biological structures and behaviors in humans and other animals, but play was never mentioned. It appeared to be frivolous with no apparent survival value. Current research is showing that play is as important as food and sleep for the developmental processes of animals, especially humans. It may actually be our most important survival behavior, supplying us with coherence, creativity, flexibility and social understanding.[482]

Stuart L. Brown presented an example of this frivolous behavior at a conference I attended in 1999. He had taken pictures for National Geographic of musk ox standing in a circle. This was not unusual, as musk ox often circle up with horns out to protect themselves and their offspring from predators. However, this time the musk ox were head in, gossip circle fashion, exposing their rears in a most vulnerable way. Suddenly one musk ox left the circle and started prancing about, and all the others followed. It looked like a game of follow the leader. This behavior was stunning in that it seemed to have absolutely no survival value and was even a bit risky.

The raven has been found to be one of the most playful of all birds. They've been spotted using plastic bags to slide down hills, playfully catching food, and even intelligently playing with wolves over a dead deer. The playfulness of ravens exposes them to a variety of risks, teaching them how to get along with much larger carnivores on whom they depend for food, and making them very flexible. These factors may have allowed them to become the most widely, naturally distributed bird in the world, inhabiting the same continents as humans and being at home in all the diverse habitats that humans also inhabit.[483,484] During play, children perceive challenge as an adventure, a learning activity, rather than a threat, thus they become flexible like the raven.

Risk appears to be part of the pleasure and challenge of play. Because play is *built into our genes*, the rewards of play must be greater and more important for survival than the risks.[485] It appears that play trains us to handle the unexpected, encouraging flexibility and creativity that becomes an advantage in new environments and situations. According to Stewart Brown, adults who had rich play lives as children, were able to handle life situations in a far more resilient and vital way.[486]

Too often we overprotect our children, inhibiting their free movement to explore and learn from their environment. If we constantly guard them out of fear that they will fall, cut, or hurt themselves or others, we limit their ability to gain confidence in the function and balance of their own body. We actually make our children unsafe because without climbing, jumping, taking risks, and fully exploring gravity and balance when they are young, close to the ground, and with more flexible cartilage than bone, they don't learn the limits of their own bodies.

BILL OF RIGHTS FOR PLAY — Joseph W. Meeker [487,488]

- All Players are equal or can be made so

- Novelty is more fun than repetition

- Rules are negotiable from moment to moment

- Risk in pursuit of play is worth it

- The best play is beautiful and elegant

- The purpose of playing is to play, nothing more.

Complex play doesn't seem to occur in fish, amphibians, or reptiles. These animals appear to be hard-wired into a format of survival/instinct reactions. Basically, if you're a reptile you run away from something bigger than you; you mate with something the same size, and eat something smaller than you. You certainly don't play with it!

Apparently, play demands two characteristics in the players: 1) warm-bloodedness and 2) a complex, highly integrated brain with the capacity to be aware of bodily sensations, experience emotions and dream; these brain capacities emotionally structure our world and formulate our imagination.[489] A developed imagination provides both the joy of play and also the ability to face our existential fears.[490]

Warm-bloodedness provides the surplus energy needed for play. Since our metabolism keeps our body temperature constant, we don't need to shut down when it's cold (hibernate) or hot (find shade). Our extensive fat storage, which both insulates and provides energy, and our insulating hair covering help to protect and maintain our energy for play. Prolonged parenting in birds and especially in mammals provides the needed protection, as well as the food necessary to free up energy for play. In humans, the most playful of all animals, play emerges within a secure, healthy, hunger-free, supportive environment, where parental involvement is abundant.[491]

Playful creatures have masses of neurons in their complex brains devoted strictly to the generation of play, even rough-and-tumble play. These distinct neural systems are located in projection areas of the thalamus and specific nuclei (parafascicular complex and posterior thalamic nuclei) in the parietal lobe of the cortex. They are linked directly to body sensations, movement, emotions and information processing within the amygdala, cerebellum, anterior cingulated cortex, right frontal insula, motor cortex and no doubt the nucleus accumbens (our pleasure center).[492] Play impulses originate in the brain and don't need to be learned.[493]

Information chemicals (neuropeptides, hormones, etc) in our bodies also affect play impulses.[494] When we play physically, our brains release brain derived neurotrophic factor (BDNF) that stimulates and orchestrates nerve-net development all over the brain. Play also releases dopamine, a chemical that induces elation, excitement and exploratory behavior, allowing us to easily coordinate our actions and physically learn from our experiences. People with Parkinson's disease or who are labeled hyperactive or ADHD have low dopamine levels, thus play can be an important deterrent to hyperactivity, learning difficulties and disease.[495,496]

Play assists the growth of the cerebellum, the main brain center for movement, and for the maturation (pruning of excess cortical brain cells) of the medial prefrontal cortex. This assists us to make subtle adjustments to our understanding and actions in our social world.[497]

Play must be crucial for the development of our huge brains and complex body/mind systems because we play more than any other animal and for a longer period of time. Neoteny means: the retention of childlike features, which we humans exhibit throughout our lives. With our remarkably malleable nervous systems, we are always in a state of development. Being playful potentially allows us to continue to take risks, be impulsive, imaginative, flexible and empathetic, creating new ideas and implementing them throughout our whole life.[498]

Play Embraces All Our Senses

Play is the rich blending of senses and emotion — energy in motion. Over 80% of the nervous system is involved in processing or organizing the sensory input we get from our bodies about the world around us. Our ability to interpret external stimuli and the sensations and actions they elicit within our own body is essential to many fundamental features of being human: emotional awareness, sentiment and sentience. Passion, motivation, empathy, ideas and intentions elicited by environmental stimuli, are key elements of our humanity. The sensual nature of play gives us the most direct access to mature our sensory/motor/emotional mind/body system.[499]

Children and adults who have access to the enriched sensory environment of nature and the freedom to explore it are very fortunate. If you examine the lives of the most creative people on the planet, you will find that they spent much of their childhood in nature. Our sensory/emotional processing system thrives on diversity:

- The solid pressure of a hug or someone next to us,
- The soft brush of grass against bare legs,
- Rough bark on fingertips,
- The smooth velvet of a new leaf,
- The solid coldness of a rock,
- The breeze blowing our hair out of place,
- And the prickly tingle of a pine cone.

Brandy Binder, a vibrant, intelligent, happy child, suddenly started having seizures from a type of meningitis at the age of four. The seizures became so frequent (over one hundred a day) that she became increasingly incapacitated. The doctors attempted to stop the seizures first through drugs, then by excising a small area of the brain, but to no avail. They finally opted to remove the whole right hemisphere of Brandy's brain. The ensuing paralysis of the left side of her body was devastating to this child who loved to dance and run.

On the advice of one very aware doctor, the family began to challenge her body and senses with lots of sensorimotor stimulation. Besides physical therapy, massage, music, being read to, and nature strolls, there was lots of play as siblings tickled and rolled her around, making her laugh. The results were miraculous. At the age of 14, Brandy was a happy, bright, good student(exhibiting only minor problems with long term memory), who rode horses, hiked and even danced.[500]

I had the good fortune to meet Brandy and her mother when she was eighteen. This physically beautiful, highly literate young woman had won two major art contests with her brilliant "right brained" paintings, and intended to become a public speaker. Brandy — and the more than one thousand people with hemispherectomies, many of whom have no intellectual deficits — went on to finish advanced degrees and score above average on intelligence tests. The accomplishments of these people have challenged neuroscience to rethink brain function.[501] Through the extraordinary power of sensorimotor stimulation, especially play, the plasticity, flexibility, redundancy and ability of the brain to reprogram itself, allow us to succeed even if some of the neocortex is lost.[502]

New research, using Stanley Greenspan's social-pragmatic (floor-play and language based) methods of intervention with severely autistic children, shows the same kind of activation and success in alleviating the symptoms of autism. Autistic children whose parents interacted with them one-on-one at least fifteen hours per week, following the child's lead in play, made good to excellent progress even within the first year of intervention.[503,504]

Our systems thrive on rich sensory challenges. Encountering new cultures, as I have over the past twenty years in more than thirty countries, demanded that I be absolutely present, that I come with the curiosity of a child, ready to step out of my judgments and habitual ruts. I was constantly experiencing different climates, foods, smells, social interactions, indigenous music and art, sleeping in different beds, and meeting remarkable people.

I was amazed at how time expanded into a sense of no time. As I became totally aware, and sensorily immersed in each new moment, I was left with a deep sense of awe and respect for the diversity I experienced, and a thirst to truly understand that diversity in my soul. I felt absolutely alive.

What a miracle to live in our senses daily, doing things in different ways, making life an adventure. Eat with the other hand or walk a different way, explore a new sport or environment, change a routine, move with your eyes closed using your other senses to guide you, play an unfamiliar musical instrument, mimic the bird songs around you, dare to be different. Sensory challenges help us stay awake and fascinated by the richness of life. You can tell if a person is living from her senses; she is confident and enthusiastic about her life in a curious, authentic way.[505]

"Do one thing each day that scares you" — *Eleanor Roosevelt*

Our senses shut down in our hurried, competitive, sleep-deprived lives when we experience only what we expect to experience while missing the ever-changing sensory landscape of our existence. This incoherent state is an embezzlement of our potential, leaving us easily fatigued and depressed. My mother was still passionately, independently taking risks to do new, novel things late into her life. A month before she died, she could still "wump" me at card games. The day before she died of pneumonia at the age of almost 99, she went to exercise class because she enjoyed the people, the chair exercises and the "Can-Can" at the end of class. She was a fantastic model for me with her playful mind and bright, independent spirit.

We always knew exactly what Mom felt, as a strong-headed redhead. She was open and honest with us, passionately expressing her opinions, which sometimes led to heated arguments. Sometimes she would purposefully take the opposite point of view just to enjoy the sport of it. I believe we are given our parents, siblings, spouses, and offspring to perturb, spar and play with us for the fun and frustration of it and the growth of our soul. A study done in the Netherlands showed that old committed couples who argued were less likely to get Alzheimer's than those who didn't.[506]

"Life is nothing if not an adventure." — *Helen Keller*

Babies need lots of space and time for free, uninterrupted play to explore new territory. Parents and caregivers can "do less" and let the baby's development unfold naturally.[507] When needed, be fully present for interactive connection, the baby's maintenance needs, and play. Experience a baby exploring your face with all her senses — it's awesome and slobbery. To a baby, your face is a much more enriched environment than any toy you could give her. For the baby's sake and your own, put the toys away, bring on the pots and pans and whisks and measuring spoons and scrubbers. Clear the floor and roly-poly play with her, jump on the bed, climb on the couch, and explore the dog. Throw away the dishwasher, get an oilcloth apron and highchair, and let that child explore the sensuous world of soap bubbles, the slippery feel of dishes and forks and dishcloths.

Bring on the mud, sand, birdseed, seashells, sticks, cardboard boxes, and stand back to give room for exploration. By the way, the stick has been entered in the Toy Hall of Fame. Eat all kinds of food with your fingers along with your child, spouse or alone, stimulating two of the most sensitive parts of your body, the fingertips and lips. Be totally aware of and celebrate everything you eat, its color, smell, texture, and delightful taste. Play with your food, stir or squeeze it into an unrecognizable paste and smear it on your body, especially your nose. These are all suggestions from my wonderful friend, teacher, and child development expert, Renate Wennekes.[508]

Our fear of dirt may prevent us from letting our children experience the whole sensory-rich environment. Researchers are now saying that our squeaky clean, antiseptic environments have weakened our immune systems, resulting in increased allergies, asthma, and auto-immune diseases such as rheumatoid arthritis and the most severe type of diabetes. The immune system organizes itself through experience, so these diseases tend to develop when the immune system lacks practice fighting bacteria and viruses.[509]

Kids need contact, not with disease causing agents, but with innocuous microbes in the soil and untreated water, to give the immune system a workout. Children growing up in big families, or on farms, or children from families who avoid antibiotics and vaccinations are much less likely to develop allergies.[510] Even insect bites help fine-tune the immune system, making it stronger and more resistant to dangerous bites from infected insects.[511]

Play Entails Movement

"If we didn't move, we wouldn't need a brain" — Robert Sylwester

"Good play involves physical activity, creativity, spontaneity, exploration, and social interaction that engages the body in fine and gross motor development and the mind in negotiations, autonomous thinking, problem solving, imagination and flexibility."
— Dr. Joe Frost[512]

Up until November 1998, I had been telling students that though we were constantly developing new nerve networks, it was doubtful whether new nerve cells developed after six months of age. We now know that growth of new nerve cells occurs until the day we die. As many as 60,000 new nerve cells per day grow in the hippocampus, the place where we start formulating memories from environmental input.[513]

Research on rats and mice show that an enriched environment, one that is large, has diverse toys and running wheels, and is shared with many other rodents they can explore and play with, is necessary for these new cells to form and remain healthy. The running wheels and cross lateral integrated movement, were the real stars though, causing the most cell growth, even in very old rats and mice.[514,515,516] Recently, Warin Krityakiarana, a Thai researcher, discovered new nerve cell growth in the spinal cords of mice as a result of exercise.[517] So, perhaps there are other places in the central nervous system where exercise is stimulating neurogenesis that we have yet to discover. These new nerve cells, activated by movement, like impressionable children, are more likely to participate in learning. They connect with existing nerve tissue, enriching the circuitry, which boosts pattern understanding and recall and participates in making new memories.[518]

Research shows the importance of integrated cross-lateral movement like walking and swimming to stimulate nerve growth, just as it did with the rats. Exercise based on developmental patterns, like Brain Dance,[519] Nurturing Pathways, Dancing Feet,[520] and On The Move,[521] as well as Feldenkrais, tai chi, yoga, Eurhythmy, Bal-A-Vis-X,[522] and Brain Gym®, to name a few, work with the integrated cross-lateral patterns that assist learning and balance. Exercise improves attention, reduces stress and anxiety, and increases cognitive function. It prompts the brain to produce greater amounts of BDNF that strengthens brain cells and encourages them to form connections the brain needs in order to learn and remember.[523]

The body grows the brain through movement with the vestibular system being the unifying factor. The vestibular system, made up of the utricles and saccules of the semicircular canals of the inner ear, cerebellum, and Reticular Activating System, connects with all the movement centers in the brain and all of our muscles. This entryway system primes the entire nervous system to function optimally. The connections between the cerebellum and the hippocampus are extensive, explaining why movement is so important to new nerve growth. The mature vestibular system organizes our mastery of gravity, which is more compelling than our need for food, touch, or even the mother-child bond.[524]   And our mastery of gravity facilitates learning in all the other arenas of life.

Watch a baby roll over or a child jump for joy, and you will notice a spiral pattern. It's the same spiral we see in the double helix of the DNA, the spiral growth in plants, or the spiral in the currents of the ocean that scientists call the Archimedian twist.[525]   Normal play movements are curvilinear, exhibiting this spiral where the body curves around and embraces the play object, whether it be an object of nature, a toy or another child. In a non-play situation, the body tends to be straight, rigid, and ready to fight or flee.[526]

Autistic children are lacking the normal spiral movements. Philip Teitelbaum's study showed that most children learn to roll over at about three months old using a spiral motion, while autistic babies exhibit no such movement. Their movements tend to be rigid, asymmetrical and unbalanced, indications that the vestibular system has not developed properly.[527]

Swinging and spinning are essential to development. The playground of the one and only school in Havelock, Iowa, where I spent summers as a child, had a merry-go-round in the schoolyard like none other in the world. It consisted of a circular wooden bench, suspended from a big central eight foot high pole by metal guy wires, so it hung freely, and boy could it spin! Kids would pile on and hold on tight while other kids would run around the outside, accelerating it to greater and greater speeds.

Now, I am hard pressed to find merry-go-rounds on any playground, and swings are even becoming rare. Parents, childcare centers, schools, and parks are demanding risk-free, scratch-free and tear-free play where safety seems to be the only concern.[528]   This over concern with physical safety might leave us with clumsy, accident-prone kids that haven't explored enough balanced movements to develop their vestibular systems, thus decreasing their ability to succeed academically, socially and physically.

A 2007 study shows that less than 15% of Americans get regular exercise. Estimates show that only 3.8% of elementary schools, 7.9% of middle schools and 2.1% of high schools provide daily physical education, and whole school districts are eliminating recess all together.[529]   These statistics support a worry of the American Academy of Pediatrics that fewer than half of all school children get enough exercise to develop healthy hearts and lungs. Less heart and lung development affects the amount of oxygen the brain and muscles receive and leaves children uncoordinated, unfocused and unable to explore and enjoy their world fully. A large accumulation of research substantiates the findings that kids and adults who are more physically active exhibit better concentration and perform better academically.[530,531,532,533,534] Some schools are having students stand up to learn, use balance boards when memorizing information, and sit on exercise balls, all of which are shown to improve academic achievement. I so appreciate people like Joe Smith, NBCT-Physical Education for early and middle childhood and movement advocate from West Virginia, who embodies communication and cooperation with his unerring dedication to children and their need to move to learn. He has doggedly kept a whole network of people abreast of the current research on the need for physical education and consistent movement in the classroom.

In November 2006, The American Academy of Pediatrics strongly recommended that free, unstructured play is healthy and essential for helping children become coordinated, focused, resilient, reach important social, emotional and cognitive developmental milestones as well as helping them manage stress.[535] In order to develop coordination, children must be allowed to explore gravity through swinging, spinning on merry-go-rounds, climbing trees, rolling down hills, walking on fences, jumping on beds, and all those wonderful, risky things we did as kids. I love to see kids being swung around by parents so both parent and child are activating their vestibular systems.

Figure 10.1 Parent swinging child – both activating their vestibular systems

We, as adults, may feel uncomfortable spinning because at puberty the fluid in the semi-circular canals thickens, so we tend to get dizzier faster and stay dizzy longer. But I have found that when I spin on a regular basis, I don't get dizzy. Spinning wakes up my brain, assists my coordination and balance, and puts me in a state of joy.[536]

I have come across many parks, playgrounds, schools and community centers that have added labyrinths to their grounds. They are even being added to church and hospital grounds. These spiral pathways, traced back over 3500 years to the Island of Crete, are thought to balance the two hemispheres of the brain. The geometric regularity and equal number of left and right turns have been found to establish a balanced (coherent) pattern for those who walk it.

Walking through the labyrinth's spiral pattern has been shown to greatly help children labeled ADHD, autistic, dyslexic and emotionally handicapped. The labyrinth requires increased focus, attentiveness, and balance just to walk, skip, or run through it. This calm, focused attention is reported to stay with the child during cognitive learning tasks.

Some added advantages of the labyrinth include:

- 1. Reaching the center is assured, so there is no failure — you can't do it wrong.

- 2. Walking the labyrinth is more about the journey than the destination, being more than doing.

- 3. The entire labyrinth is visible to the person as they walk it, so there is no stress.[537]

- 4. The circle is a symbol of wholeness and curls around the walker as they move toward and away from the center.

- 5. Walking the labyrinth quiets the mind, creates a sense of peace and gratitude and opens the walker to insights, understanding and solutions.[538,539,540]

Figure 10.2 Crete labyrinth

Movement as play is important throughout out lives as seen in the research that aerobic exercise prevents cortical decay and cognitive impairment in older adults, reducing the risk of developing dementia. Physical activity has been found to increase hippocampal volume in older adults, allowing for better learning and memory.[541] This research correlated with the research that elderly people who dance once a week decrease their chance of Alzheimer's and dementia by 79% and playing a musical instrument decreases it by 69%.[542,543] Also, because regular physical activity raises dopamine levels, it decreases by half the risk of Parkinson's disease.[544] Movement, especially if it is fun, experienced in a play context, is essential to not only our brain growth and health but also our enjoyment throughout life.

The Motor Moms and Dads Volunteer Program, developed by Nancy Sornson, recognizes the importance of building balance, bilateral motor skills, visual motor skills and spatial awareness for young children.

Figure 10.3 Labyrinth at Palm Bay Elementary, Palm Bay Florida

Play Entails Touch And Laughter

"Like clay that has been left out, we become rigid, hard and brittle if we are left untouched. Through touch of child's play we, like clay, become delightfully pliable stuff – well made, good to handle and to live with, and above all alive with use."
— O Fred Donaldson, Playing By Heart

The skin is our largest sense organ and the first to meet our environment directly. It is like a space suit, equipped to check out all the diverse senses around us through a rich assortment of nerve endings that respond to light touch, pressure, pain, heat, cold, and vibrational patterns. There are even protective touch receptors around our hair follicles, which respond to sound and air vibrations moving across the body. They literally tell us where our body ends and space begins.[545] Already at birth, touch provides safety and comfort after separation from the mother and on into later life, as we experience subsequent separations or need for connection.

Touching the skin sends messages to the brain that stimulates the production of oxytocin and endorphins. Oxytocin promotes the bonding between the mother and baby and father and baby, and endorphins produce a sense of well being at birth.[546] Traditional Chinese hospitals mandate that the mother and baby must be skin-to-skin for the first half-hour after birth to assure bonding and to bring health to the child throughout life.

In Bali, people make a poultice of garlic and coconut oil that they rub on the newborn, lovingly but with firm/vigorous pressure, to wake up the baby's senses and protect it from evil. The babies I saw loved it, and became calm, alert, and happy children.

Early touch leads to a strong immune system, better weight gain, and a healthy functioning of the hypothalamus that decreases the release of stress hormones when the situation is not life-threatening, resulting in a calm baby. Fifteen minutes of massage three times daily brings about a 45% increase in weight gain in premature babies.[547] As babies mature into children, adolescents, young adults, adults, and elderly adults the levels of oxytocin and endorphins from touch continue to give a sense of being loved, producing self-assured, self-directed, loving people.[548]

Touch is so important to the safety and the initial development of the child that without it, the child's brain may not develop well, and he or she may die.[549] When our need for touch is not met, our stress increases, bringing on the cascade of cortisol and adrenaline. Children without touch will attempt to get that need met through such self-stimulating behaviors as hitting, biting or pinching themselves or others.

Touch is the strongest anchor for validating who we are. It is ten times more important than verbal or emotional contact.[550] Humans will do anything for touch. We start by doing what we think other people want, just for a pat or a hug. If that doesn't work, we will do just the opposite to be hit or spanked, which is also touch. In either case we are getting the life sustaining touch we need for survival.[551] We often touch children and adults when they areacting in a negative, dis-empowering way, which tends to anchor that action. A better ploy would be to catch them "being good" or doing something empowering and then touch them.

In our family, Dad was the cuddler. I would run to the end of the block to meet him after work so he would carry me home on his shoulders.

I would crawl into his lap every time I got the chance; and he would put his arm around my shoulders when I needed that safety. Separation from that touch was part of the great wounding that occurred when I started into puberty. After working with a psychotherapist, I now understand the incest fear that occurs in some fathers as their daughters mature. In order to handle the incest fear, they pull away, leaving their daughters wondering what they did wrong to lose their Dad's touch and affection.

James Prescott, a researcher at the National Institute of Health, in the 1970's studied indigenous cultures that touched and carried their babies on their bodies all day as opposed to those that did not. Where infants were carried on the bodies of their mothers, the levels of violence in the culture were low (e.g. Maori, Papago, Balinese). In cultures where babies weren't carried, the violence levels were high (Comanches, Masai, Thonga).[552]

This lack of touch has been compounded in our society with fears about *how to touch*. Teachers are even asked not to touch their students, and homophobia has inhibited friends from hugging. Since rough and tumble play is so steeped in touch, this important growth activity has decreased between children and between parents and children. Thus we have become a society of people feeling separate and isolated from each other.

An unnatural phenomenon is also occurring now, with more and more people becoming touch sensitive/defensive. The first touch sensors to develop in the skin, even in utero are for pressure. Babies need the swaddling after birth to feel secure. Then as they are touched, the other sensors develop for light touch, heat and cold. Normally, by about five to seven months of age they love the game of "tickle mouse" with light touch.

When I am confronted with someone who is touch sensitive, I will make sure they know that I am about to touch them (usually on the shoulder) and then I use heavy (pressure) touch that they feel safe with. When touch sensitive autistic children are having a "bad day," I will ask if they want to be a "hotdog," which they usually accept willingly. I lay out a blanket on the floor and they roll up tight in it (swaddled). With them lying face down, I roll an exercise ball along their back, lightly at first and then with increased pressure. They not only relax, they love it.[553] The same thing is true with teenagers who, with their growth spurts have a much larger skin area where the sensors for light touch have not yet fully developed. If we touch them lightly, they pull away, but if we "bear hug" them, they love it. That strong touch helps them know the dimensions of their new body. It seems that a million worlds of separation vanish when we embrace each other.

Touch gives us the sense of belonging and safety to explore and learn from our life. Touch precedes both hearing and vision as our primary channel for learning.[554] Touch stimulates the production of NGF (nerve growth factor) aka BDNF that stimulates dendritic growth on the neurons throughout the body. Traditional Chinese Medicine recognizes touch by saying; "The sense of touch is dependent on the Heart/Mind, as this is responsible for the cognition and organization of external stimuli sensations."[555] The Institute of HeartMath showed that when people touch, there is transference of the electromagnetic energy from the heart of one person that affects the brain waves of the other person. If I have a coherent heart rate variability (HRV) pattern and reach out to hold the hand of another person, that person's brain waves will become coherent as well.[556]

Touch also provokes play. Friendly tickling is one of the easiest ways to provoke first a smile, starting at about four months of age, and laughter in young children as early as six months of age.[557] Mammals appear to have "play skin" or "tickle skin" with specialized receptors sending information to specific parts of the brain that communicate playful intentions between animals. Human "tickle skin" is located at the back of the neck, around the rib cage and the toes, where it is easiest to tickle people and get them into a playful mood.[558]

Tickling is a natural invitation to play, but when it turns uncomfortable or malicious, it can become an attack or a means of control and no longer part of play.

Laughter is the hallmark of play in action. Scientifically, it is merely a projectile respiratory movement with no apparent function, other than to let others know that we are happy.[559] Laughter appears to be genetically hardwired because even blind and deaf children laugh.[560] Amazingly, the eighty muscles in our face control all the blood flow to the brain. As the face muscles contract during laughter they raise the blood flow to the brain, creating a feeling of joy. Laughing also increases the brain's temperature, protecting it from disease organisms and affecting the release of neurotransmitters that influence emotions. Laughter can raise heart rate as much as aerobic exercise and increase one's tolerance to pain and discomfort. When we consciously or unconsciously reproduce the facial expression of another through mirroring, especially laughter, we have a similar emotional feeling.[561,562]

Neurologically, laughing and crying both come from the brain stem and are intimately connected. This may explain why I cry when I am overjoyed or touched deeply by something that makes me feel connected. And it explains those instances where we laugh so hard we cry.[563]

"Laughter is the quintessential human social signal. It solidifies relationships and pulls people into the fold." — *Albert Provine*[564]

Play Is A Social Investment

"I think play is the major mechanism whereby higher regions of the brain get socialized."— *Jaak Panksepp*

Play allows us to be effectively assimilated into the structure of our society.[565] A playful life starting in childhood and continuing throughout adulthood correlates with good social skills and flexibility, physical health, curiosity, and innovativeness.[566] Dorothy and Jerome Singer, child psychologists at Yale University, found that kids who initiate imaginative play show leadership skills in school. They cooperate more with other children and are less likely to antagonize and intimidate others.[567] Play helps to stitch individuals into the social fabric, the staging ground for their lives.[568]

In play, we learn about the world and how to be in it in a cooperative, co-creative way. Our play face lets the other player know there is trust and teaches us to accurately read facial cues in our social interactions. The game of "tag" helps to keep things equal where the chased and chaser are constantly shifting, sharing power, and relinquishing authority. This gives children and later adults the ability to work cooperatively with each other.[569] In the game of chase, the child being chased will constantly look at the chaser to make sure the other is still there, still connected, with neither child wanting to break the connection.

Figure 10.4 Family rough and tumble play.

Wrestling and rough and tumble play provide the solid touch so important to a sense of being and belonging in our bodies. It helps us develop balance and focus. It also gives us an acute awareness of where others are in relationship to ourselves. Children who haven't rough and tumbled a lot tend to be clumsy and unaware of other people's space as they bump into them or step on them unintentionally. These children struggle to stay present with others or focused for learning because they aren't solidly in their bodies.

Follow the leader lets us explore new ways to do things, thus expanding our imagination. It facilitates our understanding of how to organize our ideas to be easily followed. It also accommodates the give and take of leadership, honoring each person's special talents and ideas.[570]

Tickling, wrestling, and chasing involve negotiation, provide lessons in getting along with others, and require the restraint of aggressive impulses. These abilities help to safeguard and maintain the alliances that are needed in adulthood.[571] In true play, everyone is relaxed and aware of where others are, so they roll and connect in a way that assures no one gets hurt. If someone gets hurt, it isn't play.

Imagining physically doing something, or daydreaming about doing something activates the areas of the brain involved with actually doing the activity. In studies where people just imagined doing a task, a sport, music, dance or other skills, the brain areas involved increased in neural activity, growth and efficiency.[572] Daydreaming has often been considered a waste of time, but it might be essential to the development of not only our physical being, but our creative ability, expanding our nerve networks in accordance with our imaginative view of the world, and our place in it. The quiet times on the front porch of my cabin in Montana, as the imaginative ideas crowded into the warm afternoons, became the springboard for this book. Breeze's vivid imagination has always intrigued me. I have loved to hear her "way out" ideas, and been amazed at the physical manifestation of those ideas. Daydreaming and imaginative play have underlain many of the great discoveries and inventions of our time, allowing adults as well as children to use the amazing plasticity of the brain to create and recreate its potential, often for the good of all.

Imagination, agility, cooperation, and self-confidence are the rewards of healthy play. Early experiences of play are crucial for anchoring our spirit and bringing us home to ourselves, in order to be adept at social interactions and not only weather but grow and create out of the storms we will inevitably face throughout our lives.[573]

Figure 10.5 Fully immersed in play

Play And Creativity

"Imagination is more important than knowledge, for while knowledge points to all there is, imagination points to all there will be." — *Albert Einstein*

"Play develops the patterns and flexibility to live without anxiety in a world that continuously presents us with unique challenges and ambiguity, so we can remain plastic and creative."[574] — *Paul MacLean*

As we develop, play lays the groundwork for creative thinking in adulthood as we become more able to shift gears between subconscious and conscious processing to access more complexity and sudden insights.[575] The child's prefrontal judgment and behavior/performance monitoring centers are not developed, so the child explores all aspects of life. As that exploration leads to comparisons of differences, as well as rules of society, and a deepening of complex understanding of order out of chaos, the behavior-monitoring center of the brain develops and we fit into society's model. When we again enter that child mind during play, no matter the age, the prefrontal inhibitory center shuts down, and we can again explore the tension between order and chaos, out of which emerges all great art, creativity, and possibilities.

Our subconscious allows us to process new insights quickly without cognition or need to articulate. It is therefore our source of inspiration and central to creativity.[576] With more complexity and diversity, our play leads to the creative art of play, playing with ideas, words, music, visual art, and movement. Art, in all its forms, is one of the greatest rewards of risking to play. Reportedly, Einstein's Unified Field Theory sprung from the gift of a compass with its electromagnetic continuum that he received at the age of five.

Creativity demands the following:

Curiosity and Exploration — constantly seeing the world anew

Close Connection with Nature — the most creative people of our time spent much of their youth in nature.

Imagination — ability to see things in a new way

Playfulness — all great inventions and thoughts came from play

Risk Taking — not being afraid to fail and make mistakes

Openness & Connection — ability to integrate past experiences to create something new

Confidence — never judging yourself, seeing life as a journey

There is a niggling of excitement that precedes the germ of an idea when a book begins to be born in my consciousness, which usually strikes me in my Montana cabin around four o'clock in the morning. There is a complex of unspeakable, un-categorized feelings and thoughts full of a sense that the "missing information" is suddenly found. Then comes the questioning, the far-from-equilibrium flux that destabilizes my habitual thinking, and I search for order that fits my ideas, and grapple with the frustration when pieces don't fit or make sense. I leave it and walk in nature letting my mind relax into a totally different state of consciousness, and suddenly a piece of information or trivial observation becomes amplified, understood, the pieces fall together and order springs from chaos.

"True play is the ability to play with reality. True play drives imagination, gives resiliency, flexibility, endurance and the capacity to forego immediate reward on behalf of long-term strategies." [577] — *Joseph Chilton Pearce*

Play encourages us to test the perimeters of our knowledge and change the way we see the world. It's through the play of great artists like Einstein, Leonardo da Vinci, Thoreau, and Mozart that major paradigms have been changed. It is interesting that the term poet means change maker.[578]

"Art and play sometimes take risks that threaten the tidiness that civilization values so highly. They are sources of new experience and they encourage change, so they worry people who like things to stay put and be obedient. They are full of surprises." — *Joseph W. Meeker*[579]

Play, as our most profound change agent, is essential to our self-understanding and growth. Perhaps the only real "fountain of youth" springs from our mental and physical playfulness throughout life. Tapping our own creativity and wonder may better extend longevity than any artificial attempts to do so.

All Work and No Play

At all ages, the disappearance of natural play from our lives is usually experienced as a significant loss. Play, for both children and adults, seems to have become a highly structured, over-planned, mechanized or competitive sports play that starts very early with parent/coach orchestrated little league, extreme sports, computer games, or play with toys that intrude on imagination, the very soul of kids' play. These adulterated forms of play can easily turn into work and ego based competition.

We tend to be overprotective, not trusting our children's power, seeing them as potential victims instead of survivors. "Powerful play requires powerful and independent players." Powerful play gives children the freedom to educate themselves in the ways of the world, to truly know something by inventing it and to relate deeply with others.[580]

To understand the rewards of play, it helps to see how lack of play inhibits growth and development. When we don't play regularly throughout our lives, our social behavior as well as our health is compromised. Play begins with the mother-child connection. When baby monkeys are isolated from their mothers at birth, they miss all the developmental play that occurs through mother/baby interactions. Without play and closeness, they live in a perpetual state of fear and withdrawal. They rock back and forth (to get the movement they need) or bite themselves (for the sensory stimulation) and became violent when placed with other monkeys.[581]

Without touch, movement and play, children develop brain abnormalities associated with violence, hallucinations, and schizophrenia.[582] Isolation inhibits large areas of the brain from developing normally: the sensory system of the cerebellum that controls movement and balance, the integrative somesthetic association area in the cerebrum for touch, and the system that controls affection which is directly linked to touch and movement. Children who lack play and touch have 20 – 50% smaller brains.[583]

An absence of normal play that is positive and supportive can create violent, antisocial, mentally impaired and emotionally sterile adults. In one study about 95% of the convicted murderers it examined reported either the absence of play as children or illogical, brutal, abnormal play such a bullying, sadism and extreme teasing. In the same study, around 75% of the drunk drivers it examined reported play abnormalities.[584] The survival-based neurology and the play neurology in the brain are separate from each other. Many of these violent young men were on psycho-stimulants for depression, which are known to prompt survival-based activities, adding to their already chronic stress state and disrupting any potential for play.[585]

"The opposite of play is not work, it's depression, separation and isolation." —Bowen White[586]

The twenty-five-year-old murderer, Rene Spitz, experienced separation, isolation, and abuse in a play-less childhood. Though he was a good student, his lack of play led to depression, which also meant suppression of his impulse control, leading to pathological violence.[587] The same is true for the boys that killed at Columbine High School. Following the Columbine shooting, a woman from Pennsylvania put it this way: "Adults need to get the courage to ask: how did we come to raise children filled with fear and rage and loneliness? What can be said of a culture that forever puts the production and accumulation of meaningless material objects ahead of the spirits, hearts, and minds of its own children?"[588] Play is the way we establish a sense of self, empathy, social altruism, and compassion. Play is a fairly dependable predictor of whether a society will be peaceful, affectionate, and cooperative.

"Culture is the handmaiden of our neurobiology, and without a proper environment for physical affections, a peaceful, harmonious society may not be possible."[589] — *James Prescott*

Experiencing The Joy Of Play

How do you explain to parents, teachers, administrators, health professionals, business people, and our families, the exquisite feeling of real play? I don't know other than to have people experience it as I do. Play, imaginative physical play, is an integral part of all my workshops. Parents, elementary teachers and some brave intermediate and high school teachers take it into the classroom to the delight of everyone involved.

Regarding your own childlike nature and play, does your job enliven you, pique your curiosity, fill you with excitement, challenge you, force you to take risks, make you laugh and cry? Do the people in your life ask you to play, to be a paradigm pioneer looking at things freshly and always open?

Do you open others to all they can be, challenging them to take risks to accomplish their dreams? These are all questions I ask myself in my attempt to become a better model of my authentic nature and coherent heart. When I take conscious steps to be fully present, letting go of the "shoulds" and the multitasking, I truly feel alive. Then I have the motivation and enthusiasm (enthos = in God) to do what impassions me, knowing I am expanding beyond the limited concepts I have held of myself and the world toward love, harmony and beauty, appreciating the miracle of me and all that surrounds me.

So, I invite you to put down this book, go find a playmate, get down on the rug, grass, or whatever and play, right now, for the belonging of it.

11

Educating With The Heart In Mind

"It is paradoxical that many educators and parents still differentiate between a time for learning and a time for play without seeing the vital connection between them." — Leo F. Buscaglia

I strongly believe that play and its benefits should continue right into the educational curriculum. Play deeply anchors our ability to relate to others, have empathy, set boundaries, creatively solve problems, and learn optimally. Children learn best when they actively gain knowledge by engaging in meaningful interactions with the real world and real people. When children are given only virtual experiences and narrow, media generated scripts lacking unstructured play and creativity, there can be deficits in all areas of learning.[590,591]

In the fall of 1998, I had a day free while in Southern Germany and happened to walk into the Black Forest, only to find, there before me, a group of little "gnomes" all playing without visible adult supervision. It was a preschool, first conceived by Fredrich Fobel in Germany over 150 years ago called the Wald (forest) Kindergarten. The idea was developed because too many children were getting sick, and first Fobel and later the Scandinavians who instituted the school, felt the problem stemmed from not being outside in nature enough. The European Youth Heart Study states that youngsters need to be active at least 1.5 hours per day and just having children play outside doubles the amount of physical activity they receive. The more active children are, the healthier they are and the more they learn.[592]

Currently there are about seven hundred Wald Kindergartens in Germany in which children spend their days outdoors year-round. These schools have become mainstay preschools in Denmark and Sweden with some schools in Switzerland and Austria.[593,594]

The Wald Kindergarten I came upon that day had a group of two and a half to six year old children learning from each other and the forest with all its diverse seasonal changes and moods. Of the six hours each day five days a week, most of the time was spent in unstructured play, outside in the forest, no matter what the weather. Each Wald Kindergarten I visited had a "lean-to" or hut where children could go for a snack, a short story, or a chance to share special discoveries when the weather was especially inclement. The adult "players" provided encouragement and a safe space where the children could become strong and resilient, and develop into builders, creators, explorers and thinkers.

Games, alone or with playmates, emerged like raindrops from a moisture-laden cloud. Their unstructured play left room for all possibilities, and they hungrily experienced the options. There was lots of imagination, laughter, exploration, and discovery in the most complex environment of all — nature.

Some children climbed on logs across a stream, others wielded huge sticks that never once touched or hurt other children, while still others became enthralled by a flower, the patterns of pine needles, or the bark of a tree. There were times of active conversation when newly found treasures were shared or as imaginative games emerged, were played, and dissipated. Children moved from group play to solitary play without fear of not being included. Alone they would play, as songs floated from their concentrated lips. In a wide-eyed circle, facilitated by a teacher and her guitar, the children experienced a lesson in steady beat, using rocks, sticks, dried stems of oak leaves, and pinecones. The rain lightly fell on them as part of the ambient atmosphere of their emerging forest band of natural instruments and song.

Figure 11.1 Learning steady beat – German Forest Kindergarten

Group songs, dances and games were a part of a short morning ritual that included touching and naming toes, ears, arms, fingers, legs and the various colors they were learning. In one game they were dancing bears in the forest, coming out to *bear hug* other bears. The rich multi-sensory environment of nature was their unlimited playground. They had adult consultants on hand to appreciate their discoveries, help them pick up big logs, hug them when needed, untangle their mittens, attend to the many layers of clothing so they could urinate, and elegantly support their ability to learn.

There were few rules — the main one being "respect for all beings and things"(that meant everything). These children were learning all the rules for a successful life through their bodies, through their interactions with each other, and through their interactions with nature.

In a Swedish forest kindergarten I visited, during the half-mile walk to the forest shelter, each child was free to set his or her own pace. No adult was saying "come on, we have to get there." The children meandered as they chose. Rather than taking the trail, many of these small children climbed over huge boulders off to the side of the trail. Watching these two and three year olds attempting to get their footing on the rock, my instinct was to "help" them. The adults told me "let them be," they were developing their vestibular systems and discovering their abilities. The only time they would help a child is if the child asked for help — and then the adult would ask "how should I help you"? Thus the child had to do some deductive reasoning and communicate that to the adult.

The Swedish forest kindergarten had a mini-ropes course set up. These two to six year-olds balanced gracefully on Aspen poles braced between two trees about a foot off the ground while holding a rope suspended from above. Their vestibular systems and confidence were well developed and they were aware of each other and ready to help in a tricky situation. Again, the caregivers only helped the children if they asked, and then only in the way the child asked them to. Each caregiver was deeply loving and honestly amazed as each child taught them about the glorious world she or he was exploring.

In Denmark and Sweden, one parent is given full wages for at least a year and sometimes two to stay home with the child in those important first years. When the parents go back to their jobs the government pays for the children to go to these forest kindergartens or more traditional kindergartens. About half of Danish preschoolers go to the forest kindergartens. Studies are showing that children in the forest kindergartens are more flexible and creative in their ideas, have better concentration, motivation and cognitive skills, and are more artistic than conventional kindergartners.[595,596]

To understand abstract ideas like math and reading we must have an abundance of real, whole body experiences that create a context and activate the whole system. When children receive a lot of sensorimotor stimulation, enrichment, and reinforcement, the brain is actively building extensive and intricate neurocircuits that lead to a rich and ever-expanding understanding of the world and life. Nature and real experience generate the curiosity, questions, and discoveries that motivate the learner to search for meaning and understand at a deeper level. Deep learning occurs through active and reflective processes that change us forever.

Figure 11.2 Swedish Forest Kindergarten Ropes Course

So many of us have NDD (Nature Deficient Disorder).[597] Today, many children and young adults, with their eyes, ears, tastes and other senses trained on a commercial world and the virtual reality of our technology, are removed, as no other generation in human history, from the daily flow and rhythm of nature.[598]

Children and adults alike, lack quiet time in the woods or prairies to just listen and reflect; time to experience the wind playing in their hair, to touch the rough and smoothness of rocks, the silkiness and spikes of leaves and pine needles, the sound of cold streams rushing across bright colored rocks, and the smells of mountain maple, ash, pine, juniper, sage and wild rose. The Danes, Swedes and many Europeans consider immersion in nature essential to brain and learning development.

The first five years of life develop 90% of the child's ability to easily learn from sensorimotor experiences. The Wald Kindergarten elegantly sets up the learning apparatus for a lifetime. In this environment, children learn the interdependence and complexity of the world and themselves and how to self-regulate, take turns, pay attention, and inhibit impulsive behavior. Researchers found that these abilities were more important than cognitive intelligence for early academic success.[599]

Einstein, and most innovative thinkers, found the spaciousness of time spent in nature to be imperative for accessing their brilliant insights. After struggling long and hard with concepts, Einstein would take a simple walk in nature, being fully present to the experience in a state of coherence, and the answers came to him easily.

In my Montana forest retreat, it is so quiet I can hear my heartbeat and the soft, waterfall-like sounds of the electrical vibrations of my body. I journey daily along deer trails, through dark stands of cedar and Douglas Fir and open groves of mountain maple dappled with light, brilliant green, then red, then yellow, and along the rough limestone cliffs where Oregon grape and currants find refuge in the cracks. These places open me to ideas that remain below my awareness in the distractions of large cities and my hurried lifestyle.

I see the Archimedian spirals of the tree branches and cones that perfectly embody the golden mean of Fibonacci, a perfect pattern of mathematics and fractality in the universe, our bodies, the harmonious chords of music, and the vibrational frequencies of light. The forests around me, complex beyond the most sophisticated computer, or machine-made toy reflect the essence of each water molecule, ray of sunlight/moonlight, each wind and cloud shadow, each snow flake and raindrop, and each squirrel touch. At night I stand under the astonishing splendor of the Milky Way and other galaxies and feel at my core the wonder and awe of all possibilities. Nature has always inspired children and adults to open up to a deeper sense of their interconnectedness with everything, and set in motion the consciousness to be good stewards of this planet we are so entangled with.

> "When one tugs at a single thing in nature, he finds it attached to the rest of the world." — John Muir

In Denmark, this educational philosophy continues as children enter the Folkskol at age seven. The educators of Denmark know that children learn at their own pace. To think all children must learn all skills, within the same amount of time and exposure, defies neuroscience. Each child's diverse talents are beautifully discovered and honored. A family-like structure remains intact as the teacher stays with the same group of students until they are twelve years old. The learning is experiential, cooperative, personally and emotionally meaningful and often self-directed as students teach each other their discoveries. Individual strengths of the students are used as a foundation for further learning.

No testing occurs before age fourteen, accommodating the child's own pace and encouraging them to gain a deep understanding of what intrigues them, rather than piece-meal or "drill and kill" prescribed low level skills. No child is graded (judged) and the tests only show where more understanding of a subject is needed, thus there is no test anxiety. This educational structure naturally creates social/environmental understanding, beginning with children teaching each other and culminating with cognitive skills that assure motivated life-long learners.[600,601,602]

I love teaching; it allows me to learn along with my students, and also from their insights, and different perspectives. I prefer to teach workshops in grade schools through high schools or community college rather than the university setting with its hundreds of students in a class. I like knowing my students and hearing their unique stories and I love the freedom to make every lesson experiential. My classes are always doing experiments on themselves or their environment to better understand both. Our bodies are our most intimate connection with the earth and present time. It seems that our basic questions as humans are: "Who am I and how am I connected to everything else?" For me, experiencing the world through my body helps to deepen that understanding.

Field trips, whether on the school or college campus, or ten days in the deserts of Utah and Texas were my favorite. I always experienced something new and amazing with these groups of students. Seeing the world deeply through twenty-four other pairs of eyes left them and me changed forever. I feel the most important thing in teaching science is to get people to see with new eyes, experience life with all their senses, explore a world ever-changing, and move from self consciousness to "all consciousness." There are no real facts or absolutes, at least not in the Biological sciences. All of our new understanding comes from researchers who are willing to "step out of the box", and dare to see things in new ways.

What is the purpose of education anyway? Besides its function in integrating us into our culture, I feel it must assist us to remain curious and interested in understanding our world and ourselves more deeply. It must also provide the platform and motivation from which to explore new challenges and arrive at talents and workable solutions that further the quality and spirit of our life. And, I feel education must assist us to honor diversity and altruistically approach everyone and everything in our life with a sense of wonder and wholeness.

"The human future will be defined by our children's minds and the nature and quality of their presence on the earth. We need minds capable of inventing and creating new solutions to the world's increasingly complex problems."[603]
— Stephanie Pace Marshall

Our current education system was set up to supply workers for a competitive, industrial, information-based society following WWII. However, it is becoming obvious that it doesn't fit my idea of what education should be or what today's corporations are looking for in their workforce.

According to a study done by the National Learning Foundation, top American corporations want an agile workforce made of flexible, curious/creative, cooperative collaborators, who are altruistically motivated, aesthetically aware, reflective in their thinking, ambiguity tolerant, and open to taking risks. These are all traits that can only exist in an environment that empowers us to be authentically ourselves. Literacy, numeracy, and communication are still necessary, but only in the context of these other characteristics.[604]

Why is there now a demand for an agile workforce instead of one that follows instructions and is obedient, conforming, and competitive? A large number of the jobs available today didn't exist ten years ago. Corporations want inventive, curious people who can cooperate and take risks to come up with the work of the future. They want people who are authentic and deeply involved in life-long learning. This brings us back to what Dr. Margulis discovered, that cooperation, not competition, was the main factor in cellular evolution, the growth toward more complexity and efficiency.

With the chaos we are currently facing worldwide, it will be the agile learners, the innovators that bring us new green technologies. They will come forth with the economic plans that eliminate poverty and assure basic needs are met for all. And they will show us how to altruistically work together, as a planet, communicating and cooperating to find solutions for global warming and international disputes that have led to warfare.

Dr. Lechleitner, professor of zoology at Colorado State University, had a sign hanging over his door. Aside from his brilliant lectures and great sense of humor, that sign convinced me to pick him as my graduate advisor. It read: "If I have only made it possible for you to get a job, then I have failed. If I have given you a sense of curiosity and wonder about yourself and the world, then I have succeeded." Corporations are now catching up to Dr. Lechleitner, though they may have more interest in creativity and productivity than wonder.

Stresses Of The Cookie-Cutter Curriculum

"It surprises me how our culture can destroy curiosity in the most curious of all animals — human beings." — Paul McLean[605]

Often in the U.S., education has been treated as a separate entity from the home and family, play and work. Our wonderfully diverse children, from different backgrounds and learning styles, are immersed for a period of time, in a rapid, passive, often superficial, standardized curriculum, for the acquisition of disembodied information. This heavily cognitive education relegates play to a twenty-minute segment in the morning, during lunch, and sometimes not at all. The child's physiology is often not ready to handle reading and printing, and the lessons are often not relevant to his or her world. They spend more time sitting still, listening to the teacher, and drilling on basics, with less time for physical and social skill development. Developmental experts across the country are saying that kids need more play rather than less, more time in nature and lots of social interaction.[606,607]

With continuous homework, tests, and evaluation, the educational setting becomes stressful and devoid of curiosity, imagination and motivation. This mechanistic, uniformly delivered curriculum leaves our children with a fragmented, competitive view of the world rather than one of wholeness, connection and interdependence.

During Jim's and my separation and divorce when Breeze was seven years old, she was still expected to perform in an educational setting as if her world were not being pulled apart at the seams. Her fears of losing one or both of us disturbed every waking moment of her life, but she was still supposed to learn to read and spell well. The deep lessons of family dynamics were glossed over in lieu of learning to add and subtract. Nothing in school dealt with the context of her life, and she floundered, not having a reference point. Constant drills and tests to somehow assess her "intelligence" superseded self-exploration and discovery. Breeze was learning huge lessons that weren't acknowledged because a scheduled curriculum needed to be met. With Breeze's stress, lack of focus, and natural kinesthetic bent, the counselor labeled her ADHD and suggested we put her on Ritalin. Unwilling to accept this diagnosis, she went on, drug free, to become the perfectly wonderful person she is today as an artist, and a licensed clinical social worker, with a deep curiosity, empathy and understanding of the paradoxes and problems inherent in the human experience.

Brain research reveals that all learning is driven by emotion, so, information that accommodates our emotional nature and is contextually important for us is what we will most remember.[608] During this transition in our lives, *The Education of Little Tree*[609] assisted our connection and learning. As Breeze and I read it to each other, we would laugh and cry and empathetically relate to the human experiences this young boy was going through. At the elementary school where I worked as a Special Ed. counselor, we actually had a program that addressed loss and divorce called "Banana Splits." Students who were interested could come for forty-five minutes every week to discuss their situation with other students and me. Often, I remained quiet and the children counseled each other with great wisdom, and it helped them be more focused in their classes.

Child development experts agree that the only thing shown to optimize a child's intellectual potential is a secure, trusting relationship with at least one person who truly sees them and acknowledges their value and feelings.[610,611,612] *The Loving Guidance* work of Becky Bailey[613] and the *Love and Logic* work of Jim Fay and Bob Sornson[614] are brilliant in the way they honor the child and address their emotional needs while setting humane boundaries.

In our current "culture of neglect,"[615] working parents have little time for exploration, cuddling, interactive communication, and play with their children. The electronic babysitters (TV, computer, etc.) take over, leaving the child without healthy models of how to govern themselves personally and socially in lieu of a sitcom humanity that lacks honoring and safety.[616] With the lack of a safe emotional home environment rich in coherent human interactions where children feel a sense of personal power and optimism about their future, they are left disconnected and fearful.[617]

Any trauma will inhibit learning, and today children are faced with many traumas. I believe that is why it has been estimated that 80% of all school children are considered to have some learning disability.[618] Learning is our most natural state, so when 80% of children are considered learning disabled, it's time to change what we're doing to bring them knowledge about their world and themselves.

One of the most important things a teacher can do is to make an emotional connection with each student. Students must feel safe, accepted and included if they are to learn. Just standing at the door each day to greet them, noticing something about them ("I see you are wearing green today") and welcoming them to the classroom starts the process.[619,620] Using integrative movement sprinkled throughout the class time helps to keep their brains active, and asking different students to lead the movement activities increases self-esteem and responsibility.

Three decades of research show that high achievers in school have received praise, not for their intelligence or talent, but for their creativity, effort and persistence. A person who wants to facilitate growth in another might say; "Wow, you figured that out, you must have been really motivated to see all the possibilities and stay with it," instead of "you really did good, you must be smart." When students have drawn something or come up with something new, rather than saying "that is good or beautiful," which is a judgment, say "that is interesting, tell me about it" or "tell me how you did it." Recognizing their achievement for its quality of motivation and effort encourages learners to focus, be persistent and take more risks while exploring their world.[621]

Studies show that the top performers in music, mathematics and sports gain their mastery, not from genetic talent, but from motivated effort and continually tackling challenges that lie just beyond their competency. Curiosity, motivation and practice can explain the feats of famous people like Mozart and Tiger Woods. Motivation appears to be more important than innate ability, thus experts are made, not born.[622] Both Mozart and Tiger Woods came from homes where parents modeled enthusiasm and passion for music or golf and their children could not help but mirror and learn from that love of music or golf in their lives.[623] Once motivated, the learner has the potential to fully develop special gifts that, if mined, can enrich and expand everybody's wisdom and life. Enthusiastically exposing children and ourselves to the richness of explorers, and master artists and athletes helps to feed our creative nature and image of all we can be, for a lifetime.

"I have no special talents. I am only passionately curious" — Albert Einstein

As an example of what our hurried society is missing, *The Washington Post*, as part of an experiment on perception, stationed Joshua Bell, a world-renowned violinist, in a Washington, DC metro station during rush hour. Bell, incognito, dressed in ordinary clothes, played some of the most beautiful music in the world as thousands of people went through the station. Amazingly, only six people stopped to listen awhile, the most interested being a three-year-old child who was eventually hurried along by his parents. This lack of enthusiasm and passion for even the small pieces of beauty in our world are very telling.

We so want our children to "succeed" that we tend to push them into educational molds that focus on a narrow band of reality, devoid of enthusiasm, awe and beauty, and do it way too early. Our educational paradigm encourages lots of homework to the exclusion of playtime, down time and deep human connection. In so doing, we have ignored the research showing that in Intermediate and High School, homework and testing can hone organizational skills, encourage time management, and develop the ability to learn autonomously. But in grade school, where the joy and passion of learning should be nurtured, it is causing burned-out children with self-doubt and a decreased desire to learn.[624] And, if they don't fit the mold, acting out or not acting at all, they may be labeled, isolated and/or drugged into conformity.

Fewer skills, deeper understanding, and greater learning success in the early years of school, are emphasized by Bob Sornson, founder of the Early Learning Foundation. His *Essential Skills Inventories (K-3)* help focus teachers on the skills and behaviors that need time for learning, practice, play, and deep understanding, with the assumption that some children will need more time to master basic skills before they are pushed along to be challenged by more complex skills.

Pills And The Learning Brain

About four million Americans and nearly 10% of ten year-old boys take stimulant medications (dexamphetamines like Ritalin) for ADHD.[626] Concerns about Ritalin's widespread use brought together several hundred doctors, experts, and educators in November 1998 at the National Institute of Health in Bethesda, MD to discuss this drug. Their consensus was that for the great majority of children, taking Ritalin has very few benefits beyond simply masking the problems and controlling the behaviors, and even these effects disappear as soon as the drug wears off.[627] Participants expressed concern about the side effects, which include decreased appetite, insomnia, tics, and depression. It was associated with depression in 43% of school children younger than ten and 50% between the ages of ten and nineteen.[628,] Ritalin and other psycho-stimulants can actually decrease our sensory-seeking behavior, thus decreasing our motivation to explore our world actively. None of these drugs has been found to assist academic achievement, psychological well being or social behavior.

Taking Ritalin for several days damages dopamine-rich cells in the brain area called the caudate as well as the habenula. The habenula maintains the connection to cells that produce serotonin and helps regulate dopamine transmission to the brain by slowing its release elsewhere.[629] Dopamine is vital for learning and considered the most important biochemical we produce for motivation and curiosity, allowing us to be creative, while serotonin assists us to focus and learn from a state of calm. Ritalin sits on the dopamine receptor sites, causing dopamine to go elsewhere and serotonin to decrease, thus the body and focus slow down for a time. The motivational drive that makes one creative, unique, happy, and curious decreases. The same occurs with other stimulant drug use, television, and video games, reducing our need to acquire stimulation through our own actions.[630] Studies show that ADHD children turn into everyday, normal children under safe, pleasurable, sensory-rich conditions where there is a lot of integrative movement and play, without drugs.[631]

During integrated movement, imaginative time and play, the production of dopamine is high, and many areas of the brain are actively reprogramming themselves with more complex neural-networks.[632] In a major study, children who spent forty minutes per day taking part in active games and playing tag made the greatest improvement on standardized achievement tests. Also, their levels of executive function, the ability to plan, organize, think abstractly, and control themselves were much higher.[633,634]

When the research so strongly shows that integrated movement, supportive touch, and play grow brain areas necessary for increasing focus, creativity and learning for a lifetime, without detrimental side effects, why do we use potentially harmful drugs?[635]

From data on arts in the curriculum and their effect on SAT scores, we immediately find that acting and drama increased students' linguistic and mathematical scores at least 30 points compared with students that didn't take drama or acting. In drama classes, students may move, express themselves, learn to embody various emotions and work with others to create something interesting. Students taking music score at least 40 points higher than those who don't, and visual art, again between 20 – 30 points higher. And the more years students are involved in arts in the curriculum, the more profound the effects they have on all learning, creativity and social development. We are making a big mistake if we take the arts out of the curriculum. The data says it all.

Course	Verbal Mean Scores				Math Mean Scores			
	2001	2002	2004	2005	2001	2002	2004	2005
Acting/Play Prod.	541	539	539	543	531	530	527	532
Art History/Appr.	518	515	516	518	518	517	516	519
Dance	512	509	503	503	510	508	501	503
Drama Study/Appr.	534	531	528	530	523	522	517	520
Music Study/Appr.	539	537	536	538	538	537	533	537
Music Performance	533	530	530	534	535	535	532	537
Studio Art/Design	525	522	524	527	528	528	527	526
NO ARTS	476	473	473	478	494	494	492	498

Years of Study	Verbal Mean Scores				Math Mean Scores			
	2001	2002	2004	2005	2001	2002	2004	2005
More than 4	544	538	533	534	545	541	536	540
4 years	535	536	539	543	530	534	535	541
3 years	518	513	512	514	518	516	512	516
2 years	506	504	505	508	513	514	512	517
1 year	497	495	497	501	510	510	510	515
.5 year or less	484	484	483	485	500	502	498	502

Figure 11.3 SAT scores and participation in the arts[636]

In Danish, Balinese and tribal African schools, I saw exuberant, focused, spirited, joyful, cooperative, respectful, non-competitive, relaxed children. There was no inflexible agenda and no rush to fulfill a curriculum. No child was being graded or judged. There was no stress, no threat, no fear, nothing but that very moment in time and all the possibilities of learning. Hyperactivity and learning disabilities were scarce and accommodated through movement and a sense of belonging, leaving the children motivated to learn everything. Is there a place for childhood and natural, relaxed learning in an anxious, over-technological society worried about jobs, the marketplace, and its children's chances of academic success?[637] It may be time to change our paradigm for learning, for the sake of our children and ourselves.

Communities of Learning

"A child should never be given a toy that has no purpose, or given actions to carry out which have no meaning. Nothing that one does with an infant should be purposeless. If it is so, then it's whole life will be purposeless."
— *Hazarat Inyat Khan*

Hazrat Inyat Khan and Susan Kovalik, creator of The Center for Effective Learning,[638] believe all learning must be directly related to the child's real world. Each part of Susan Kovalik's curriculum starts out with a hands-on, in the field experience, out of which arise the questions and contexts that students will use to expand their knowledge. Nothing about the curriculum is superfluous, and every part is related directly to the interest of the child.

What changed the school failure dynamics for Breeze was her interest in theater and acting. We were blessed in Kona, Hawaii with an active community theater that encouraged and welcomed young people. The theater somehow made sense to her life, with its rich, moving stories of people that misunderstood each other, loved deeply, made mistakes, and found the essence in life. The plays became healing for her as she started to put them into context in her own life.

Her two peak performances came as Helena in *Midsummer Night's Dream* and Emily in *Our Town*. She was highly resistant to reading her social studies book, yet when the auditions were announced, Breeze got the Shakespeare text of *Midsummer Night's Dream* from the library, read the whole thing in one sitting and spent hours telling me about the characters. These characters allowed her to finally laugh at her life's dramas (like Helena longing for love), realize the tenuous nature of relationships, and gain a deep sense from *Our Town* of what is most precious in life. It was contextual learning, and she was the director, choosing the curriculum that taught her what she was most interested in. It also gave her a strong sense of community and belonging.

Susan Kovalik builds a nurturing community of belonging through her adoption of the Tribes work, created over 30 years ago by Jeanne Gibbs as a Drug Prevention program. Students learn to know and honor each other as part of a tribe or classroom community. For any group to function well each member must feel included. Jeanne Gibbs points out that, if a kid doesn't feel included, he will grab influence any way he can, thus disrupting the coherence of the group. For inclusion to occur, each person must 1) be acknowledged, 2) have their expectations be heard, and 3) feel they belong to the group. Such a community then actively: 1) celebrates each achievement, 2) calls forth the personal gifts of each member, and 3) supports the group through challenges, including curriculum content and tests in school.[639]

Identity and life purpose need an intimate community in order to develop; otherwise we don't have a true sense of our unique gifts. Community is the stabilizer of one's identity.[640] According to Breeze, if you don't have an audience in the theater, you don't exist as an actor. The same is true of life.

To expand pleasure, acknowledgment, and respect, programs like Susan Kovalik's have instituted social skills training for the whole school community: janitors, cooks, office staff, as well as teachers, administrators and students. The important skills of active listening, truthfulness, trustworthiness, respectful speech (no put-downs), and being your personal best, become habits for all members of the community. Because stress can occur when no solid perimeters or consequences are set, clear and humane lifeskills that provide structure, boundaries and consequences are also a part of this program.[641,642]

Students learn how to manage themselves and the consequences of making poor choices. If a child makes a poor choice, he is educated as to how it affects others and how to more lovingly and successfully obtain what he wants. This approach is far more effective than harsh consequences, bribes, shaming, food or point rewards.[643]

Rudolf Steiner, founder of Waldorf Education, felt that consistent structure and boundaries were very necessary for the developing child up through the age of eleven, so she or he would have a solid framework of safety on which to explore and learn in her or his environment.[644]

The *Lifeskills* concept really hit home for me. After the divorce, my sense of guilt at fracturing our family left me overly permissive with Breeze. Whatever she wanted I gave her and bowed to her every whim. When she overstepped her boundaries, I set consequences and never followed through on them. I would physically be with her, but my mind was on my job or how to make ends meet or the confusion I felt about my life. She became a "bratty" child, unruly and unmanageable. Desperately wanting my own time, I relished the times when she would be invited to play with friends at their homes. Finally when a friend would not let her children play with Breeze and told me it was because Breeze was "spoiled," I was at first shocked, then thankful for the guidance. I hadn't set consistent boundaries or followed through on consequences. I hadn't taught her to make choices to manage herself socially and personally with others.

Through this behavior, Breeze was unconsciously asking for the consistent boundaries that would make her safe. In our culture we tend to be lenient and permissive with children when they are young and need the safety of consistent boundaries and rules, and we clamp down on them when they get older and it's appropriate for them to develop healthy independence. Breeze was also asking me to be totally there with her instead of just physically. A psychologist once told me that people only need fifteen minutes of one-on-one human connection each day to feel safe. Children, especially, are aware of when we are not totally present; but so are our spouses, friends, other family members, and our world at large. When I can come out from under the haze of "doing," and coherently be with someone, the deep connection that occurs between us is like a laser, where all else falls away and even without words we both feel safe and understood.

Learning begins in utero as we connect to the full potentiality of life in a safe, secure environment if our mother is usually coherent during pregnancy. If that is not the case, then we, as masters, have created the opportunity to learn through our dramas, to gain greater understanding and to evolve our souls in other ways. All of life is part of the process toward understanding our oneness with the field of consciousness and growing in empathy and altruism toward ourselves and others.

In our hurried, success-driven society, parents often work hard to give their children everything, but they miss what children and they as parents need most: a deep sense of belonging, open communication, play, reflective down time and models of passionate living. Without these, our children and we feel isolated, unmotivated, and learning becomes secondary to survival.

In these times of global transformation, the importance of a holistic and inclusive learning environment is essential in order to respond to the complex and intricate problems we face that defy simplistic solutions. Education must embrace the understanding that it is often through the polarities and seemingly different ways of knowing that genuine understanding and wisdom can be created. When our children become our teachers and we trust their innate altruism and wisdom, we empower them to make right choices, follow their truth, learn how to have healthy relationships, explore the wonder and beauty of the earth, and optimally grow in love, harmony and beauty.

12

The Future Of Our Creative Nature

*"The love of God, unutterable and perfect, flows into a pure soul
the way that light rushes into a transparent object. The more love that it finds,
the more it gives itself; so that, as we grow clear and open,
the more complete the joy of heaven is. And the more souls who resonate
together, the greater the intensity of their love, and, mirror-like,
each soul reflects the other." — Dante Alighieri Purgatorio XV.67-75.*

Dante's insights summarize for me the essence of our evolution toward a higher state of consciousness. As we become more coherent, we are able to tap into the unified field to expand our understanding. That expanded understanding allows us to experience more light, more love, more joy and mirror that back to all we encounter. It appears that love is about understanding our oneness and the moment-to-moment beauty, power and wonder of all creation. This union, where we resonate from that coherent, present place, altruistically realizing our connection to, our impact on, and the gifts and magnificence of all beings, is a place to start to recreate our world.

"How we approach each other will shape everything, including our own evolving self and the cosmos in which we participate." — Richard Tarnas[645]

Barbara Kingsolver[646] writes about being taken aback in Spain at the overwhelming respect and love people instantly show for children. People would stop on the street or anywhere to be absolutely present with and say wonderful things to her young daughter. I also saw this in Africa, as huge smiles would break out on the faces of people when they saw a baby or child, followed by wonderful sounds and joyful touching. A Balinese person hearing someone yell at or spank a child would be mortified. Children are our most cherished gifts and teachers, still so attuned to their vibrational nature and enthusiastically exploring wholeness.

These cultures see the future in their children, honoring them to grow up healthy, happy, and connected so they will add to the culture and take loving care of the adults and society that raised them. Cherished children, allowed to explore the depth of their being with coherent, passionate adults, grow into cherished adults, embodying the greater intensity of love described by Dante.

In Western society, with our bid for independence within the nuclear family stronger than the embrace of an extended family and community, we often tend to confine our love to our immediate family. Childless couples often ignore children altogether, seeing them as a nuisance or a threat to their peace of mind. This kind of shortsighted thinking isolates us from the rich, pleasurable human experiences that manifest a compassionate, altruistic global community. Our children, as the pilots of our future, will either grow up compassionate and willing to run our services, teach us, enrich our world through wisdom, art and music, *or they won't*.

At times I feel we get lost in intellectualism, technology, consumerism, competition, alienation and isolation — a fracturing of our wholeness and infinite potential. Our sense of inadequacy that arises from this fracturing doesn't go away as we get older, and we act out on the world's stage what is unresolved in our own psyche.[647] We take on the survival role of "lost child" as described by Sharon Wigschneider-Cruze. In this state we lose touch with our emotions, trust, and intimacy that connect us with our magnificence and that of others, while intellectualizing everything. In our mistrust of self and others, we set up rigid criteria of how another person or thing should operate to make us feel safe. The world and others become something to compete with, manipulate, harm, or feel victimized by.[648] We cannot feel at ease.

The revolutions of the past forty to sixty years: gender equality, racial equality, technology, ending the cold war, global economy, and the internet have helped us order our lives to this point. Willis Harman described the next revolution as the New Copernican Revolution where we move from competition to the collaboration and communication necessary for intelligent evolution. Gary Schwartz describes intelligent evolution as: "an intelligently guided process that promotes the creative expression and evolution of ever more complex and interconnected systems."[649] It is a revolution/evolution to regain a true sense of self as both independent and connected to all that is; where we compassionately support and facilitate connection in others so our planet can heal. For this to happen we must be able to fully understand our vibrational, authentic nature. Authenticity and altruism must permeate how we respond each moment to every being and situation.[650]

"And when we look for the existence of independence in the universe, what we find instead is interdependence and interconnectedness. What physics calls the vacuum or void is actually filled with incomprehensibly complex dynamic networks of highly organized – and organizing fields of force."[651]
— Gary Schwartz

Happiness is not a destination but instead lies in an understanding that we are the masters of our lives, "fields of force" enjoying the journey as we accept our mastery to create the perfect lessons for our soul's evolution. Happy, coherent people tend to accept everyone as a teacher and actively engage in experiences that are fascinating, motivating, challenging and absorbing. Being present in the "flow" of life aligns with the Eastern concept of "mindfulness," consciously being in the present. Both Fritz Perls and Carl Rogers described psychological health as being totally engaged in the present moment as vibrational wholeness, without self-consciousness. According to research, when people volunteer to help others they find themselves much happier, fully engaged, with a sense of satisfaction, gratefulness, appreciation and self-esteem at having been a part of something worthwhile.[652] The New Copernican Revolution could usher in our happiest and most exciting time yet.

Heart Song

"There are only two ways to live your life, as though nothing is a miracle, or as though everything is a miracle." — Albert Einstein

"The next phase of our evolution will take us into the experiences of the multisensory human and the nature of authentic power. This requires the heart"
— Gary Zukav, Seat of the Soul

We might learn from the wisdom of the ancients who gave the world its first technology as well as great works of art, music, and philosophy. At the center of these ancient cultural beliefs is the heart. The heart has always been the starting point for all yogic traditions and is the center of balance, the yin and yang, in Oriental traditions.

In traditional Chinese medicine, the Mind (Shen) equals Heart, which is said to be the "residence" and governor of the mind. The Chinese characters for thought, thinking, and pensiveness all have the character for "Heart" as their radical. Thinking, consciousness, sleep, insight, memory, cognition, intelligence, wisdom, and ideas are all dependent on the heart. Intelligence is insight and reflection, raising self-knowledge and self-recognition above cognitive intelligence.[653] If the heart is strong, its owner will be strong and act wisely.[654,655]

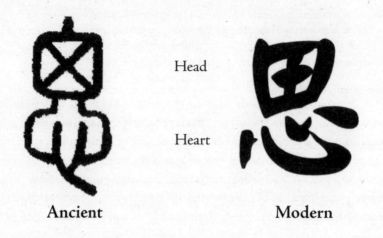

Head

Heart

Ancient   Modern

Figure 12.1 Chinese character for thinking

These ancients supply us with wisdom that can guide us out of our current chaos into a higher state of order and understanding. According to Theodore H. Bullock "The unparalleled abilities of the human mind arise not from neurons but from the coherence of brain waves,"[656] which we now know are orchestrated by the heart. When Marie Louis Van Franz of the Jungian Institute was asked, "Is there hope for humanity"? She answered: "I don't know, it is a matter of the heart."[657]

A Reflection Of Love

"What we're all striving for is authenticity,
a spirit-to-spirit connection." — Oprah Winfrey

Paul Solomon tells about deciding to become a great healer. For his initial training his teacher had him get five tomato plants and keep them alive and healthy. He watered them faithfully and gave them plenty of sunlight. But, alas, all the tomato plants died. Undaunted, he got more tomato plants, cared for them, but they also died. After killing fifteen tomato plants, he decided he didn't want to be a healer after all.[658]

In a plant store, several months later, he became intrigued with a small cactus garden. Reasoning that cacti were very hardy and hard to kill, he bought the garden and kept in the front entryway of his home. Everyday as he came into or left his home he found himself taking time to observe the cactus plants, noting their unique structures and how they had changed. His curiosity made him more their student than their caretaker. The cactus plants thrived and bloomed in this developing relationship.

Paul had discovered that to become a healer wasn't necessarily about caring for and helping others. It was more about being fully present, curious, and experiencing others as universes of unique wisdom, guides to new learning, new possibilities and reflections of our own unique nature and potentiality.

As a biologist, I felt totally unprepared when asked to become the "Special Education" counselor for a local elementary school. Being a mother and exploring the Brain Gym® work with intermediate students for a year was the extent of my counseling experience. Fortunately, before I began working in this capacity, I attended an in-service for school counselors. The keynote speaker just happened to be the warden at the maximum-security male prison in Oahu. He shared with us his remarkable perspective: that every time an inmate would walk through his door, he would say to himself: "What has this person come to teach me, and what is the dance we are to do to together?" His wisdom touched me deeply and made it easier to just be myself, and see every child that came through my door as my teacher.

Helping is an interesting concept. When I ask for help, and someone is willing to accommodate what I need, it is a great blessing. However, I can feel diminished when someone says or implies "you need help and I can help you," when I haven't asked for their help. Their statement denotes an inadequacy in me, that something is broken and that they have more wisdom than I have to "fix" it. If we experience life as a journey, then with each decision, the choices we make will somehow lead to our soul's evolution. We most honor another person, all that they are in the moment, if we are curious and interested to learn from them, as Paul Solomon did. When we see other people as light beings, entangled with our vibrations, and master creators of their own unique reality for their highest growth, we may be more ready to open our hearts to them for the dance we are to do together?

Being fully present and clearly seeing both the humanity and divinity of another person is the greatest gift we can give to them and ourselves. During these times of authentic relationship, there is a significant increase in oxytocin production created within our bodies, forging a bond of safety, closeness and understanding. As a result, both heart and brain come into coherent patterns.[659] It seems that just authentically looking into another person's eyes stimulates oxytocin release and we are able to accesses our frontal lobes, the seat of our highest emotions: love, compassion and altruism.[660]

With That Moon Language

Admit something: Everyone you see, you say to them,
"Love me."
Of course you do not do this out loud;
Otherwise, Someone would call the cops.
Still though, think about this,
This great pull in us to connect.
Why not become the one who lives with a full moon in each eye
That is always saying,
With that sweet moon Language,
What every other eye in this world
Is dying to Hear.
                                                    — *Hafiz*[661]

When we don't make eye contact, especially when a bond feels tenuous or we are not connected with our own wholeness, we can be left feeling isolated and separate. When we aren't fully present with our spouse or children as they speak, we break the connection. Fully seeing and affirming another sets up the trust and deep connection necessary for all of us to see each other's wonder.

I love the tradition of Dances of Universal Peace, in which people look into another's eyes and sing to them of their shared divinity. It "opens the heart" because it produces such a strong sense of connectedness, not only with each other but within one's self. Many traditions use similar rituals to bring people together as a strong community; the Coffee Hour after the Methodist church service, the Pow Wows on the Crow reservation, sewing circles, barn dances, sing-alongs, meditation groups, the family card games, pick-up soft-ball games, etc.

Our greatest stress comes from isolation, disconnection, and abandonment, especially from those we love. When I become stressed, I lose access to my dominant eye and have a hard time really seeing people to reconnect. Once, during a misunderstanding with Breeze, she suggested we do *infinity 8's* for the eyes together. She cupped the fingers of her right hand with the fingers of my right hand, our thumbs together. We both watched our thumbs as we did the eye movements following the infinity symbol (coming up in the center) to integrate our brains. We changed to the left hand, and when we finally put both hands together, instead of looking at our thumbs, we looked into each other's eyes. The change was instant!! In this coherent state I could again see and connect to this precious person whom I love so deeply and the misunderstanding faded away.

A story is told of an Aikido master on his way home to the suburbs of Tokyo when a drunk got onto his subway car. The drunk was filthy, and in his intoxicated state was yelling, swinging, kicking and hitting people as he came down the aisle. The Aikido expert, now standing at the end of the subway car, prepared himself to stop this drunk when suddenly an old man stood up between the aggressor and himself. The old man opened his arms, looked the drunk in his eyes and said in a gentle voice, "What's the matter my friend? Come, let's talk." Instantly the aggressor stopped and began to sob, telling the old man of the struggles that had brought him to this point.[662] So simple and profound is the moment of love.

It may be time for us to look each other in the eyes, totally present and curious about the magnificent assembly of vibration and light we are a part of and co-create with. See each being, each soul on his way to becoming both a reflection and a guide for our journey, a blessed gift. Let's open our arms to embrace the gift each moment brings. It is a time to not only know but trust our power to passionately step beyond our limited reality into our true nature and a life of possibilities. We can then lay down our hectic lifestyles, play, work, sing and fully absorb all the wonder, beauty and lessons our current existence has to offer. As we move toward our potential, reflectively, the world will become a more coherent place.

Decade Of The Evolving Soul

"We are not human beings in search of a spiritual experience. We are spiritual beings in search of a human experience." — *Pierre Teilhard de Chardin*

The scientific community deemed the 1990's the decade of the brain, and focused much energy on understanding this remarkable organ. Assigning the brain the role of master controller fit our ordered, linear, intellectual, non-emotional paradigm well. But what if, as the ancient yogis, doctors of traditional Chinese medicine, and current scientific researchers claim, the master controller is actually the holographic body, the intricate, coherent interplay of the heart, emotions, senses and movement with reciprocal space. With our new understanding, perhaps we should deem this decade, *The Decade Of The Evolving Soul*.

According to William Tiller, the self consists of our physical neural-sensory atoms that interface with the personality and soul in reciprocal magnetic space, bridged by our emotions, intentions and desires. As we evolve, we become a more resonant vehicle for the soul self to interface with our physical reality. We evolve as our material reality is perturbed by the presence of free will. Thus, "consciousness is a byproduct or emergent property of spirit entering dense matter."[663]

With this clearer understanding of soul, I can envision the possibility of a world of people who truly love and experience their own power as masters of their lives, seeing and reflecting that power to all other beings. The emphasis on existence then, might be community, coherence, cooperation and communication rather than commerce, competition and warfare.

The Decade of the Evolving Soul could be a period of understanding our universal connection, via vibrational patterns, with everything and everyone else, repositioning our stance from being masters of the earth attempting to exploit and subdue it with our technology, to being its protectors and stewards. Might we then see our planet as an energetic extension of ourselves, a living, vibrationally entangled part of us, so vital to our journey?

Our success would no longer be measured by our performance on tests, early reading, performing technological wonders on computers at ever-earlier ages, our possessions, income or fame. All beings would be cherished as sacred entities, gifts, and teachers to us, being highly sensitive and sensible to the vibrational patterns within and around them. We would live in that state of awe and wonder, so prevalent when we are truly present in each moment. There would be lots of play, music, curiosity, co-creativity, gratitude, and enthusiasm for the challenges of the journey ahead.

We might then be open to exploring a vibrational reality far beyond the current reality we have honed, so shaped and limited to a miniscule portion of our known vibrational spectrum. We might learn to easily access the non-local information field and work with all the creative, sentient minds to expand the possibilities of coherence in a universal energy web — conceivable but inaccessible to our current technology.

Welcome to your authentic Creative Nature, which makes possible fearless exploration into the universal field of intelligence, which many know as God.

Notes

Preface Notes

[1] Spretnak, Charlene. *The Resurgence of the Real.* Addison Wesley, Reading, MA, 1997.

[2] Taylor, Jill Bolte. *My Stroke of Insight.* Viking, New York, 2008.

[3] MacNeilage, Peter F., Lesley J. Rogers and Giorgio Vallortigara. *Evolutionary Origins of Your Right and Left Brain. Scientific American,* June 24, 2009.

[4] His Holiness the Dalai Lama. *The Universe In A Single Atom: The Convergence of Science and Spirituality.* Morgan Road Books (Broadway Books), 2005.

Chapter One Notes

[5] Pert, Candace. *The Learning Brain Conference,* August, 2001, Toronto, Canada.

[6] Prescott, James. *Discovering the Intelligence of Play.* Video. Touch the Future, TTFuture@aol.com 1997.

[7] *World Book Dictionary*, Doubleday and Co., New York, 1983, p. 402.

[8] Tiller, William. *Science and Human Transformation: Subtle Energies, Intentionality and Consciousness.* Walnut Creek, CA : Pavior Publications, 1997, p. 196.

[9] McTaggart, Lynn. *The Field, The Quest for the Secret Force of the Universe.* Quill Publications, New York, 2002, Chapter 3, p. 39

[10] Creath, K. & G. E. Schwartz, *What biophoton images of plants can tell us about biofields and healing. Journal of Scientific Exploration,* 2005, vol.19(4):531-50.

[11] S. Cohen and F. A. Popp: *Biophoton emission of the human body, Journal of Photochemistry and Photobiology,* 1997, vol. 40:187-9

[12] K. Korotkov, et al. *Assessing biophysical energy transfer mechanisms in living systems: The basis of life processes, The Journal of Alternative and Complementary Medicine,* 2004, vol. 10(1): 49-57.

[13] Odent, Michelle. *Primal Health, A Blueprint for Our Survival.* Century Hutchinson, Ltd., London, 1986, p. 30.

[14] Selye, Hans. *The Stress of Life.* McGraw-Hill, New York, 1956. Gabriel, Gerald. *Hans Selye: The Discovery of Stress,* Brain Connection.com. www.brainconnection.positscience.com/topics/?main=fa/selye.

[15] McEwen, Bruce. *Stress.* Review Article, *New England Journal of Medicine,* January, 1999.

[16] Hannaford, Carla. *Smart Moves, Why Learning Is Not All In Your Head (2nd ed.).* Great River Books, Salt Lake City, UT, 2005, pp. 175-196.

[17] Marano, Hara Estroff. *Depression: Beyond Seratonin. Psychology Today,* March/April 1999, pp. 33-34, 72.

[18] Elkind, David. *The Hurried Child: Growing Up Too Fast Too Soon.* Addison-Wesley Pub., Reading, MA, 1988, p. 3.

[19] Morgan, Marlo. *Mutant Message From Forever. Perennial Press/Harper Collins,* 2004, p. 213.

[20] David Dobbs. *Human See, Human Do; A Revealing Reflection. Scientific American Mind,* April/May 2006, pp. 22-27.

[21] Giacomo Rizzolatti, & Corrado Sinigaglia, *Mirrors in the Brain: How Our Minds Share*

Action, Emotions and Experiences. Oxford University Press, 2007.

[22] Baily, Jean. Coordinator of child and adolescent mental-health services at Lutheran Medical Center in Brooklyn, NY. In: *Time Magazine*, July 5, 1999, p. 58.

[23] Revonsuo, Antii. *Research on Consciousness.* **Journal of Consciousness Studies,** March 2001.

[24] Rubic, Beverly, ed. *The Interrelationship Between Mind and Matter,* **Temple University Symposium,** Report of Group 2, Philadelphia, 1999. www.start.gr/user/symposia/group22. htm.

[25] Russell, Peter. **From Science To God, A Physicists Exploration of the Light of Consciousness.** Elf Rick Pub., U.K., 2000. Russell, Peter. **The Consciousness Revolution, A Transatlantic Dialogue with Stan Grof and Ervin Laszlo,** Element Books, London, 1999.

[26] Douglas, Kate. *The Subconscious Mind: Your Unsung Hero.* **New Scientist,** December 1, 2007.

[27] Dijksterhuis, Ap. *Our Superior Subconscious.* **New Scientist**, May 5, 2007, p.35

Chapter Two Notes

[28] Chopra, Deepak. **Consciousness Conference** in Denver, CO. July, 1998.

[29] Diamond, Mariam. **Magic Trees Of The Mind.** Dutton, New York, 1998, p. 66.

[30] Alesandra Piontelli. *Infant observation from before birth.* **International Review of Psychoanalysis.** 1987, vol. 16: 413-426.

[31] Ludwig, Janus & Jason Aronson. **The Enduring Effects of Prenatal Experience: Echoes From The Womb.** Ludwig Janus-Jason Aronson, Inc., New Jersey, 1997, p. 612.

[32] Heinberg, Richard, *Creativity Begins in the Womb.* **Shift: at the Frontiers of Consciousness,** Institute of Noetic Sciences, Petaluma, CA, March-May 2005, No. 6, pp. 16-17.

[33] McCarty, Wendy Ann. **Welcoming Consciousness; Supporting Wholeness from the Beginning of Life.** 2004. E-book at www.wondrousbeginnings.com

[34] Bower, Thomas. *The perceptual capacities of young children,* **The Magical World Television Series,** July 16, 1984.

[35] William Condon & Louis Sander. *Neonate movement is synchronized with adult speech: Interactional participation and language acquisiton.* **Science.** Jan. 1974, vol. 11: 99-101.

[36] Verney, Thomas R and Pamela Weintraub. **Pre-Parenting: Nurturing Your Child From Conception.** Simon & Schuster, New York, 2003.

[37] McCarty, W. A. *The power of beliefs; what babies are teaching us.* **Journal of Prenatal & Perinatal Psychology & Heath,** 2002, vol. 16(4): 341-360.

[38] Gerhard Rottman. *Unterscuchungen uber die Einstellung zur Schwangerschaft und zur Fotolens Entwickling.* In **Prenatale Psychologie.** ed. G.H. Grober, Munich, Kindler, 1974.

[39] Gerhard Amendt & Michael Schwartz. **Das Leben Unerwunschter Kinder.** Frankfurt/ Main, Fischer, 1992.

[40] Bergh, B. *The influence of maternal emotions during pregnancy on fetal and neonatal behavior.* **Pre- and Parinatal Psychology**, 1990, vol. 5: 119-130.

[41] Valman, H.B. & J. F Pearson. *What the Fetus Feels.* **British Med. J.,** January 26, 1980.

[42] Sontag, Lester W. **War and the Maternal-Foetal Relationship**. 1944, p. 40. And Lester W. Sontag, *Physiological Factors and Personality in Children.* **Child Development Journal,** December, 1947, vol. 18(4).

[43] Rosenblith, J.F. *Relations Between Graham/Rosenblith Neonatal Measures and Seven Year Assessments.* **Paper presented at International Conference on Infant Studies,** Montreal, 1990.

[44] Nordberg, L., et al. *Psychomotor and mental development during infancy: Relations to psychosocial conditions and health: Longitudinal study of children in a new Stockholm suburb.* **Acta Paediatrica Scandinavica.** 1989, (Suppl. 353), 3- 35.

[45] Frida E. & M. Weinstock. *Prenatal stress increases anxiety related behavior and alters cerebral lateralization of dopamine activity.* **Life Science,** 1988, vol. 42: 1059-1065.

[46] Van Der Bergh, Bea, et al. *ADHD Deficit as measured in Adolescent Boys with a Continuous Performance Task is Related to Antenatal Maternal Anxiety.* **Pediatric Research,** January, 2006, vol. 59 (1): pp. 78-82.

[47] Veldman, Frans. *Confirming affectivity in the dawn of life.* **International Journ. Of Prenatal and Perinatal Psychology and Medicine,** 1994, vol.6: 11-26.

[48] Lawlor, Robert. **Voices of the First Day; Awakening in the Aboriginal Dreamtime.** Inner Traditions Pub., Rochester, VT, 1991.

[49] Newberg, A. and Waldman, M. **Why We Believe What We Believe: Uncovering Our Biological Need For Meaning, Spirituality And Truth.** Free Press, New York, 2006.

[50] Zion, Leela C and Betty Lou Raker. *The Physical Side of Thinking.* C.C. Thomas, Springfield, IL, 1986. Also: Zion, L. and Frank Alexander, *The Physical Side of Learning: A Parent-Teacher's Guidebook Of Physical Activities Kids Need To Be Successful In School.* Front Row Experience, Byron, CA, 1994.

[51] Rudman, Laurie and Richard Ashmore. *Group Processes and Integroup Relations Journal,* 2007. Cited in **Scientific American Mind,** April/May 2008, p.39.

[52] Corey Binns. *The Hidden Power of Culture.* **Scientific American Mind.** August/September 2007, p. 9.

[53] Sylvester, R. *Neurotheology, Brain Science and Religious Belief.* **Brain Connection.** March 2002.

[54] Newberg, Andrew and Waldman, Mark Robert. **Born To Believe: God, Science, and the Origin of Ordinary and Extraordinary Beliefs.** Free Press, New York, 2007.

[55] Baron, Andrew S. and Malzarin R. Banaji. *Buried Prejudice,* **Scientific American Mind,** April/May 2008, pp. 35-37.

[56] Dasgupta, Nilanjana. *Mechanisms Underlying Malleability of Implicit Prejudice and Stereotypes: The Role of Automaticity Versus Cognitive Control.* In: **Handbook of Prejudice, Sterotyping and Discrimination,** ed. Todd D. Nelson, Psychology Press, New York, 2009.

[57] Bremyer, Jay. **The Dance Of Created Light, A Sufi Tale.** New Falcon Pub., Tempe, AZ, 1996, p. 164.

[58] Kayser, Christopher. *Listening with Your Eyes.* **Scientific American Mind,** April/May 2007, pp. 24-29.

[59] Hainline, Louise. *The Development of Basic Visual Abilities.* In: **Perceptual Development, Visual, Auditory and Speech Perception in Infancy,** ed. Alan Slater, Psychology Press, East Sussex, UK, 1998, pp. 5-42.

[60] Goddard Blythe, Sally. **What Babies and Children Really Need.** Hawthorn Press, Gloucestershire, UK, 2008, pp. 169-170.

[61] Wilson, Frank R. **The Hand; How It's Use Shapes the Brain, Language, and Human Culture.** Pantheon Books, New York , 1998. Introduction.

[62] Cohen, Mark S. *Visual Perception.* **Brain Journal,** Feb. 27, 1996. **Science News,** vol. 149. p. 155, March 1, 1996.

[63] Sereno, et al. *Borders of Multiple Visual Areas in Humans Revealed by Functional MRI.* **Science,** 1995, vol. 268, pp. 889-893.

[64] Russell, Peter. Science and Consciousness Conference. 1999.

[65] Rock, I. **The Nature Of Perceptual Adaptation.** Basic Books, New York, 1967.

[66] Sibatani, Atuhiro. *The Japanese Brain, The Difference Between East and West May Be The Difference Between Left and Right.* **Science 80**, December, 1980, pp. 22-27.

[67] Hebb, D. O. *The Organization Of Behavior.* John Wiley and Sons, New York, 1949, pp. 289-294.

[68] Tiller, William A. *Science Of Human Transformation: Subtle Energies, Intentionality and Consciousness.* Pavior Pub., Walnut Creek, CA, 1997, p. 148.

[69] Gopnik, Alison, Andrew N. Meltzoff, and Patricia Kuhl. *The Scientist in the Crib.* William Morrow and Company, New York, 1999.

[70] Haesler, Sebastian. *Programmed for Speech.* **Scientific American Mind**, June/July 2007, pp. 67-71.

[71] Ramachandran, Vilayanur S & Diane Rogers-Ramachandran. *Touching Illusions.* **Scientific American Mind**, December 2007/January 2008, p. 16

[72] Nicolelis, Miguel A. L. and Sidarta Riberio. *Seeking the Neural Code.* **Scientific American.** December 2006, pp. 70-77.

[73] Norretranders, Thor. *The User Illusion, Cutting Consciousness Down to Size.* Penguin, New York, 1999.

[74] Myers, David. *The Powers and Perils of Intuition.* **Scientific American Mind.** June/July 2007, pp. 24-31.

[75] Melzack, Ronald. *Phantom Limbs.* **Scientific American Reports**, September, 2006, vol.16 (3): 53-59.

[76] Biello, David. *Explaining Out-of-Body Experiences.* **Scientific American**, November 2007, p. 34.

[77] Bremyer, Jay. 1996, p.176

[78] Tiller, William. 1997.

[79] Douglas, Kate. *The Subconscious Mind: Your Unsung Hero.* **New Scientist**, Dec., 1, 2007.

[80] Sousa, David A. *How the Brain Learns.* **The National Association of Secondary School Principals.** Reston, VA, 1995, p. 10.

[81] Blakslee, Sandra. *Scientist At Work: Rodolfo Llinas, In a House of Ailments, Seeing a Brain Out of Rhythm.* **The New York Times**, December 2, 2008.

[82] McNab, Fiona & Torkel Klingberg. *Your Inner Spam Filters.* **Scientific American Mind**, June/July 2008, pp. 76-77.

[83] Tsien, Joe Z. *The Memory Code.* **Scientific American**, July 2007, pp. 52-59.

[84] Sylwester, Robert. *A Celebration Of Neurons.* ASCD Publication, 1995, Chapter 4.

[85] Levine, Amir. *Unmasking Memory Genes.* **Scientific American Mind**, June/July 2008, pp. 49-51.

[86] Fields, R. Douglas. *Making Memories Stick.* **Scientific American**, February 2005, pp. 75-81.

[87] Ross, Philip E. *The Expert Mind.* **Scientific American**, August 2006, pp. 64-71.

[88] Ellenbogen, Jeffrey M., et al. *Time delay plus slumber equals memory boost.* **Proceedings of the National Academy of Science**, May, 2007. **Science News**, April 28, 2007, vol. 171, pp. 260-261.

[89] Higgins, Edmund S. *The new genetics of mental illness.* **Scientific American Mind,** June/July 2008, pp. 41-47

[90] Goleman, Daniel. *Emotional Intelligence.* Bantam Books, New York, 1995.

[91] Levin, Amir, June/July 2008, pp. 50-51.

[92] Doidge, Norman. *The Brain That Changes Itself: Stories of Personal Triumph from the Frontiers of Brain Science.* James H. Silberman Books, (Penguin Books), 2008, pp. 45-92. (Michael Merzenich).

[93] Lashley, K. S. *In Search of the Engram.* **Symposia of the Society for Experimental Biology.** 1950, vol. 4, p. 478.

[94] Pribrum, Karl. *Karl Pribrum Interview with Judith Hooper.* **Omni Magazine,** October 1982.

[95] Lashley, K. S. 1950, pp. 454-482.

[96] Gerber, Richard. *Vibrational Medicine.* Bear & Co., Santa Fe, NM, 1988, pp. 45-48.

[97] Pribrium, Karl. *Languages Of The Brain.* Prentice Hall, Englewood Cliffs,NJ, 1971.

[98] Pribrum, Karl H. *Brain And Perception; Holonomy and Structure in Figural Processing.* Lawrence Erlbaum Assoc., New York, 1991.

Pribrium, Karl H. *Origins: Brain and Self Organization.* Lawrence Erlbaum Assoc., New York, 1994.

[99] Pert, Candace. *Molecules Of Emotion, Why You Feel the Way You Feel.* Simon & Schuster, NewYork, 1999, pp. 135-148.

[100] Ibid.

[101] Schwartz, G. E. & L. G. Russek. *Do All Dynamic Systems Have Memory? Implications of the Systemic Memory Hypothesis for Science & Society,* In: **Brain And Values: Behavioral Neurodynamics.** K. H. Pribram & J. S. King, eds. Lawrence Erlbaum Assoc., Hillsdale, NJ, 1997.

[102] Pearsall, Paul. *The Heart's Code.* Broadway Books, New York, 1998.

[103] Pert, Candace. 1999, p. 148.

[104] Bremyer, Jay, p. 164.

[105] Ibid. pp. 166, 164.

[106] Pribrim, Karl. 1982, p. 72.

Chapter Three Notes

[107] Lakoff, George & Mark Johnson. *Philosophy In The Flesh.* Basic Books, New York, 1999.

[108] Capra, Fritjof. *The Tao of Physics: An Exploration of The Parallels Between Modern Physics and Eastern Mysticism.* Shambhala, Boston, 2000.

[109] Russell, Peter. *Science and Consciousness Conference,* Albuquerque, NM, April, 1999.

[110] McTaggart, Lynne. *The Intention Experiment.* Free Press, New York, 2007, pp. xviii -xix

[111] Barrow, J.D. *The Book of Nothing.* Jonathan Cape, London, 2000, p. 216.

[112] Laszlo, E. *The Interconnected Universe, Conceptual Foundations of Transdisciplinary Unified Theory.* World Scientific Publications, Singapore, 1995, p. 28.

[113] Clarke, A.C. *When will the real space age begin?* Ad Astra, May-June 1996, pp. 13-15.

[114] Tiller, William. *Science And Human Transformation: Subtle Energies, Intentionality and Consciousness.* Pavior Pub., Walnut Creek, CA, 1997, p. 46.

[115] Rivlin, Robert and Karen Gravelle. *Deciphering The Senses: The Expanding World of Human Perception.* Simon & Schuster, New York, 1984, p. 11.

[116] Ibid.

[117] Ibid.

[118] Werblin, Frank and Botond Roska. *The Movies in Our Eyes.* **Scientific American,** April 2007, pp. 73-79.

[119] Goldsmith, Timothy H. *How Birds See.* **Scientific American,** July 2006, pp. 69-75.

[120] McKay, B. and M. Persinger. *Geophysical variables and behavior: LXXXVII. Effects of*

synthetic and natural geomagnetic patterns on maze learning. **Perceptual and Motor Skills,** 1999, vol. 89, (3 pt1): 1023-4.

[121] V.N. Oraevskii, et al. *Medico-biological effects of natural electromagnetic variations,* **Biofizika,** 1998, 43 (5): 844-8.

[122] E. Stoupel. *Relationships between suicide and myocardial infarction with regard to changing physical environmental conditions.* **International Journal of Biometeorology,** 1994, 38(4): 199-203. E. Stoupel, et al. *Suicide-homicide temporal interrelationship, links with other fatalities and environmental physical activity,* **Crisis,** 2005, 26: 85-9.

[123] A. Raps, et al. *Geophysical variables and behavior; LXIX. Solar activity and admission to psychiatric inpatients,* **Perceptual and Motor Skills,** 1992, 74: 449.

[124] Flavia, **Seeing.** Portal Publications, Ltd., Novato, California, 1999.

[125] McCraty, Rollin & Institute of HeartMath. HeartMath Research Center. **Research Overview, Exploring the Role of the Heart in Human Performance,** 1997, p. 3. HeartMath Research Center, 14700 West Park Ave., P.O. Box 1463, Boulder Creek, CA, 95006. (831)338-8500. www.Heartmath.org.

[126] Russek, L. B. and G. E. Schwartz. *Interpersonal Heart-Brain Registration and the Perception of Parental Love: A 42 Year Follow-up of the Harvard Mastery of Stress Study.* **Subtle Energies,** 1994, vol. 5(3): pp. 195-208.

[127] Moss, T., **The Body Electric.** Jeremy P. Tarcher, Los Angeles. 1979, p. 219.

[128] Armour, J. A. and J. Ardell (EDS). **Neurocardiology.** Oxford University Press, New York, 1994.

[129] Russek, L. B. and G. E. Schwartz. *Energy cardiology: a dynamical energy systems approach for integrating conventional and alternative medicine.* In: **Advances,** 1996, vol. 12(4): pp. 4-24.

[130] Pert, Candace B. **Molecules of Emotion.** Simon & Schuster, New York, 1999.

[131] Cantin, M. & J. Genest. *The Heart as an Endocrine Gland.* **Scientific American,** 1986, vol. 254, p. 76.

[132] Armour, J. A. and J. Ardell (eds.). 1994.

[133] Armour, J. A. 1991, pp. 1-37.

[134] Pearce, Joseph Chilton. **Evolution's End, Claiming the Potential of Our Intelligence.** Harper & Row, San Francisco, 1992, p. 104.

[135] Pearsall, Paul. **The Heart's Code.** Broadway Books, New York, 1998, p. 78.

[136] Tortora, Gerard J. & Nicholas P. Anagnostakos. **The Principles Of Anatomy And Physiology (6th ed.)** Harper & Row, New York, 1990, pp. 590-591.

[137] Russek, L. G. & G. E. Schwartz. 1996. pp. 4-24.

[138] Shermer, Michael. *Why you should be skeptical of brain scans.* **Scientific American Mind,** October/November 2008, pp. 66-71.

[139] Coulter, Dee Joy. **Enter The Child's World.** Coulter Pub., Longmont, CO. Sound cassette, 1986.

[140] Pomeranz, B, J.B. Macaulay, & M.A. Caudill. *Assessment of autonomic function in humans by heart rate spectral analysis.* **American Journal of Physiology,** 1985, vol. 248: H151-H158.

[141] Tiller, William, Rollin McCraty, Mike Atkinson. *Cardiac Coherence: A new, noninvasive measure of autonomic nervous system order.* **Alternative Therapies,** January 1996, vol. 2, no.1, p. 52.

[142] McCraty, Rollin, et al. *The Effects of Emotions on Short-Term Power Spectral Analysis of Heart Rate Variability.* **American Journal of Cardiology,** 1995, vol. 76(14): 1089-1093.

[143] Russek and Schwartz. 1996, pp. 4-24.

[144] Ragan, P. A., W. Wang & S. R. Eisenberg. *Magnetically Induced Currents in the Canine Heart: A Finite Element Study.* **IEEE Transactions in Biomedical Engineering,** 1995, vol. 42, pp. 110-115.

[145] McCraty, Rollin. Personal conversation with Rollin McCraty, Director of Research, Institute of Heartmath ®, 2000.

[146] Armour, J. A. & J. Ardell (eds.) 1994.

[147] Portner, Martin. *The Orgasmic Mind*. **Scientific American Mind**, April/May 2008, p. 70.

[148] Armour. J. A. *Anatomy and function of the intrathoracic neurons regulating the mammalian heart.* IN: I. H. Zucker and J. P. Gilmore (eds.), **Reflex Control Of The Circulation.** Boca Raton, FL, CRC Press, 1991, pp. 1-37.

[149] McCraty, Rollin. *Influence of cardiac afferent input on heart-brain synchronization and cognitive performance.* **International Journal of Psychophysiology,** 2002, 45(1-2): 72-73.

[150] McCraty, Rollin. 1997, p. 3

[151] McCollough, Andrew W. and Edward K. Vogel. *Your Inner Spam Filter.* **Scientific American Mind,** June/July 2008, pp. 76-77.

[152] Rodriquez, Eugenio, et al. *Perception's shadow: long-distance synchronization of human brain activity.* **Nature,** February 4, 1999, vol. 397, pp. 430-433.

[153] McCraty, Rollin, William A. Tiller, and Mike Atkinson. *Head-Heart Entrainment: A Preliminary Survey.* In: *Integrating the Science and Art of Energy Medicine:* ISSSEEM Fifth Annual Conference Long Program and Proceedings. Boulder, CO ISSSEEM, 1995, pp.26-30.

[154] McCraty, Rollin. Research on alpha brain rhythm synchronization assisting cognitive learning following the HeartMath Instututes Cut-Through technique that brings the heart into coherence. Phone conversation, February, 2000.

[155] D. I. Radin and M. J. Schlitz, *Gut feelings, intuition, and emotions: An exploratory study,* **Journal of Alternative and Complementary Medicine,** 2005, 11(5): 85-91.

[156] Tiller, William. 1997, p. 278.

[157] Dean I Radin, *Event-related electroencephalographic correlations between isolated human subjects,* **The Journal of Alternative and Complementary Medicine,** 2004, 10(2): 315-23.

[158] S. Fahrion, et al. *EEG amplitude, brain mapping and synchrony in and between a bioenergy practitioner and client during healing.* **Subtle Energies and Energy Medicine,** 1992, vol. 3 (1): 19-52.

[159] Kendall, H., Kendall, F, Wadsworth G. **Muscle Testing and function.** Williams & Wilkins, Baltimore, 1971.

[160] Monti, Daniel A., et al. *Muscle Test Comparisons of Congruent and Incongruent Self-Referential Statements.* **Perceptual and Motor Skills Journal,** 1999, vol. 88: 1019-1028.

[161] Jahn, R. G. and B. J. Dunne. *Science of the Subjective,* **Technical Notes.** Princeton University, New Jersey, March 1997. Research done at the Princeton Engineering Anomalies Research program at Princeton University (P.E.A.R).

[162] Brain Gym®/Educational Kinesiology Foundation, www.braingym.org.

[163] Hannaford, Carla. **Smart Moves, Why Learning Is Not All In Your Head (2nd ed.).** Great River Books, Salt Lake City, UT, 2005.

[164] Grinbert-Zylberbaum, J. et al. **Human communication and the electrophysiological activity of the brain.** *Subtle Energies and Energy Medicine,* 1992, vol. 3 (3): pp. 25-43.

[165] Dossey, Larry. **Healing Words: The Power of Prayer and the Practice of Medicine.** HarperCollins, New York, 1993, p. 291.

[166] Czikszentmihalyi, Mihaly. **Creativity: Flow and the Psychology of Discovery and Invention.** Harper Collins, New York, 1996, pp. 57-123, 259.

[167] Dunne, B. J. and R. G. Jahn., *Consciousness And Anomalous Physical Phenomena,* **Technical Notes.** Princeton University Press, 1995.

[168] Lacey, John I & Beatrice C. Lacey. *Two-way communication between the heart and the brain: Significance of time within the cardiac cycle.* **American Psychologist**, Feb. 1978, pp. 99-113.

[169] Adapted and expanded from the original Yum Solution developed by my good friends in Hawaii, Candle and Iao.

Chapter Four Notes

[170] Jung, Carl. **Collected Works**, Princeton University Press, 1978.

[171] Bohm, David, B. Hiley and P. N. Kaloyerou. *An Ontological Basis for Quantum Theory.* **Physics Reports**, 1987, vol. 144 (6): 323. And, Bohm, David & F. David Peat. **Science, Order and Creativity.** Bantum Books, New York, 1987.

[172] Tiller, William A. **Psychoenergetic Science: A Second Copernican-Scale Revolution.** Pavior Pub., Walnut Creek, CA, 2007, p.115.

[173] A. Einstein, B. Podlsky, and N. Rosen. *Can Quantum-Mechanical description of physical reality be considered complete?* **Physical Review**, 1935, vol. 47:pp. 777-780.

[174] Aspect, A., J. Dalibard, and G. Rogen. *Experimental tests of Bell's inequalities using time-varying analyzers.* **Physical Review Letter**, 1982, vol. 49: pp. 1804-7.

[175] Aspect, Alan. *Bell's inequality test more ideal than ever.* **Nature**, 1999, vol. 398: 189-90.

[176] Mansfield, Victor. *A Physics of Peace, Nonlocality, Emptiness, and Compassion.* **Elixir Journal, International Sufi Order**, Spring 2007, p. 53.

[177] Bohm, David, B. Hiley and P. N. Kaloyerou. 1987, p. 323.

[178] Bohm, David & David Peat. 1987.

[179] Tiller, William A., **Science Of Human Transformation: Subtle Energies, Intentionality and Consciousness.** Pavior Pub., Walnut Creek, CA, 1997, pp. 70-75.

[180] Tiller, William A. 2007.

[181] Goswani, Amit, **What The Bleep Do We Know!?**, DVD, Captured Light & Lord of the Wind Films, LLC, 2004.

[182] Clarke, Arthur C. **Technology and the Future.** Harper Books, New York, 1972.

[183] Goswani, Amit. *Quantum Physics, Consciousness, Creativity....* **Science of Consciousness Conference,** Albuquerque, NM, April, 1999.

[184] Dean I. Radin,. *Event-related electroencephalographic correlations between isolated human subjects,* **The Journal of Alternative and Complementary Medicine**, 2004, 10(2): 315-23.

[185] Dossey, Larry. **Larry Dossey in Conversation with Michael Toms.** Audio-tape. Aslan Pub., Lower Lake, CA, 1994.

[186] Pearce, Joseph Chilton. **Science and Consciousness Conference**, Albuquerque, NM, April, 1999.

[187] Shearer, A. **Effortless Being.** Mandala University Paperbacks, London, 1989, p. 9.

[188] Radin, Dean. **The Conscous Universe: The Scientific Truth of Psychic Phenomena.** Harper Edge, 1997.

[189] D. I. Radin, *For whom the bell tolls; A question of global consciousness.* **Noetic Sciences Review**, 2003, vol. 63: pp. 8-13 and 44-45. R.D. Nelson, et al., *Correlation of continuous random data with major world events,* **Foundations of Physics Letters,** 2002, vol. 15(6): pp. 537-50.

[190] D. I Radin. *Exploring relationships between random physical events and mass human attention: Asking for whom the bell tolls.* **Journal of Scientific Exploration,** 2002, vol. 16(4): pp. 533-47.

[191] R. D. Nelson. *Coherent consciousness and reduced randomness: Correlation's on September 11, 2001* **Journal Scientific Exploration,** 2002, vol.1 6(4): pp. 549-70.

192 Bryan J. Williams. *Exploratory block analysis of field consciousness effects on global RNG's on September 11, 2001.* http://noosphere.princeton.edu/williams/GCP911.html.

193 Mander, Jerry. *Four Arguments for The Elimination of Television.* Quill Pub., New York, 1978.

194 Wallis, Claudia. *Kindergarten Rage, Does Kindergarten Need Cops?* **Time Magazine,** December 12, 2003.

195 Christakis, D.A. et al. *Early Television Exposure and Subsequent Attentional Problems in Children.* **Pediatrics Journal,** September 2004, (13): pp. 708-713.

196 Pearce, Joseph Chilton. **Evolution's End, Claiming the Potential of Our Intelligence.** Harper & Row, San Francisco, 1992, pp. 169-170.

197 Pearce, Joseph Chilton. **Educational Kinesiology Gathering,** Vancouver, B.C., July, 1999.

198 Mander, Jerry. 1978.

199 Orme-Johnson, David. International peace project in the Middle East; The effect of the Maharishi Technology of the Unified Field. 1988, vol. 34(4): 776-813. And Orme-Johnson, David W., *EEG coherence during Transcendental consciousness.* **Electroencephalography and Clinical Neurophysiology,** 1977, vol. 43 (4): 581-582.

200 Haeglin, J. et al. *Effects of group practice of the Transcendental Meditation program on preventing violent crime in Washington, D.C.: Results of the National Demonstration Project, June-July 1993,* **Social Indicators Research,** 1999, 47(2): 153-201.

201 McTaggart,Lynne. **The Intention Experiment. Using Your Thoughts to Change Your Life and the World.** New York, Free Press. 2007, pp. 181-196.

202 Prigogine, Ilya and Isabelle Stengers. **Order Out Of Chaos: Man's New Dialogue With Nature.** Random House, New York, 1984.

203 Zeilinger, A. *Probing the limits of the quantum world.* **Physics World,** March 2005. (online journal. www.physicsweb.org/articles/world/18/3/5/1.)

204 Resch, J., et al. *Distributing entanglement and single photons through an intra-city, free-space quantum channel.* **Optics Express,** 2005, 13(1): 202-9.

205 McTaggart, Lynne. 2007, p.17.

206 Recanzone and Merzenich: Michael Kilgard, **Learning Brain Expo 2001,** Austin, Texas, July, 2001.

207 Zubieta, Jon-Kar. *Placebo Power.* **Scientific American Mind,** 2005, vol.16(4), p.10.

208 Kong, Jian et al, and Dagfinn Matre. *Intrinsic Remedies for Pain.* **Journal of Neuroscience,** January 11, 2006. In: **Science News,** vol. 169, January 21, 2006, pp. 37-38.

209 Rana, Jamal S., et al. *Longevity of the Placebo Effect in the Therapeutic Angiogenesis and Laser Myocardial Revascularization Trials in Patients With Coronary Heart Disease.* **The American Journal of Cardiology,** June 15, 2005, vol. 95 (12): 1456-1459.

210 Enserink, M. *Can the Placebo Be the Cure?* **Science,** 1999, vol. 284: 238-245.

211 Tiller, W. A. *Human psychophysiology, macroscopic information, entanglement & the placebo effect.* **Journal of Alternative and Complimentary Medicine,** 2006, vol. 12 (10): pp. 1015-1027.

212 Lo, Shui-Yin, *The Foundation Project Video from the Quantum Health Research Institute,* Pasadena, CA.

213 **Quantum Touch.** www.QuantumTouch.org. "About QT."

214 Rubic, Beverley. *Subtle Information: A Unifying Concept for Matter and Consciousness.* **Toward A Science of Consciousness Conference,** Albuquerque, NM, April, 1999.

215 Conner, M., G. Schwartz, et al. *Oscillation of amplitude as measured by an extra low frequency magnetic field meter as a biophysical measure of intentionality,* presented at the **Toward a Science of Consciousness, Conference,** Tucson, AZ, April, 2006.

216 Green, E. E.. et al. *Anomalous electrostatic phenomena in exceptional subjects.* **Subtle Energies,** 1993, vol.2: p. 69.

217 Tiller, W.A., et al. *Towards explaining anomalously large body voltage surges on exceptional subjects, part I: The electrostatic approximation.* **Journal of the Society of Scientific Exploration.** 1995, vol. 9(3) :p. 331.

218 Dossey, Larry. *How Healing Happens: Exploring the Nonlocal Gap.* **Alternative Therapies in Health and Medicine,** 2002, vol. 8(2): pp. 12-16, 103-110.

219 Tiller. 2007, pp. 88-91.

220 Tiller, W.A., W. E. Dibble, Jr., & J. G. Fandel. **Some Science Adventures With Real Magic.** Pavior Pub, Walnut Creek, CA, 2005. And: White Papers at www.tillerfoundation.com.

221 M. Murphy, et al. *The Physiological and Psychological Effects of Meditation: A Review of Contemporary Research With A Comprehensive Bibliography,* **1931-1996.** The Institute of Noetic Sciences, Petaluma, CA, 1997.

222 E. P. Van Wijk, et al. *Anatomic characterization of human ultra-weak photon emission in practitioners of Transcendental Meditation TM and control subjects.* **Journal of Alternative and Complementary Medicine,** 2006, vol. 12(1): pp. 31-36.

223 K. Reece, et al. *Positive well-being changes associated with giving and receiving Johrei healing.* **Journal of Alternative and Complementary Medicine,** 2005, vol. 11(3): 455-457.

224 B. Rubic, et al. *In vitro effect of reiki treatment on bacterial cultures: Role of experimental context and practitioner well-being.* **Journal of Alternative and Complementary Medicine,** 2006: 12(1): 7-13.

225 Tiller, W. White Papers, 2009.

226 Emoto, Masaru. Hidden **Messages From Water.** I.H.M. General Research Institute, Hado Kyoikusha Co. Ltd, Tokyo, Japan, 2002, p. 72

227 Ibid.

228 McTaggart, Lynne. 2007. p.25

229 Tiller, William A., Walter E. Dibble, Jr., and Michael J. Kohane. *Exploring Robust Interactions between Human Intention and Inanimate/Animate Systems.* Presented at **Toward a Science of Consciousness Conference—Fundamental Approaches.** May 25-28, 1999, United Nations University, Tokyo, Japan. Information available through Ditron, LLC, P.O. Box 70, Excelsior, MN, 55331, USA.

230 Tiller, William A., Walter E. Dibble, Jr. and Michael J. Kohane. **Conscious Acts of Creation, The Emergence of a New Physics.** Pavior Publishing, Walnut Creek, CA, 2001.

231 Ibid. pp. 175-182.

232 Tiller, W and Walter E. Dibble, Jr. *New Experimental Data Revealing An Unexpected Dimension To Materials Science And Engineering.* **Material Research Innovation,** 2001, vol.5: pp. 21-34.

233 Tiller, William. 2007, pp. 145-163

234 McTaggart,Lynne. *The Field: The Quest for the Secret Force of the Universe.* HarperCollins, New York, 2001, pp. 205-207.

235 Dean Radin, *Beyond Belief: Exploring Interaction Among Body And Environment.* **Subtle Energies and Energy Medicine,** 1992, vol. 2(3), pp. 1-40.

236 D. Radin, et al. *Effects Of Healing Intention On Cultured Cells And Truly Random Events,* The Journal of Alternative and Complementary Medicine, 2004; vol. 10: pp. 103-112.

237 Goswani, Amit. *The Self-Aware Universe.* Tarcher/Putnam, New York, 1995. **What the Bleep Do We Know?,** DVD, Captured Light & Lord of the Wind, Films, 2004. www. whatthebleep.com. Grinberg-Zylberbaum, J, Delaflor M, Attie L, Goswani, Amit. *The Einstein-Podolsky-Rosen Paradox In The Brain; The Transferred Potential.* **Physics Essays.** 1994, vol. 7(4): pp. 422-428.

Chapter Five Notes

[238] Satir, Virginia. *Becoming Whole.* **New Dimensions Radio** 6/14/84, #1881. 1984.

[239] Roush, Wade. *Defining the First Steps on the Path Toward Cell Specialization.* **Science,** October 27, 1995, vol. 270: pp. 578-579.

[240] Tortora, Gerard J. and Nicholas P Anagnostakos. **Principles Of Anatomy And Physiology.** *6th ed.* Harper and Row, N. Y., 1990, p. 933.

[241] Tiller, William. **Science and Human Transformation: Subtle Energies, Intentionality and Consciousness.** Pavior Publications, Walnut Creek, CA,1997, pp. 172-175.

[242] Tiller, William. **Psychoenergetic Science: A Second Copernican-Scale Revolution.** Pavior Pub., Walnut Creek, CA, 2007, pp. 128-133.

[243] Tiller, William. White Papers at www.tillerfoundation.com. 2009.

[244] Burr, Harold S. *The Fields Of Life.* Ballantine Books, New York, 1972.

[245] Kirlian, S.D., and V.K. Kirlian. *Photography and Visual Observation by Means of High Frequency Currents.* **Journal of Scientific and Applied Photography,** 1964, vol. 6: 397-403.

[246] Kirlian, Semyon and V. Kirlian. *Photography and Visual Observations by Means of High Frequency Currents.* **Journal of Scientific and Applied Photography,** 1961, vol. 6: 145-148.

[247] Korotkov, Konstantin G. **Human Energy Field: Study With GDV Bioelectrography.** Backbone Publishing Co., Fair Lawn, NJ, 2002.

[248] Sheldrake, Rupert. *The Hypothesis of A New Science Of Life, Morphic Resonance.* Park Street Press, Rochester, VT, 1995, p. 13.

[249] Popp, F. A., *Evidence of non-classical (squeezed) light in biological systems* **Physics Letters A,** 2002, vol. 293(1-2): 98-102.

[250] Popp, F. A., et al. *Further analysis of delayed luminescence in plants* **Journal of Photochemistry and Photobiology,** 2005, vol. 78: pp. 235-44.

[251] Gerber, Richard. *A Practical Guide to Vibrational Medicine,* HarperCollins, New York, 2001.

[252] Gerber, Richard. **Vibrational Medicine,** Bear and Company, Santa Fe, NM, 1988, pp. 51, 60, 111-112.

[253] New Dimensions Radio, **Great Thinkers of the Past 20 Years.** 1999.

[254] Gerber, Richard. 1988, p. 60.

[255] Ingebar, Donald E. *The Architecture of Life.* **Scientific American,** January 1998, pp. 48-57.

[256] Yogananda, Paramahansa. **Scientific Healing Affirmations.** Self-Realization Fellowship. 9th ed., 1990.

[257] Steiner, Rudolf. *Outline of Occult Science.* Anthroposophical Literature Concern, Inc., Chicago. 1922, p. 174.

[258] Elinasto, Jaan. *A 120-Mpc perodicity in the three-dimensional distribution of galaxy superclusters.* **Nature,** 1997, vol. 385: 139-141.

[259] Szalay, Alexander, S. **Texas Symposium of Relativistic Astrophysics, Chicago,** John Hopkins U. , Baltimore, December, 1996.

[260] Jenny, Hans. **Cymatics** (Videotape), Macromedia, P.O. Box 1223, Brookline, MA 02146, 1986.

[261] Jenny, Hans. **Cymatics.** Basilius Presse, AG, Switzerland, 1974.

[262] Halpern. Steven. **Sound Health, The Music and Sounds that Make Us Whole.** Harper & Row, San Francisco, 1985, pp. 33-39.

[263] Braden, Gregg. **Awakening To Zero Point. The Collective Initiation.** Radio Bookstore Press, Belleview, WA, 1997, pp. 70-71.

264 Jenny, Hans. 1986.

265 Halpern, Steven. 1985, pp. 32-36.

266 Manners, Peter. *The Future of Cymatic Therapy.* In: *Technology Tomorrow,* June, 1980.

267 Manners, Peter Guy. **Cymatics Therapy: Sound and Vibratory Pattern Research.** Bretforton, England, 1976.

268 Emoto, Masaru. **Messages From Water, World's First Pictures of Frozen Water Crystals.** I.H.M. General Research Institute, Hado Kyoikusha Co., Ltd., Tokyo, 2001.

269 Nijhuis, J. G.,(ed.) **Fetal Behavior: Developmental And Perinatal Aspects.** Oxford U. Press, 1992, p. 133.

270 Bernard, J, and Sontag, L. *Fetal reactions to sound.* **Journal of Genetic Psychology,** 1947, vol. 70: 209-210.

271 Ingebar, Donald E. 1998, pp. 48-57.

272 Schumann, Winfried O. *Uber die strahlungslosen Eigenschwingungen einer leitenden Kugel, die von einer Luftschicht und einer Ionospharenhulle umgeben ist.* **Zeitschrift und Naturfirschung,** 1952, 7a: 149-154.

273 Schumann, W. O. and H. Konig. *Uber die Boebactung von Atmospherics bei geringsten Frequenzen.* **Naturwiss** 44, 1954, pp. 183-184.

274 Tesla, Nikola. *The Transmission of Electrical Energy Without Wires As a Means of Furthering World Peace,* **Electrical World and Engineer,** January 7, 1905, pp. 21-24.

275 Valet, Jean-Pierre, Yohan Goyodo, and Laure Meynadier. *Geomagnetic dipole strength and reversal rate over the past two million years.* **Nature,** June 9, 2005, vol. 435: pp. 802-805.

276 Glatzmaier, Gary and Peter Olson. *Probing the Geodynamo.* **Scientific American,** April 2005, pp. 51-57.

277 Price, C., O. Pechony, E. Greenbert. *Schumann resonance in lightning reserch.* **Journal of Lightning Research,** 2006, vol. 1: 1-15.

278 Balser, M. and C. Wagner. **Observations of earth-ionosphere cavity resonances.** **Nature,** 1960, vol. 188, pp. 638-641.

279 Halpern, Steven. 1985, p. 38.

280 Ludwig, W. **Informative Medizin,** VGM Verlag Fuer Ganzheitsmedizin, Essen, 1999.

281 Konig, H.I. *Bioinformation – Electrophysical Aspects.* **Electromagnetic Bioinformation.** F. A. Popp, G. Becker, H.L. Konig, and W. Peschka (eds.), Urban und Schwarzenberg, 1979, p. 25.

282 Ludwig, W. 1999.

283 Pasti-Dickenson, Ingrid. **BRCP EMR,** 2003, i.dickenson@earthbreathing.co.uk.

284 Becker, Robert O. *Exploring new horizons in electromedicine.* **Journal of Alternative and Complimentary Medicine,** 2004, vol. 10(1): pp. 17-18. And: Feinstein, David and Donna Eden. *Six Pillars of Energy Medicine, Clinical strength of a complementary paradigm.* **Alternative Therapies in Health Medicine,** 2008, vol. 14(1): pp. 44-54.

285 Schafer, R. Murray. **The Tuning Of The World.** Knopf, New York, 1977.

286 Overbye, Dennis. *Music of the Heavens Turns Out to Sound a Lot Like a B Flat.* **New York Times, Science Times,** September 16, 2003, p. D3.

287 Mendelsohn, Robert S., M.D. **Confessions Of A Medical Heretic.** Warner Books, New York, 1979.

288 Swicord, Mays. 1984. Biophysicist with the National Center for Devices and Radio-Logical Health at the FDA. In: **Science News,** April 24, 1984.

289 Newnham, J. P., et al. *Effects of Frequent Ultrasound during Pregnancy: A Randomized Controlled Trial.* **The Lancet,** October 9, 1993, vol. 342, pp. 887-891.

290 Campbell, J.D., et al. *Case-Controlled Study of Prenatal Ultrasound Exposure in Children*

with Delayed Speech. *Canadian Medical Association Journal,* 1993, vol. 149(10): pp. 1435-1440.

291 Devi, P.U., et al. *Effect of fetal exposure to ultrasound on the behavior of the adult mouse. Radiation Research* (QMP), 1995, vol. 141(3): pp. 314-317.

292 Ewigman, B., et al. *Impact of prenatal ultrasound screening on perinatal outcome.* **New England Journal of Medicine,** Sept. 16, 1993, vol. 329, pp. 821-7. LeFevre, M, et al., *A randomized trial of prenatal ultrasound screening: Impact on maternal management and outcome.* **American Journal of Obstetrics. and Gynecology,** Sept. 15, 1993, vol. 169: pp. 483-489.

Chapter Six Notes

293 Long, Charles H. **Alpha: The Myths of Creation.** George Braziller, New York, 1983.

294 Lorenz, Edward N. *Predictability: Does the Flap of a Butterfly's Wings in Brazil Set Off a Tornado in Texas?* Paper presented at annual meeting of the American Association for the Advancement of Science, Washington, DC, December 29, 1979.

295 Poincare, Henri. **The Value of Science: Essential Writings of Henri Poincare.** Random House, New York, 2001.

296 Prigogine, Ilya. **From Being to Becoming.** W. H. Freeman, San Francisco, 1980.

297 Margulis, Lynn and Dorion Sagan. **Microcosmos.** Summit Books, New York, 1986.

298 Briggs, John and F. David Peat. **Turbulent Mirror.** Harper & Row, New York, 1989, pp. 19-29.

Chapter Seven Notes

299 Morgan, Marlo. **Mutant Message From Forever.** Perennial Press/Harper Collins, 2004, p. 210.

300 Goleman, Daniel. **Emotional Intelligence.** Bantam Books, New York, 1995.

301 Stokes, Gordon and Daniel Whiteside. **Tools Of The Trade.** Applied Kinesiology Press, Tucson, AZ, 1985.

302 Friston, K. J. *Functional and effective connectivity in neuro-imaging: a synthesis.* **Human Brain Mapping,** 1994, 2: 56-68.

303 Ramachandran, Vilayanur S. and Lindsay M. Oberman. *Broken Mirrors, A Theory of Autism.* **Scientific American,** November, 2006, p. 69.

304 Dobbs, David. *Mastery of Emotions.* **Scientific American Mind,** February/March, 2006, pp. 44-49.

305 Bechara, Antoine, et al. *Role of Emotions in Cognitive Function,* **Journal of Neuroscience,** July 1, 1999. **Science News,** July 24, 1999, vol. 156, p 59.

306 Lipton, Bruce. **The Biology of Belief, Unleashing the Power of Consciousness, Matter and Miracles.** Mountain of Love/Elite Books, Santa Rosa, CA, 2005.

307 Blakeslee, Sandra and Matthew Blakeslee. *Where Mind and Body Meet, Conscious physical sensation and conscious emotional awareness come together in the right frontal insula.* **Scientific American Mind,** August/September 2007, pp. 44-51.

308 Damasio, Antonio R. *Looking for Spinoza.* **Scientific American Mind,** Feb/March 2006, pp. 27-29.

309 Hawkins, David R. *Power vs Force, The Hidden Determinants of Human Behavior.* Veritas Publishing, Sedona, AZ, 1995, p. 237.

310 De Waal, Frans B. M. *Do Animals Feel Empathy?* **Scientific American Mind,** December 2007/January 2008, pp. 28-35.

311 Rizzolatti, Giacomo, Leonardo Fogassi and Vittorio Gallese. *Mirrors in the Mind.* *Scientific American*, November 2006, pp. 54-61. And: Giacomo Rizzolatti and Corrado Sinigaglia, *Mirrors in the Brain; How Our Minds Share Actions and Emotions.* Oxford U. Press, 2008.

312 Iacoboni, Marco, et al. *Grasping the Intentions of Others with One's Own Mirror Neuron System.* *PloS Biology,* March, 2005, vol. 3 (3): 529-535.

313 Ramachandran. V.S. *The Edge, Mirror Neurons and the Brain in a Vat.* 2006. http://www.edge.org/3rd_culture/ramachandran06/ramachandran06_index.html.

314 Iacobonni, Marco. *Mirroring People: The New Science of How We Connect with Others.* Farrar, Straus & Giroux, New York, 2008.

315 Zahn-Wasler, Carolyn. *Becoming Compassionate: The Origins and Development of Empathetic Concern.* *Shift, At the Edge of Consciousness, Institute of Noetic Sciences,* December 2006-February 2007, no. 13, p. 21.

316 Ibid. pp. 23-25.

317 Nowicki, S. and M. Duke. *A measure of nonverbal processing ability in children between the ages of 6 and 10.* Paper presented at the American Psychological Society meeting. 1989.

318 Ramachandran, Vilayanur S. and Lindsay M. Oberman. *Broken Mirrors: a theory of autism.* *Scientific American*, November 2006, 295(5): 62-69.

319 Greenspan, Stanley & Serena Wieder. *Engaging Autism, Using the Floortime Approach to Help Children Relate, Communicate, and Think.* Merloyd Lawrence Books, Cambridge, MA, 2009.

320 Solomon, Rick. *The P.L.A.Y Project, Play and Language for Autistic Youngsters.* University of Michigan Medical Center. http://www.playproject.org.

321 Mottron, Laurent and Michelle Dawson. *Hidden Smarts, Abstract thought trumps IQ scores in autism.* *Science News,* July 7, 2007, vol. 172, pp. 4-5.

322 Gross, J.J. and O.P. John. *Individual Differences in Two Emotion Regulation Processes: Implications for Affect, Relationships and Well-Being.* *Journal of Personality and Social Psychology*, 2003, vol. 85(2): 348-362.

323 Kubler-Ross, Elizabeth. *On Death And Dying,* 1969. www.elizabethkublerross.com/pages/Quotes.html.

324 Leung, Kok Yuen. *Traditional Chinese Teachings.* College of Acupuncture course. 1971.

325 Taylor, S.E., Klein, L.C. et al. *Female Responses to Stress: Tend and Befriend, Not Fight or Flight.* *Psychological Review*, 2000, vol. 107(3): 41-49.

326 Morgan, Marlo. 2004.

327 Kevin Ochsner, Silvia Bunge, John Gabrieli and J.J.Gross. *Control your anger!* *Scientific American Mind*, 2005, vol. 16 (4): 69-71.

328 Koenig, M, et al. *Damage to the Prefrontal Cortex increases utilitarian moral judgement.* *Nature*, April 11, 2007, vol. 446: pp. 908-911.

329 Lutz, Antoine, et al. *Long-Term Meditators Self-Induce High-Amplitude Gamma Synchrony during Mental Practice.* In: *Proceedings of the National Academy of Sciences, USA*, November 16, 2004, vol. 101 (46): 16, 369-16, 373.

330 Merzel, Dennis Genpo. *Big Mind Big Heart, Finding Your Way.* Big Mind Publishing, Salt Lake City, UT, 2007.

331 Luskin, Fred. *Forgive For Good.* Harper, San Francisco, 2002.

332 Farrow, Tom & Peter Woodruff. *Neuro-Imaging of Forgability.* In: *Handbook of Forgiveness, Anthology of Scientific Studies,* ed. Everette Worthington, Routledge (Taylor & Francis Group), New York, 2005.

[333] Tolle, Eckhart. **Realizing The Power of Now.** Sounds True Audio Learning Course, 2007.

[334] Sergo, Peter. *Mental Illness in America.* **Scientific American Mind,** February/March 2008, p.15.

[335] Marano, Hara Estroff. *Depression: Beyond Serotonin.* **Psychology Today,** March/April 1999, p. 32.

[336] DeQuervain, D.J., B. Roozendall and James McGaugh. *Stress and glucocorticoids impair retrieval of long-term spatial memory.* **Nature,** 1998, vol. 394: 787-790.

[337] Teeguarden, Iona M. **A Complete Guide to Acupressure.** Japan Publications, Tokyo and New York, 1996.

[338] Marano, Hara Estroff. 1999, p. 34.

[339] Drevets, Wayne C., et al. *A functional anatomical study of unipolar depression.* **Journal of Neuroscience,** 1992, vol. 12: 3628-41.

[340] Sapolsky, Robert. *Taming Stress.* **Scientific American,** September 2003, pp. 87-91.

[341] Blumenthal, James A. *Exercise steps up as a depression buster.* **Psychosomatic Medicine,** September 2007, and in *Science News,* Oct. 13, 2007, vol. 172, p. 237.

[342] Barber, Charles. **Comfortably Numb, How Psychiatry is Medicating a Nation.** Pantheon Books, New York, 2008.

[343] Healy, David. **Let Them Eat Prozac.** New York University Press, 2004.

[344] Barber, Charles. *The Medicated Americans.* **Scientific American Mind,** February/March 2008, pp. 45-51.

[345] Ornish, Dean. **Love and Survival: 8 Pathways to Intimacy and Health.** Harper Collins, New York, 1998.

[346] Canli, Turhan. *The Character Code.* **Scientific American Mind,** February/March 2008, pp. 53-57.

[347] Phelps, Elizabeth A, and Joseph E. LeDoux. *Contributions of the Amygdala to Emotion Processing: From Animal Models to Human Behavior.* **Neuron,** October 20, 2005, vol. 48(2): 175-187.

[348] Bremner, J. Douglas. *Does stress damage the brain?* **Biological Psychiatry,** 1999, vol. 45(7): 797-805.

[349] Drevets, Wayne C., et al. *Depression and the Prefrontal Lobes.* **Nature,** April 24, 1997. In: *Science News,* April 26, 1997, vol. 151: p. 254.

[350] McEwen, Bruce. *From Molecules to Mind; Stress, Individual Difference, and the Social Environment.* **Annals of the New York Academy of Sciences.** 2001, no. 935. McEwen, Bruce and Elizabeth Norton, *The End of Stress As We Know It.* National Academies Press, 2002. Bremner, J. Douglas, et al, *Hippocampal volume reduction in major depression.* **American Journal of Psychiatry,** 2000, vol. 157(1).

[351] Redford, B. Williams, et al. *Depression.* **Science News,** July 1997, vol. 152, p. ll.

[352] Carrigan, Catherine. **Healing Depression.** Heartfire Books, Santa Fe. NM, 1997.

[353] Cohen, S. & T.A. Wills. *Stress, social support, and the buffering hypothesis.* **Psychological Bulletin,** 1985, vol. 98: pp. 310-357.

[354] DeKeukelaere, Lisa. *Optimism Prolongs Life.* **Scientific American Mind,** February/March 2006, p. 7

[355] Krackhards. D. *The strength of strong ties: The importance of Philos in organizations.* In: N. Nohria & R. Eccles (eds.), **Networks And Organizations: Structure, Form And Action.** Harvard Business School Press, Boston, 1993.

[356] DeAenlle, Conrad. *Is All This Zippy Technology Actually Ruining our Lives?* **International Herald Tribune,** October 8, 1999, p. 9.

357 Middleton-Maz. J. *Boiling Point; The High Cost of Unhealthy Anger to Individual and Society.* Health Communications, Inc., Deerfield Beach, FL, 1999.

358 Niehoff, D. *The Biology of Violence: How Understanding the Brain, Behavior, and Environment Can Break the Vicious Circle of Aggression.* Free Press, 1999.

359 Bremner. 1999, pp. 797-805.

360 van Praag, Henriette, Gerd Kempermann, & Fred H. Gage. *Running Increases Cell Proliferation And Neurogenesis In The Adult Mouse Dentate Gyrus.* **Nature Neuroscience,** March, 1999, vol.2 (3): pp. 266-270.

361 Ornish, Dean. 1998.

362 Fry, Christopher. *Three Plays: The Firstborn, Thor with Angels, A Sleep of Prisoners.* Oxford University Press, New York, 1951, p. 209.

Chapter Eight Notes

363 Nadell, C.D. B.L. Bassler, S.A. Levin. *Observing bacteria through the lens of social evolution.* **Journal of Biology,** 2008, vol. 7, p.27.

364 Bassler, Bonnie L. and R. Losick, *Bacterially speaking.* **Cell,** 2006, vol. 125, pp. 237-246. And: Camilli, A and B.L. Bassler. *Bacterial small-molecule signaling pathways.* **Science,** 2006, vol. 311, pp. 1113-1116.

365 Backster, Cleve. *Evidence of a Primary Perception in Plant Life.* **The International Journal of Parapsychology,** Winter, 1968, vol. 10.

366 Backster, Cleve. *Biocommunications Capability: Human Donors and In Vitro Leukocytes.* **The International Journal of Biosocial Research,** 1985, vol. 7 (2), 132-146.

367 Backser, Cleve. **Primary Perception: Biocommunication with Plants, Living Foods, and Human Cells.** White Rose Millennium Press, 2003.

368 Mather, Jennifer. *Cephalopod Consciousness and Behavioral Evidence.* **Consciousness & Cognition,** March, 2008, vol.17 (1), 37-48.

369 Patton, Paul. *One World, Many Minds.* **Scientific American Mind,** December 2008/January 2009, pp. 72-79.

370 Pepperberg, Irene Maxine. *The Alex Studies. Cognitive and Communicative Abilities of Gray Parrots.* Harvard University Press, 2002.

371 Scholtyssetk, Christine. *Bird Brains? Hardly.* **Scientific American Mind,** April/May 2006, pp. 51-55.

372 Benda, William & Rondi Lightmark. *People Whisperers.* **Shift: At the Frontiers of Consciousness.** Noetic Sciences Publication. June-Aug 2004, pp. 30-35.

373 Fauna Communications Research Institute in Hillsborough, NC. http://groups.yahoo.com/group/drjoncat/message/115. **J. Am Vet Med Assoc,** 1999, vol. 214(9): 1136-41. And: Dr. David Williams, **Alternatives for the Health-Conscious Individual** (online newsletter).

374 Friedmann, E. & S. A. Thomas. *Pet ownership, social support and one-year survival after acute myocardial infarction in the Cardiac Arrhythmia Suppression Trial (CAST).* **American Journal of Cardiology,** 1995, vol. 76.

375 deWaal, Frans B.M. *Do Animals Feel Empathy?* **Scientific American Mind.** December 2007/January 2008, pp. 28-35.

376 Langford, Dale J. *Social Modulation of Pain as Evidence for Empathy in Mice.* **Science,** June 30, 2006.

377 Iacoboni, Marco, et al. *Grasping the Intentions of Others with One's Own Mirror Neuron System.* **In PloS Biology,** 2005, vol.3(3): 529-535. http://iacoboni.bmap.ucla.edu/.

378 Sebanz, Natalie, Harold Bekkering, Gunther Knoblick. *Joint Action: Bodies and Minds*

Moving Together. **Trends in Cognitive Sciences,** February 20, 2006. And: Sebanz, Natalie. *It Takes 2 to…,* **Scientific American Mind,** December 2006/January 2007, pp. 52-57.

[379] Chartrand, Tanya. Chartrand Automaticity Lab at Duke University. http://faculty.fuqua.duke.edu/blab/publications.html

[380] Hauser, Marc D. **Moral Minds: How Nature Designed Our Universal Sense of Right and Wrong.** Harper Collins, 2006.

[381] Choi, Charles. *Speaking in Tones.* **Scientific American,** September 2007, p. 25.

[382] Campbell, Don. *The Mozart Effect for Children,* William Morrow, New York, 2000.

[383] White, David. Science and Spirituality, Summer Conference, Denver, Colorado. July, 1999.

[384] Halpern, Steven. **Sound Health, The Music and Sounds that Make Us Whole.** Harper & Row. San Francisco, CA, 1985, p. 32.

[385] deWaal, Frans and Amy Pollech, *Talk To The Hand.* **Science News,** May 5, 2007, vol. 171, pp. 275-76.

[386] Berard, Guy. **Hearing Equals Behavior.** Keats Pub., Inc. New Canaan, Connecticut, 1993, pp. 15-37.

[387] McDermott, Jeanne. *The Solid-State Parrot.* **Science 83',** 1983, pp. 59-65.

[388] Goddard-Blythe, Sally. **What Babies and Children Really Need.** Hawthorn Press, Gloucestershire, UK. 2008, pp. 179-212.

[389] Haesler, Sebastian. *Programmed for Speech.* **Scientific American Mind.** June/July 2007, pp. 67-71.

[390] Jourdain, Robert. **Music, The Brain and Ecstasy.** Avon Books, New York, 1997, p. 275.

[391] Maestripieri, Dario and Jessica Whitham. *Understanding Baby Talk.* **Scientific American Mind,** December 2007/January 2008, p. 10.

[392] Taggart, Cynthia Crump. *The Effect Of Instruction On The Music Potential Of Young Children.* Suzuki Assoc. of America Conference, 1998.

[393] *Time Magazine,* February 14, 2000, Number Section, p. 25.

[394] Healy, Jane M. **Endangered Minds, Why Children Don't Think and What We Can Do About It.** Simon & Schuster, New York, 1990, pp. 86-104.

[395] Berard, Guy. 1993.

[396] Halpern, Steven. 1985, p. 82.

[397] Goddard-Blythe, Sally. 2008, pp. 26-29, 139-176.

[398] Livingston, Richard. *Winter Diseases And Dyslexia.* **J. of the American Acad. of Child and Adolescent Psychiatry,** May 1993. In: **Science News,** May 1, 1993, vol. 143, p. 278.

[399] Diamond, Marion C. **Magic Trees Of The Mind.** Dutton/Penguin Group, New York, 1998, pp. 80-120.

[400] Paulesu, Eraldo and Elise Temple. *Dyslexia.* **Science,** March 16, 2001.

[401] Berard, Guy. 1993.

[402] Johansen, Kjeld. *Frequency specific left hemisphere stimulation with music and sounds in dyslexia remediation.* 3rd European Music Therapy Conference, June 17-20, 1995, Aalborg, Denmark.

[403] Trowbridge, Anthony. *Ecology of Knowledge Network.* Paper given at the **Science and Vision Conference,** Human Sciences Research Center, Pretoria, South Africa. January, 1992. interafrika@mweb.co.za.

[404] Parry, Glenn Apapicio. *Native Wisdom in a Quantum World.* **Shift: At the Frontiers of consciousness,** December 2005/February 2006, pp. 29-33.

[405] Peat, F. David. **Infinite Potential: The Life and Times of David Bohm.** Addison Wesley, Reading, MA, 1997.

406 Bohm, David. *On Dialogue.* Routledge, New York, 1996.

407 Nichols, Michael. *The Lost Art Of Listening.* Guilford Press, New York, 2009.

408 Tomatis, Lena A. *The multi-disciplinary aspects of audio-psycho-phonology.* Paper presented at the 5th International Congress of Audio-Psycho-Phonology, Toronto, May, 1978.

409 Ladinsky, Daniel. *The Gift, Poems By Hafiz, The Great Sufi Master.* Penguin/Arkana, New York, 1999, p. 99.

Chapter Nine Notes

410 Campbell, Don. *Mozart Effect For Children.* William Morrow, New York, 2000.

411 Ibid.

412 Goddard, Sally. *What Babies and Children Really Need.* Hawthorn Press, Early Years Series, Gloucestershire, UK, pp. 208-212.

413 Papansek, Hanus. *Musicality in infancy research; biological and cultural origins of early musicality.* In: *Musical Beginnings, Origins and Development of Musical Competence.* Irene Deliege and John Slovoa (eds.), Oxford University Press, 1996, pp. 37-51

414 Brewer, Chris and Don Campbell. *Rhythms Of Learning.* Zephyr Press, Tuscon, AZ, 1991, p. 20

415 Campbell, Don. *The Mozart Effect, Tapping The Power of Music to Heal the Body, Strengthen the Mind and Unlock the Creative Spirit.* Avon Books, New York, 1997, pp. 103-104.

416 Campbell, Don. *Effects of intense noise during fetal life upon postnatal adaptability.* J. of Acoustical Soc. of America. 1970, vol. 47, pp. 1128-1130.

417 The Committee on Hearing, Bioacoustics & Biomechanics of the National Research Council. *Prenatal effects of exposure to high-level noise.* National Academies Press, Wash. DC ,1982.

418 Campbell, Don. 2000

419 Hamby, William. Ultimate Sound Pressure Level Decibel Table. 2004.

420 Tomatis, Alfred A. *The Ear And Language.* Stoddart Pub., Toronto, 1997. *The Conscious Ear: My Life of Transformation through Listening.* Station Hill Press, Barrrytown, NY, 1992.

421 Campbell, Don. 2000, p. 54

422 Levintin, D. J. & V. Menon. *Musical structure is processed in "language" areas of the brain: A possible role for Brodmann Area 47 in temporal coherence.* NeuroImage, 2003, vol. 20(4): 2142-2152.

423 Hodges, Donald. *Implications of Music and Brain Research.* Music Educators Journal Special Focus Issue: Music and the Brain, 2000, vol. 87: pp. 2, 17-22.

424 Pearce, Joseph Chilton. *The Magical Child.* Plume (Penguin), New York, 1992.

425 LeCanuet. J.P., et al. *Fetal cardiac, and motor responses to octive-band noises as a function of cerebral frequency, intensity and heart rate variability.* Early Human Development, 1988, vol.18: pp. 81-93.

426 Condon, William F. *New Dimensions Synthesis of Great Interviews.* New Dimensions Radio, San Francisco, 1999.

427 Condon, William F. and Louis Sander. *Statistical studies on the effects of intense noise during fetal life.* J. of Sound Vibrations, 1973, vol.27; pp. 101-111. Also, F.N. Jones & Tauscher, J., *Residence under an airport landing pattern as a factor in autism.* Archives of Environmental Health, 1978, vol. 35; pp. 10-12.

428 Pearce, Joseph Chilton. 1977, p. 71

[429] Ayers, A. Jean. *Sensory Integration And The Child; 25th Anniversary Edition.* Western Psychological Services, Los Angeles, CA, 2005.

[430] Hernandez-Peon, R. *Neurophysiology of Attention.* In: J. J Vinkin & G. W. Bruyun(eds.) **Handbook Of Clinical Neurology.** Amsterdam, North Holland Pub., 1969.

[431] Ridgeway, Roy, *The Unborn Child, How to Recognize and Overcome Prenatal Trauma.* Wildwood House, Ltd., London, 1987, p. 20.

[432] Ibid. p. 17.

[433] Liley, A.M. *The Foetus as a Personality.* **Self and Society,** June, 1977.

[434] Tiller, William, Rollin McCraty, Mike Atkinson. *Cardiac Coherence: A new, noninvasive measure of autonomic nervous system order.* **Alternative Therapies,** January 1996, vol. 2 (1): p. 52.

[435] Odent, Michelle. **Primal Health, A Blueprint for our Survival.** Century, London, 1986, p. 30.

[436] Rodriquez, Eugenio. et al. *Perceptions Shadow; long-distance synchronization of human brain activity.* **Nature,** February 4,1999, vol. 397; pp. 430-433.

[437] Redmond, Layne. *Primal Sound: The Beat of the Drum.* **New Dimensions,** July-August, 1999, p. 20.

[438] Schwartz, Peter John, et al. *Infant Deaths Linked to Odd Heartbeat.* **New England Journal of Medicine,** June 11, 1998.

[439] Prescott, James. **Discovering The Intelligence Of Play.** Touch The Future Foundation, Video, 1997.

[440] Weikert, Phyllis S., & Elizabeth B. Carlton. **Foundations In Elementary Education: Movement.** High/Scope Press, Ypsilanti, MI, 1995.

[441] Weikert, Phyllis S. Personal correspondence during a course in Michigan, April, 2000.

[442] Ibid.

[443] *The Yellow Emperior's Classic of Internal Medicine, Simple Questions (Huang Ti Nei Jing Su Wen)* People's Health Pub. House, Beijing. 1979, p. 28. First Published ca. 100 BC.

[444] Campbell, Don. 2000.

[445] Levitin, Daniel J. *This Is Your Brain on Music; The Science of a Human Obsession.* Dutton, New York, 2006, pp. 5-6.

[446] Weinberger, N.M., *The Musical Infant.* **Musica Research Newsletter,** Spring 1994.

[447] Balaban, M.T., L. M. Anderson & A. B. Wisniewski. *Lateral asymmetries in infant melody perception.* In: **Developmental Psychology,** 1998, pp. 34-48.

[448] Burns, M. T., *Music as a tool for enhancing creativity.* **Journal of Creative Behavior,** 1998, vol.22: pp. 2-69.

[449] Wiggins, J. H., *Children's strategies for solving compositional problems with peers.* **Journal of Research in Music Education,** 1994, vol. 42: 232-252.

[450] Kratus, J. *Relationships among children's music audition and their compositional processes and products.* **Journal of Research in Music Education,** 1994, vol. 42: 115-130.

[451] Jourdain, Robert. **Music, The Brain and Ecstasy.** Avon Books, New York, 1997, p. 4.

[452] Levintin, Daniel J. 2006, p. 7.

[453] Cockerton, T, Moore, S. and Norman, D., *Cognitive test performance and background music.* In: **Perceptual and Motor Skills.** 1997, vol. 85: 1435-1438.

[454] Hughes, J. R., Daaboul,Y., Fino, J.J. & Shaw, Gordon. *The "Mozart effect" on epileptiform activity.* In: **Clinical Electroencephalography,** 1998, vol. 29: 109-119.

[455] Sachs, Oliver. **Musicopilia: Tales of Music and the Brain,** Knopf, New York, 2008.

[456] Parsons, L.M., M.J. Martinez, D.A. Hodges. *Brain basis of piano performances.*

Neuropsychologia, vol. 43, pp. 199-215. Brown, S., M.J. Martinez, L.M. Parsons. *Music and language side-by-side in the brain: a PET study of generating melodies and sentences.* **European Journal of Neuroscience**, 2006, vol. 23: pp. 2791-2803.

[457] Szmedra. L. & D. W. Bacharach. *Effect of music on perceived exertion, plasma lactate, norepinephrine, and cardiovascular hemodynamics during treadmill running.* **International Journal of Sports Medicine**, 1998, vol. 19: 3 2-37.

[458] **The College Board, Profile of College-Bound Seniors National Report for 2005.**

[459] Cutietta, Robert, et al. *"Spin-offs", The Extra-Musical Advantages of a Musical Education.* **United Instruments, Inc., Future of Music Project.** 2000

[460] Campbell, Don. **Sound Spirit.** The Mozart Effect Resource Center, P.O. Box 800, Boulder, CO 80306. www.mozarteffect.com. 2008.

[461] Goddard, Sally. 2008, pp. 209-210.

[462] Beaulieu, John. **Sound In The Healing Arts.** Station Hill Publishers, London,1987.

[463] Kindermusik: P.O. Box 26575, Greensborough, NC 27415, Phone: 800-628-5687. www.kindermusik.com. Musikgarten: 409 Blandwood Ave., Greensborough, NC 27401. Phone: 800-216-6864. Music With Mar: 149 Garland Circle, Palm Harbor, FL 34683. Phone: 727-545-4627. www.musicwithmar.com.

[464] Schlaug, Gottfried, and Gaser Christian. *Musical Training During Childhood May Influence Regional Brain Growth.* Paper presented at the 53rd Annual Meeting of the *American Academy of Neurology,* Philadelphia, PA, May 16, 2001.

[465] Pantev, C, et al. *Increased cortical representation in musicians.* *Scientific Correspondence,* **Nature.** 1998, vol.396(128): 811-813.

[466] Hodges, Donald. *Neuromusical Research: A Review of the Literature.* IN **Handbook of Music Psychology,** D. Hodges, ed., 2nd edition, 1996, pp. 203-290.

[467] Hodges, Donald. 2000. pp. 17-22.

[468] Menon, V and D. J. Levitin. *The rewards of music listening; Response and physiological connectivity of the mesolimbic system.* **NeuroImage** 2005, vol. 28(1): 175-184.

[469] Weinbeiger, Normal M. *Music and the Brain.* **Scientific American,** November, 2004, pp. 90-95.

[470] Sachs, Oliver. 2008.

[471] Levitin, D. J. and V. Menon. *The neural locus of temporal structure and expectancies in music: Evidence from functional neuroimaging at 3 Tesla.* **Music Perception,** 2005, 22 (3): 563-575.

[472] Brewer, Chris. **Soundtracks for Learning: Using Music in the Classroom.** LifeSounds Educational Services, 2008. www.musicandlearning.com. (336)207-7505

[473] Johnson, Michael. Musician and teacher in Salt Lake City, Utah. Personal conversation.

[474] Mithen, Steven. **The Singing Neanderthals: The Origins of Music, Language, Mind and Body.** Harvard University Press, 2006.

[475] Levitin, Daniel J. 2006.

[476] Khan, Hazrat Inayat. **The Heart of Sufism.** Shambhala, Boston, 1999, p. 275.

[477] Limb, Charles J., James F. Battey, and Allen R.Braun. *Improvisation in Jazz Musicians.* **Public Library of Science (PloS)** one. February 27, 2008.

Chapter Ten Notes

[478] Henig, Robin Marantz. *Taking Play Seriously.* The New York Times, Feb. 17, 2008, http://www.nytimes.com/2008/02/17/magazine/17play.html.

[479] Wenner, Melinda. *The Serious Need for Play.* **Scientific American Mind,** Feb/March 2009, pp. 22-29.

[480] Brown, Stuart L. *Through the Lens of Play.* **Revision,** 1995, vol. 17(4): 4-12.

[481] Teitel, Jay. *The Kidnapping of Play.* **Night,** April 1999, p. 57.

[482] Sutton-Smith, Brian. *The Ambiguity of Play.* Harvard University Press, Cambridge, 2001.

[483] Heinrich, Bernd and Thomas Bugnyar. *Play In Ravens.* **Scientific American,** April 2007. pp. 65-71

[484] Bugnyar, Thomas and Bernd Heinrich. *Pilfering Ravens, Corvus corax, Adjust Their Behaviour to Social Context and Identification of Competitors.* **Animal Cognition,** October, 2006, vol. 9(4): 369-376.

[485] Brown, Stuart L. 1999. *Play, Learning Without Limits, Exploring the Intelligence of Play.* Touch The Future Conference, Monterey, CA, January 1999.

[486] Brown, Stewart, and Christopher Vaughn. **Play: How It Shapes the Brain, Opens the Imagination, and Invigorates the Soul.** Avery (Penguin), New York, 2009.

[487] Meeker, Joseph W. *Comedy and a Play Ethic.* **ReVision,** 1995, vol 17, no. 4.

[488] Meeker, Joseph. **The Comedy Of Survival; Literacy Ecology and a Play Ethic.** University of Arizona Press, Tucson, AZ, 1997.

[489] Brown, Stewart L. *Animals at play.* **National Geographic,** 1994, vol.186(6): n2-35.

[490] Sutton-Smith. 2001.

[491] Panksepp, Jaak. **Affective Neuroscience, The Foundations of Human and Animal Emotions.** Oxford University Press, 1998, pp. 281-282.

[492] Burghardt, Gordon M. **The Genesis of Animal Play: Testing the Limits.** MIT Press, 2005.

[493] Panksepp. 1998, p. 281.

[494] Ibid. pp. 280-281.

[495] Siviy, Stephen M., Kelly A. Harrison, and Ian S. McGregor. *Fear, Risk Assessment and Playfulness in the Juvenile Rat.* **Behavioral Neuroscience,** 2006, vol. 120(1): 49-59.

[496] Schmidt, Konrad & Wolfgang Oertel. *Fighting Parkinson's.* **Scientific American Mind,** February/March 2006, pp. 64-69.

[497] Pellis, Sergio M. & Vivian C. Pellis. *Rough and Tumble Play and the Development of the Social Brain.* **Current Directions in Psychological Science,** April 2007, vol. 16(2): 95-98.

[498] Montague, Ashley. **Growing Young.** Bergin & Garvey, New York, 1989, p. 292.

[499] Goddard-Blythe, Sally. **What Babies and Children Really Need.** Hawthorn Press, Gloucestershire, UK, 2008, pp. 169-171.

[500] Roberts, Debra, Documentary Editor, **Brandy Binder Story.** ABC News 20/20, October 3, 1997

[501] Ross, Philip E. *Half-Brained Schemes, What's all that gray matter good for, anyway?* **Scientific American,** January 2006, pp. 24-26.

[502] Kenneally, Christine. *The Deepest Cut, How can someone live with only half a brain?* **The New Yorker,** July 3, 2006, pp. 36-42.

[503] Greenspan, Stanley. **The Child With Special Needs: Encouraging Intellectual and Emotional Growth.** Merloyd Lawrence Books, Cambridge, MA, 1998.

[504] Solomon, Rick. **The P.L.A.Y Project, Play and Language for Autistic Youngsters.** University of Michigan Medical School. March 10, 2005. www.playproject.org.

[505] Wennekes, Renate & Angelika Stiller. **Developmental Kinesiology Intengration of our Senses.** Institut fur kinesiologische Lernforderung, Neuenkirchen-Vorden, Germany. Course, July, 1999.

506 Ibid.

507 Mason, Ruth. *Giving Babies the Best Start in Life.* In *Exchange Everyday*, January 8, 2008. www.childcareexchange.com/eed/. exchangeeveryday@ccie.com.

508 Wennekes, Renate & Angelika Stiller. 1999.

509 Cohen, R. Irun. *Tending Adam's Garden, Evolving the Cognitive Immune Self.* Elsevier Academic Press, London, 2000.

510 Carpenter, Siri. *Modern Hygiene's Dirty Tricks, the clean life may throw off a delicate balance in the immune system. Science News,* Aug. 14, 1999, vol. 156, pp. 108-110.

511 Sacks, David L & Shaden Kamhawi. *Fly bites help guard against Leishmania.* May 1999 meeting of the American Society of Microbiology in Chicago.

512 Frost, Jay L., S.C. Worthan and S. Refifel. *Play and Child Development.* Prentice Hall, Upper Saddle River, NJ, 2001.

513 Eriksson, Peter S., Fred H. Gage, et al. *Neurogenesis In the Adult Human Hippocampus. Nature Medicine,* November, 1998, 4(11): 1313-1317.

514 vanPragg, Henriette, et al. *Running increases cell proliferation and neurogenesis in the adult mouse dentate gyrus. Nature Neuroscience,* March, 1999, vol. 2 (3), 266-270.

515 Gould, Elizabeth, et al. *Learning enhances adult neurogenesis in the hippocampal formation. Nature Neuroscience,* March, 1999, vol. 2 (3): 260-265.

516 Vastag, Brian. *Brain Gain, Constant sprouting of neurons attracts scientists, drugmakers. Science News,* June 16, 2007, vol. 171, pp. 376-380.

517 Krityakiarana, Warin. *Effects of Exercise on the Intact Adult Spinal Cord.* Noted in *Brain Research and Instruction Newsletter*, Janet Zadina. February 2, 2009. www.brainresearch. us.

518 Fields, R. Douglas. *New Brain Cells Go to Work. Scientific American Mind,* August/September 2007, pp. 31-35.

519 Gilbert, Anne Green, *Brain Dance, Variations for Infants through Seniors.* VHS/DVD. 2003 www.creativedance.org.

520 Roberts, Christine. *Nurturing Pathways, Growing the Mind Through Movement.* And: *Nurturing Pathways, Dancing Feet.* Book and DVD, 2004. www.nurturingpathways.com.

521 Lyman, Peggy and John M. Feierabend. *Move It! Expressive Movements with Classical Music.* DVD, CD and Booklet. GIA Publications, Chicago, IL, 2003. www.giamusic.com.

522 Hubert, Bill. *Bal-A-Vis-X, Rhythmic Balance/Auditory/Vision eXercises for Brain & Brain-Body Integration.* Bal-A-Vis-X, Wichita, KS, April 2001.

523 Ratey, John. *Spark: The Revolutionary New Science of Education and the Brain.* Little, Brown & Co. , January, 2008.

524 Ayers, A Jean. 1982. *Sensory Integation and The Child.* Western Psychological Services, Los Angeles, 1982.

525 Brown, Stuart L. 1995, p 6.

526 Brown, Stuart L. *Taking Play Seriously. New York Times,* nytimes.com. February 17, 2008. Robin Marantz Henig, column writer.

527 Teitelbaum, Philip. *Physiological Psychology: Fundamental Principals.* Prentice Hall, Englewood Cliffs, NJ, 1997.

528 Randall, Kay. *Child's Play, Demise of play bodes ill for healthy child development, research says.* Interview with Dr. Joe Frost, Parker Centennial Professor Emeritus in the University of Texas at Austin College of Education's Department of Curriculum and Instruction. January 10, 2007. www.utexas.edu/features/2007/playgrounds.

529 Trost, Steward G. *Physical Education, Physical Activity and Academic Performance. Active Living Research,* Research Brief. San Diego State University, Fall 2007

[530] Brownlee, Christen. *Buff and Brainy, Exercising the body can benefit the mind.* **Science News**, March 4, 2006.

[531] Summerford, Cathie. *What is the Impact of Exercise on Brain Function for Academic Learning.* **Teaching Elementary Physical Education**, May 2001, pp. 6-8.

[532] Vail, Kathleen. *Mind and Body, New research ties physical activity and fitness to academic success.* **American School Board Journal**, March 2006, pp. 30-33.

[533] Field, Tiffany, Miguel Diego, and Christopher E. Sanders. *Exercise is positively related to adolescents' relationships and academics.* **Adolescence**, Spring, 2001, vol. 36(141): 105-110.

[534] Barros, Ronina M., *The 3 R's? A Fourth Is Crucial, Too: Recess.* **The New York Times**, Health, February 24, 2009, p. D5.

[535] *New AAP Report Promotes Play.* **Exchange Every Day** www.ccie.com/eed. November 2, 2006. www.aap.org/stress.

[536] Hannaford, Carla. **Smart Moves, Why Learning Is Not All In Your Head, (2nd ed.).** Great River Books, Salt Lake City, UT, 2005, pp. 117-119, 124-125.

[537] White, Sally S., **Building A Labyrinth on a Shoestring budget.** Physical Education Department, Palm Bay Elementary, 1200 Allamanda Rd., NE., Palm Bay, FL 32905. 1998. Also: *The St. Louis Labyrinth Project,* c/o Robert Ferre, 3124 Gurney Avenue, St. Louis, MO 63116. Phone (800) 873-9873.

[538] Artress, Lauren. *Walking the Labyrinth.* **Elixir: Consciousness, Conscience, & Culture.** Autumn 2007, Issue 5, p. 76.

[539] Goodstein, Laurie. *Reviving Labyrinths, Paths to Inner Peace.* **New York Times,** May 10, 1998.

[540] Westbury, Virginia. **Labyrinths, Ancient Paths of Wisdom and Peace.** Da Capo Press (Perseus Books Group), 2001.

[541] Erickson, Kirk, Arthur F. Kramer, et al. *Aerobic fitness is associated with hippocampal volume in elderly humans.* **Hippocampus**, Wiley-Liss (A Wiley Co.), Published Online: January 2, 2009. Also: Sharon Begley, *Old Age, Old Brain? Maybe Not.* **Newsweek,** February 25, 2009.

[542] Verghese, Joe, et al. *Leisure Activities and the Risk of Dementia in the Elderly.* **New England Journal of Medicine,** 2003, vol. 348(25), pp. 2508-2515.

[543] Churchill, James, et al. *Exercise, Experience and the Aging Brain.* **Neurobiology of Aging.** 2002, vol.23 (5): pp. 941-955.

[544] H. Chen, Alberto Ascherio, et al. *Physical Activity and the Risk of Parkinson's Disease.* **Neurology**, 2005, vol. 64(4): 664-669.

[545] Pyfer, J., Johnson R., *Factors affecting motor delays.* In: *Robert L. Eason, Robert L., Theresa L. Smith, Fernand Caron.* **Adapted Physical Activity, From Theory To Application.** Human Kinetics Publishers, Champaign, IL, 1983. Also, Crowe, Walter C., David Auxter & Jean Pyfer. **Principles & Methods of Adapted Physical Education and Recreation.** C.V. Mosby Co., St. Louis, 1991.

[546] Sylwester, Robert. **A Celebration Of Neurons: An Educator's Guide To The Human Brain.** Association for Supervision and Curriculum Development, Alexandria, VA, 1995, p. 158.

[547] Goddard. 2008, p. 47.

[548] Sylwester. 1995, p. 37.

[549] Ackerman, Diane. **A Natural History Of The Senses.** Vintage Books, New York, 1990, pp. 76-77.

[550] Ibid. p. 77.

[551] Wegscheider-Cruse, Sharon. *The Family Trap.* **Family Reconstruction: The Living Theater Model.** Science and Behavior Books, Palo Alto, CA, 1997.

552 Prescott, James. *Nurturing in Indigenous People.* **Psychology Today,** December, 1979. Prescott, James W. and Michael Mendizza. *The Origins of Love & Violence, Bonding & Brain Development. Historical Video & Selected Publications.* Touch the Future & Institute of Humanistic Science. www.ttfuture.org www.violence.de. DVD. 2003.

553 Ayres, A. Jean. *Sensory Integration and Learning Disorders.* Western Psychological Services, Los Angeles, 1972, p. 58.

554 Goddard, Sally. 2008, p. 45.

555 Maciocia, Giovanni. *The Practice Of Chinese Medicine.* Churchill Livingston Pub., Edinburgh, London. 1994, p. 200.

556 McCraty, Rollin, Mike Atkinson, Dana Tomasino and William A. Tiller, *The Electricity of Touch: detection and measurement of cardiac energy exchange between people.* In: K. H. Pribram, ed. *Brain and Values: Is a Biological Science of Values Possible,* Lawrence Erlbaum Associates, Inc., Mahwah, NY, 1998, p. 7

557 Penksapp. 1998, p. 287-310.

558 Ibid. p. 289.

559 Ibid. pp. 287-290.

560 Ibid. p.33.

561 Zajonc, Robert B., *The Face of Emotion. Science,* April 5, 1985. In: *Science News,* June 6, 1985, vol. 128.

562 Rizzolatti, Giacomo, Leonardo Fogassi and Vittorio Gallese. *Mirrors in The Mind.* **Scientific American,** November, 2006, pp. 54-61.

563 Penksapp. 1998, p. 280.

564 Provine, Albert. *Laughter, A Scientific Investigation.* Viking Penguin, New York, 2000.

565 Penksapp. 1998, p. 280

566 Brown, Stewart. 1995, p. 11

567 Singer, Dorothy and Jerome. *The House Of Make-Believe, Childrens Play and the Developing Imagination.* Cambridge, Harvard U. Press, 1990.

568 Penksapp. 1998, p. 280.

569 Brown, Stewart. 1995, pp. 4-12.

570 Pellegrini, Anthony D., Danielle Dupris & Peter M. Smith. *Play in Evolution and Development. Developmental Review,* June 2007, vol. 27(2): 261-276.

571 Singer, Dorothy and Jerome. 1990.

572 Doidge, Norman. *The Brain that Changes Itself.* Penguin Books, NY, 2007, pp. 199-214.

573 Singer, J.L. and D.G. Singer. *Imaginative Play and Human Development; Schemas, Scripts and Possibilities.* In: D. Bergen(ed.), *Play as a Medium for Learning and Development.* Association of Childhood Education International, 1998, pp. 63-66.

574 McLean, Paul D. *The Triune Brain In Evolution, Role in Paleocerebral Functions.* Plenum Press, New York, 1990, p. 559.

575 Penksapp. 1998, p. 281.

576 Dijksterhuis, Ap. *The Subconscious Mind: Your Unsung Hero. New Scientist,* December 1, 2007.

577 Pearce, Joseph Chilton. *Evolution's End, Claiming the Potential of Our Intelligence.* Harper & Row, San Francisco, 1992, pp. 160-162.

578 Kemp, Martin. *Seen/Unseen: Art, Science and Intuition from Leonardo to the Hubble Telescope.* Oxford University Press, 2005.

579 Meeker, Joseph W. 1995, p. 23.

580 Tietel, Jay. 1999, pp. 59-60.

581 Prescott, James, Harry Harlow, Bill Mason & Chris Berkeson. At Hazelton Labs, Falls, Church, VA. *Rock A Bye Baby, A Time Life Documentary,* (1970).

582 Prescott, James. *Discovering the Intelligence of Play.* Video. Touch The Future Foundation, Nevada City, California, 1997.

583 Perry, Bruce. *Secrets To Academic Success.* In: *Time Magazine,* Claudia Wallis article, October 19,1998.

584 Brown, Stewart. *Discovering The Intelligence of Play.* Video, 1997.

585 Penksepp. 1998, pp. 283-17.

586 White, Bowen. *Why Normal Isn't Healthy.* Touch The Future Conference, Monterey, CA, January 1999.

587 Brown, Stewart. 1997.

588 Brinson, Cynthia. *Comment in USA Today,* April 23, 1999. Doylestown, PA.

589 Prescott, James W. 1979.

Chapter Eleven Notes

590 Healy, Jane M. *Your Child's Growing Mind: Brain Development and Learning from Birth to Adolescence.* New York, Broadway Books, New York, 2004.

591 Michnick-Golinkoff, Roberta, Kathy Hirsh-Pasek, and Diane Eyer. *Einstein Never Used Flashcards: How Our Children Really Learn — and Why They Need to Play More and Memorize Less.* Rodale Books, New York, 2004.

592 Anderson, L.B., et al. *Physical activity and clustered cardiovascular risks in children: a cross-sectional study. Lancet,* July 22, 2006, vol. 368 (9522): 299-304.

593 Esterl, Mike. *German Tots Learn to Answer Call of Nature. The Wall Street Journal,* April 14, 2008, p. A1.

594 Wald Kindergarten, Patrick Friedrich, Zartenerstr. 7, 79199 Kirchzarten, Germany. Phone: 07661/627272.

595 Hafner, Peter. *Natur-und Waldkindergarten in Deutschland: Eine Alternative zum Regelkindergarten in der vorschulischen Erziehung.* Dissertation, Heidelberg University, Germany, 2002.

596 Mills, Andrea. *Forest for a classroom, For these Waldkinder the best educational environment is the woods – rain or shine. Mothering Magazine,* November-December 2008, pp. 74-77.

597 Low, Richard. *The Last Child In The Woods, Saving Our Children from Nature-Deficit Disorder.* Algonquin Books, Chapel Hill, NC, 2005.

598 Nader, Ralph. *The Seventeen Traditions.* Harper Collins, New York, 2007.

599 Sachan, Dinsa. *Behave Yourself! Kids who can control their impulses do better in school. Scientific American Mind,* August/September 2007, p. 11.

600 Ministry of Education and Research, International Relations Division. *Characteristic Features of Danish Education.* Copenhagen, Denmark. 1992, pp. 1-39.

601 Siegler, Robert S. & Elsbeth Stern. *Natural Learning. Journal of Experimental Psychology: General.* December, 1998.

602 Kohn, Alfe. *The Schools Our Children Deserve: Moving Beyond Traditional Classrooms and Tougher Standards.* Houghton-Mifflin, Boston, 1999.

603 Pace-Marshall, Stephanie. *A Decidedly Different Mind. Shift: At the Frontiers of Consciousness Journal,* Sept/Nov 2005, No. 8, pp. 11-15.

[604] Messier, Paul, Barbara Given and Charlene Engel. *National Learning Foundation Mission Statement.* Presented in February 1994. National Learning Foundation, 11 Dupont Circle, N.W., Suite 900, Washington, DC 20036-1271.

[605] McLean, Paul. Personal Communication.

[606] Dickinson, Amy. *KinderGrind.* **Time Magazine,** Education Section, November 8, 1999.

[607] Kirn, Walter and Wendy Cole. *What Ever Happened to Play?* **Time Magazine,** April 30, 2001, p. 56.

[608] Chaloner, Barry. *Brain Research Sheds New Light on Student Learning.* Director of the Center for Early Intervention. November 11, 2003. www.cec.sped.org/AM/Template.cfm?Section=Home&TEMPLATE=/CM/ContentDisplay.cfm&CONTENTID=6271.

[609] Carter, Forrest. *The Education of Little Tree.* Delacorte Press (Random House), New York, 1976.

[610] Mate, Gabor. **Scattered, How ADD Originates and What You Can Do About It.** Dutton, New York, 1999.

[611] Kluger, Jeffrey and Alice Park. *The quest for a Super Kid.* **Time Magazine,** April 30, 2001, p. 53.

[612] Benson, Peter. **All Kids Are Our Kids (2nd ed.).** Jossey Bass, San Francisco, 2006.

[613] Bailey, Becky. **I Love You Rituals, Activities to Build Bonds and Strengthen Relationships.** Loving Guidance, Inc., Oviedo, FL. www.beckybailey.com

[614] Fay, Jim and Bob Sornson. **Meeting The Challenge, Using Love and Logic to Help children Develop Attention and Behavior Skills.** The Love and Logic Press, Inc., Golden, CO, 2000. www.loveandlogic.com.

[615] DeGrandpre, Richard. **Ritalin Nation: Rapid-Fire Culture and the Transformation of Human Consciousness.** Norton, New York, 1999.

[616] Elkind, David. **The Hurried Child: Growing Up Too Fast Too Soon.** Addison-Wesley, Reading, MA, 1988, p. 4.

[617] Benson, Peter. 1997. **All Kids Are Our Kids, What Communities Must Do To Raise Caring And Responsible Children And Adolescents.** Jossey-Bass, San Francisco. 1997, p. 314.

[618] National Center on Health Statistics. U. S. Dept. of Health and Human Services, Presidential Bldg. 6525 Belcrest Rd, Hyattsville, Md. 20782.

[619] Fay, Jim. 2000.

[620] Sornson, Robert. **Creating Classrooms Where Teachers Love to Teach And Students Love to Learn.** The Love and Logic Press, Inc., Golden, CO, 2007.

[621] Dweck, Carol S. *The Secret to Raising Smart Kids.* **Scientific American Mind,** December 2007/January 2008, pp. 37-43

[622] K. Anders Ericsson, et al., eds. **The Cambridge Handbook of Expertise and Expert Performance.** Cambridge University Press, New York, 2006.

[623] Ross, Philip. *The Expert Mind.* **Scientific American,** August 2006, pp. 64-71.

[624] Michele Donley, Sheila Gribben, et al., *The Homework Ate My Family.* **Time Magazine,** January 25, 1999, pp. 56-61.

[625] Morse, Jodie, Alice Park and James Willwerth. *Troubled Kids.* **Time Magazine,** Special Report, May 31, 1999, pp. 34-49.

[626] Szabo, Liz. *ADHD Treatment is Getting a Good Workout.* **USA Today,** March 27, 2006.

[627] DeGrandpre, Richard P. 1999, p. 200.

[628] Ibid.

[629] Ellison, Gaylord, *Amphetamine, Cocaine: New Brain Link*. **Science News,** Jan. 16, 1992, vol. 142, p. 44.

[630] Rapaport, Judith L., et al. *Dextriamphetamine: Cognitive and Behavioral Effects in Normal Prepubescent Boys*. **Science,** 1978, vol. 199, 560-63.

[631] DeGrandpre, Richard. 1999, p. 195.

[632] Doidge, Normal. **The Brain That Changes Itself.** Viking Penguin Books, New York 2007, pp. 196-214.

[633] Davis, Catherine L. *Play and Standardized Testing*. **Research Quarterly for Exercise and Sport,** December 2007.

[634] Liebertz, Charmaine. *Learning to Focus*. **Scientific American Mind,** 2005, vol. 16(4), p.91.

[635] McKearney, J. W. *Asking Questions about Behavior*. **Perspectives In Biology And Medicine,** 1977, p. 116.

[636] The College Board, **Profile of College-Bound Seniors National Report for 2001, 2002, 2004, & 2005.**

[637] Diller, Lawrence. **Running On Ritalin, A Physician Reflects On Children, Society And Performance In A Pill.** Bantam, Doubleday, Dell Pub., New York, 1999.

[638] Kovalik, Susan. The Center for Effective Learning. www.thecenter4learning.com.

[639] Gibbs, Jeanne. **Tribes, A New Way of Learning and Being Together.** Center Source Systems, LLC, Windsor, CA, 2001.

[640] Bohm, David. **New Dimensions Radio**, San Francisco, CA, 1998.

[641] Susan Kovalik and Associates. The Center for Effective Learning. www.thecenter4learning.com.

[642] Bailey, Becky. 1997, pp. 165-180.

[643] Bailey, Becky. 1997, pp. 129-150.

[644] Steiner, Rudolf **The Steiner Books**, Rudolf Steiner Publications. Blauvelt, NY, 1973.

Chapter Twelve Notes

[645] Tarnas, Richard. *Romancing the Cosmos*. **Shift: at the Frontiers of Consciousness – Noetic Sciences,** No. 9, Dec. 2005-Jan. 2006, no. 9, p. 37.

[646] Kingsolver, Barbara. **High Tide In Tucson, Essays from Now or Never.** Harper Perennial, New York, 1995, pp. 99-107.

[647] White, Bowen. **Why Normal Isn't Healthy.** Touch the Future Conference, Monterey, CA, Jan. 1999.

[648] Wegscheider-Cruze, Sharon. **The Family Reconstruction: The Living Theater Model.** Science and Behavior Books, Palo Alto, CA, 1997.

[649] Schwartz, Gary. *Intelligent Evolution*. **Shift: At the Frontiers of Consciousness.** Noetic Sciences Pub., June-August 2006, no.11, p. 12

[650] Vasconcellos, John. *The First Person... The Time is Ripe: Are We?* Touch the Future Conference, Monterey, CA, Jan., 1999.

[651] Schwartz, Gary and William L. Simon. **The G.O.D. Experiments.** Atria Books, (Simon & Schuster), New York, 2006.

[652] Wiederman, Michael. *Why It's So Hard To Be Happy*. **Scientific American Mind.** February/March, 2007. pp. 36-43.

[653] Maciocia, Giovanni. **The Practice Of Chinese Medicine.** Churchill Livingston Press, Edinburgh, London. 1994, pp. 198-202.

654 *The Yellow Emperor's Classic of Internal Medicine, Simple Questions* (Huang Ti Nei Jing Su Wen), People's Health Pub. House, Beijing, 1979, p. 58. First Pub. C. 100 BC.

655 *The Spiritual Axis (Ling Shu Jing)*, People's Health Pub. House, Beijing, p. 128. First Pub. ca. 100 BC.

656 Bullock, Theodore, H., et al. *The Neuron Doctrine, Redux.* **Science**, November 4, 2005, vol. 310, p. 791-793.

657 Marion Woodman Foundation Movie, *The Way of the Dream.* Based on Conversations with Jungian Analyst, Dr. Marie-Lovine von Franz. Windrose Films, Mandala Book Shop, 190 Central Ave., London, Ontario, Canada. N6A 1M7.

658 Solomon, Paul. Audio Tape. Edgar Casey Foundation, Virginia Beach, VA, 1985.

659 Turner, Rebecca, et al. *Psychiatry, Summer 1999.* In: *Science News*, vol. 156, Aug 7, 1999, vol.156, p. 90.

660 Schwartz, Gary and Linda Russek. Science and Consciousness Conference. Tucson, AZ, March 1996.

661 Ladinsky, Daniel. *The Gift, Poems By Hafiz, The Great Sufi Master.* Translations by Daniel Ladinsky. Penquin/Arkana, New York, 1999.

662 Dobson, Terry. *A Kind Word Turneth Away Wrath.* In: *Aikido And The New Warrior*, Richard Strozzi, ed., North Atlantic Books, Berkeley, CA, 1985, pp. 65-59.

663 Tiller, William. *Psychoenergetic Science: A Second Copernican-Scale Revolution.* Pavior Publishing, Walnut Creek, CA, 2007, p. 149.

Index

biophotons 24

birds 135, 173

Blackfoot Indians 147

blastocyst 96

blood viscosity 56

bobtail squid 134

Bohm, David 74, 78, 148, 149

Bohmian dialogue 148

Bohr, Niels 77, 148

boundaries 27, 207–208

brain 19, 40–45, 62 –65, 88, 93, 116–117 126, 141, 151–152, 155, 162, 173, 178, 181–182, 190

Brain Dance 178

Brain Gym® 45, 65, 67, 82, 92, 123, 128, 178, 213

brain stem 42, 151, 185

brain waves 53, 58, 65, 69, 92, 102, 185, 212

breath 82, 157, 166

Brewer, Chris 145, 165

Broca's area 141

Brown, Stuart L. 171–172

Buddhism 79, 100

Bullock, Theodore H. 212

Burr, Harold 97

C

calf muscle 47

Cameron, Julia 121

Campbell, Don 138

cats 135–137

caudate 204

cell differentiation process 96

cerebellum 116, 153, 155, 164, 166, 173, 174, 178, 190

cerebrum 153, 190

chakra system 91–92

chanting 140, 163, 166

chaos 16, 104–106, 111–115

Chaos Theory 105

China 44, 57, 71, 89–91, 104, 122, 149, 160, 183, 185, 211, 215

Chinese medicine 57, 71, 90, 104, 160, 185, 211, 215

Chladni, Ernst 98–99

cholesterol 58, 70, 136

classroom 69, 164–166, 180, 191, 202, 206

cochlea 100, 152–153

cognitive skills 82, 196, 198

coherence 21–30, 48, 56–73, 90–95, 103, 107, 115, 130, 161, 164–165, 170–171, 197, 206, 212, 216

Columbine High School 129, 191

communication 34, 81, 106–107, 114, 126, 129, 136–138, 148, 201, 208

community 94, 118, 125, 126, 129, 167, 206, 207, 210, 214, 216

competition 106, 133, 190, 199, 210, 216

computer 71, 84, 130, 141, 142, 190, 201

concentration 180, 196

conception 28, 33, 34, 96, 100, 151, 157

conditioning 17, 31, 37, 39, 40, 49, 55, 83, 95, 122

confidence 22, 27, 118, 165, 172, 187, 195

connection 34, 58, 117, 126, 127, 129, 130, 138, 142, 201, 202, 208, 214,

Connor, Melinda 91

consciousness 28, 29, 41, 64, 79–80, 94, 123, 135, 209, 216

consciousness, collective 84–87, 148

consumerism 71, 127, 210

Cooper, Michael 70

cooperation 106–107, 114, 115, 133, 134, 137, 138, 147, 148, 180, 187, 199, 216

Copenhagen Interpretation 77

core muscles 38, 155

coronary artery disease 56

corpus callosum 164

cortex 42, 64, 66, 67, 119, 123, 124, 125, 126, 141, 153, 155, 164, 168, 173, 174

cortical brain cells 174

heart disease 57, 58, 126
heart entrainment 60, 66
heart field 59, 69
heart rate 25, 58, 60, 157, 158, 162, 185
heart rate variability pattern 61, 62, 65
heart transplants 47
Heisenberg, Werner 51, 52, 75, 77
helping 213
Herizinga, Johan 171
hippocampal volume 182
hippocampus 42, 126, 131, 135, 153, 178
histones 42, 44, 45
histones acetyltransferases 42
histones methyltransferases 44
Holland, Ernst Runair 97
holograms 46, 47, 78
homeopathy 89
Hook Ups 67, 68, 69, 70, 123
hormonal system 57
hormones 26, 33, 47, 58, 62, 64, 173
hyperactivity 25, 34, 173, 205
hypothalamus 125, 126, 183

I

ICA (Intrinsic Cardiac Adrenergic) 59, 62
ice crystals 93
imagination 170, 173, 187, 189, 194
imaginative games 22, 186, 187, 194
immune system 25, 143, 177, 183
inanimate objects 71, 84, 85, 94, 147
incest fear 184
incoherence 22–24, 28, 58, 60–62, 65, 66, 69, 73, 85, 86, 94, 115, 159
India 65, 148
indigenous peoples 18, 19, 56, 147, 160, 167, 184
Inequalities Theorem 78
infants 33, 37, 86, 102, 103, 119, 141, 142, 155, 159, 160, 184
information field 19, 74, 79, 81, 82, 85, 95, 103, 150, 216

information molecules 47
Ingebar, Donald 98
inner ear 139, 143, 151, 153, 155, 178
innovators 199
insight 18, 20, 44, 49, 123, 145, 146, 147, 181, 188, 197, 211
insomnia 203
inspiration 30, 44, 188
instantaneous information transfer 78
instinctive emotions 117
insula 117, 119, 173
integrated movement 45, 49, 91, 178, 202, 204
intellectualism 71, 125, 147, 210
intentions 17, 21, 33, 48, 49, 66, 71, 74, 79, 81, 87–98, 103, 113, 115, 145, 215
intention experiments 89
interference patterns 19, 46, 48, 74–76, 93
intimacy 130, 145, 210
intuition 29, 57, 65, 70, 72, 81, 138, 150
in utero 24, 26, 47, 100, 151, 155, 157, 160, 184, 208
ionosphere 101
isolation 58, 117, 126, 127, 143, 190, 191, 210, 214

J

Jacobi, E. 102
Japanese 39, 40, 93, 103
Jenny, Hans 99
Jordain, Robert 161
Jung, Carl 74

K

Kenya 110, 111, 112
Khan, Hazrat Inyat 206
Kindermusik 163
Kingsolver, Barbara 209
Kirlian, Semyon 97
Konig, Herbert 102
Korotkov, Konstantin G. 97

P

Carla Hannaford, Ph.D. is a biologist and educator with more than forty years of teaching experience, including twenty years teaching biology at the university level and four years as a counselor for elementary and intermediate school children with learning difficulties.

She is an internationally recognized educational consultant, having presented more than six hundred lectures and workshops in thirty-five countries over the past two decades. She was selected as a guest educator with the AHP-Soviet Project in 1988, has been recognized by Who's Who in American Education, and has received awards from the University of Hawaii and the American Association for the Advancement of Science for outstanding teaching in science. She has advised ministries and departments of education in the United States, Russia, South Africa, Singapore, and Scotland.

Her first book, *Smart Moves; Why Learning Is Not All In Your Head*, first published in 1995 and updated in 2005, (Great River Books) has been translated into thirteen languages. She is also the author of *The Dominance Factor, How Knowing Your Dominant Eye, Ear, Brain, Hand & Foot Can Improve Your Learning*, (Great River Books, 1997) and *Awakening The Child Heart, Handbook for Global Parenting*, (Jamilla Nur Publishing, 2002.) She authored and co-produced the video *Education in Motion*, and co-presented her work with Candace Pert and Susan Kovalik on the video *Emotions: Gateway to Learning*. She has contributed hundreds of articles to educational and science journals and magazines and been featured in scores of radio and TV interviews in the U.S. and abroad.

She lives with her musician husband Ahti Mohala in Hawaii and Montana.